Cosima Wagner

By the same author

Chopin: A Biography
The Bed and the Throne: The Life of Isabella d'Este
Puccini: A Biography
Richard Strauss: The Life of a Non-Hero
Opera as Theatre
The World Treasury of Grand Opera
Beethoven: Biography of a Genius
The Eagles Die: Franz Joseph, Elisabeth and Their
  Austria
Gentle Genius: The Story of Felix Mendelssohn
Toscanini

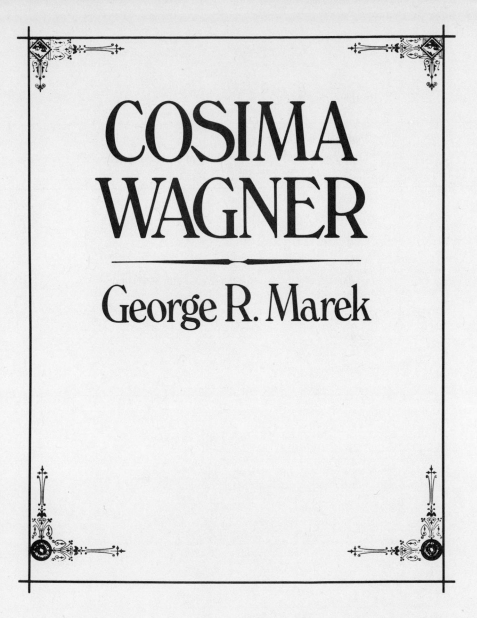

COSIMA WAGNER

George R. Marek

HARPER & ROW, PUBLISHERS, NEW YORK
Cambridge, Hagerstown, Philadelphia, San Francisco
London, Mexico City, São Paulo, Sydney

FIRST EDITION

Designer: Gloria Adelson

Library of Congress Cataloging in Publication Data

Marek, George Richard, 1902–
  Cosima Wagner.
  Bibliography: p.
  Includes index.
  1. Wagner, Cosima Liszt, 1837–1930. 2. Opera producers and directors—Germany—Biography. 3. Wagner, Richard, 1813–1883. 4. Composers—Germany—Biography. 5. Wives—Germany—Biography.
  ML429.W133M4   782.1′092′4   [B]   80-7591
  ISBN 0-06-012704-X

81 82 83 84 85 10 9 8 7 6 5 4 3 2 1

To Richard and Margot

Contents

Illustrations

Foreword

Anybody who wanders into the thicket of Wagnerian literature must be grateful to Ernest Newman. It was he who hewed a path through the brambles of exaggerations and the undergrowth of mystifications planted by "official" Bayreuth biographers (Karl Glasenapp, Julius Kapp, Houston Stewart Chamberlain, etc.). He modified as well the highly colored portraits of such writers as Paul Bekker, Henry T. Finck, Max Koch, Ferdinand Pohl, Guy de Pourtalés, etc., who loved Wagner too well but not wisely. An astonishing quantity of documents has come to light since Newman published his fourth and last volume of *The Life of Richard Wagner* in 1946. The thicket has grown denser: hardly a year passes when a new book about Wagner is *not* published. Still, Newman's work remains valid; and it includes a brief but carefully reasoned sketch of Cosima.

Considering the importance of the role Cosima Wagner played in her husband's life, and considering how provocative and striated her personality was, it is curious that more has not been written about her. Her "official" biographer was Richard Count Du Moulin Eckart, who published a two-volume work in 1929 (the year before she died) and 1931; it is a paean unashamed. The best one can say about it is that it contains a heap of casual facts—while often suppressing the truth—but shows a cavalier disregard for dates and sources of quotations. Nor does it give an estimate of her character: Cosima here is all white and shining. A short biography by Max Millenkovich-Morold, published in 1937, is better. Add two small and inconsequential attempts—*Twilight of the Swans* (1973) by Douglas Sutherland and *Cosima Wagner*

(1969) by Alice Hunt Sokoloff—and that's about all there is.

When her diary was published in 1976—"a historical document of unsurpassable interest," Peter Gay called it—it created new curiosity about her and Wagner and their life together. It explained much, opening fresh perceptions. Yet this huge document, with its thousand daily details, needs an overall view, a synthesis, an interpretation, to be fortified by Cosima's letters and the testimony of those who knew her.

I have loved Wagner's music since as a boy of thirteen I first heard *Die Walküre* from a corner of the third gallery of the Imperial Royal Opera House in Vienna, a corner from which I could see only a tiny segment of Hunding's hut. The years have not dimmed that love, though often enough I have been irritated by the composer's philosophical writings, such as "What Is German?" or "State and Religion." With Cosima, however, I have concerned myself only relatively recently. This book attempts a study of who she was and what she contributed.

It is impossible to tell Cosima's story without encroaching on, and connecting it with, Wagner's story. If the reader will here come across a few well-known facts, he or she must forgive me. I hope I have brought enough fresh material to the task of presenting a full view of a woman who made herself indispensable to an artist and, by force, love and cunning, carved a unique place in the chronicle of music.

In undertaking this task I owe a great debt to Dr. Dietrich Mack, coeditor of Cosima's diary, editor of an anthology of her letters titled *Cosima Wagner, das zweite Leben,* author of *100 Jahre Bayreuther Festspiele.* He made available to me some as yet unpublished letters —yes, there are still quite a few such—took time to discuss many details, criticized the manuscript, and gave me guidance at every stage. Others who helped were Dr. Manfred Eger, director of the Wagner Museum in Bayreuth, Friedelind Wagner, Wayne D. Shirley of the Library of Congress, Henry Pleasants of London, Rigbie Turner of the Pierpont Morgan Library, Sir Robin Mackworth-Turner of the Royal Archives of Windsor Castle, and Robert W. Gutman, author of *Richard Wagner,* a book that has become controversial but is important.

I am especially grateful to Frances Lindley, a good friend and a rare editor who shows one how to make a book better.

George R. Marek

New York
March 1980

CHAPTER I

Orphan with Living Parents

Oₙ SEPTEMBER 1, 1933, Thomas Mann was in Lugano, a voluntary exile from Hitler's Germany. Seven months previously, he had given a lecture at the University of Munich, based on his essay "The Sufferings and Greatness of Richard Wagner." He repeated the lecture in Amsterdam, Brussels, and Paris. Away from Germany, he became fully cognizant of what was happening in his beloved country and he determined that he would not return to "the hell run amok." Whatever the sacrifice, he had to divorce himself from the Third Reich. His citizenship was promptly taken away, his house, car, bank account in Munich, confiscated. Uprooted and plunged into melancholy, he did not know where to find his future home. Yet amidst his perplexity, he was still preoccupied with the most German of German composers; the subject of Wagner was still vibrating in his mind. He noted in his diary:

> September 1, 1933. Conversation about a novel to be written dealing with the Wagner-Cosima-Liszt-Nietzsche relationship. A highly interesting theme. A most complicated, many-layered, European-German subject. . . . The daughter of Liszt, intellectually mundane and born not-German (not to say un-German), she filled Wagner's aura with Catholic incense. Yet she either inspired or herself wrote those anti-Semitic and German-nationalistic articles by the old Wagner. . . .

Two days later, he began to read the correspondence of Liszt and Marie d'Agoult. But the novel was never written.

Later, Henry Handel Richardson, the fine Australian author of *Maurice Guest, Ultima Thule, The Fortunes of Richard Mahony,* did make the attempt. *The Young Cosima* was published in 1939. It was not a successful novel.

One need not summon the aid of fiction to tell the story of this woman who invigorated Wagner's creativity and thereby earned immortality for herself; this "weaker vessel" who went after what she wanted with such strong determination; this unbending tall creature who, learning self-worship from a flamboyant father and a vain mother, yet dissolved into selfless devotion. Brilliantly gifted, she could be obtuse to a child's needs. Intensely perceptive, she could be blind to the truth. Widely cultured, she was guilty of numerous misjudgments. Essentially honest, she fled into lies. The elements of her character often collided. She was a jigsaw puzzle the pieces of which were not easy to assemble.

That is now possible, at least more easily possible, not only because the diary she kept from 1869, her thirty-second year, until Wagner's death in 1883, when she was forty-six, is available, but also because in recent years many of her letters have surfaced from the archives. When she died, Olin Downes, the music critic of *The New York Times,* wrote: "It is probable that the real Cosima is known less than any of the other dramatic figures of the Wagnerian past. It is probable, furthermore, that she will remain the most enigmatic and by no means the least significant of them all." She *was* significant. She is no longer quite the enigma she was. But first and last, she remains as fascinating as an enigma usually is.

"Happy families are all alike; every unhappy family is unhappy in its own way." Cosima came from an unhappy family—which wasn't even a family. She was the second child born to Franz Liszt and Marie Catherine Sophie de Flavigny, Countess d'Agoult. Theirs was a great passion, the passion of two beautiful people, and like many a great passion, it was to end in a great hatred.

In 1833, when the two first met, Liszt was twenty-two and already "a genius to swoon over." She was six years older than he, married to a dry, conventional, and wealthy court official twenty years her senior, and the mother of three children, one of whom had recently died. Though inwardly dissatisfied, she had led a life of smooth respectability, until . . . until, as she wrote, "the door opened and a wondrous apparition appeared before my eyes—a tall and extremely slender figure, a pallid face with great eyes of the deepest sea green."

What those eyes looked at was a woman straight and white as a willow tree, with glittering blond hair, clothed in a Paris creation which had cost no less than one thousand francs, her physical radiance set off by the artfully planned interior of her home. She was inordinately proud of being a member of French High Society—to which she only half belonged since her mother had been a Bethmann, a family of bourgeois German bankers who may or may not have been converted Jews—but she swiftly decided that she needed Liszt more than Society, more than marriage, more than the tributes offered by her Parisian courtiers, who gave her an unmistakable look as they bent to kiss her hand. She left her husband as well as the Paris she loved to live with the artist who "burns and illuminates like an angel's sword." Around that liaison stood the deities of the Romantic Age, Byron and Musset and George Sand, intoning defiance of the "conventions."

Then and later, Liszt was irresistible to women. They used to steal into his hotel room and scoop up the water he had washed in. In Rome, at a party at the Villa Medici, "it was impossible to count the ravishing, celestial women who came to fall trembling like poor little larks at the feet of the terrible enchanter." Marie wanted the terrible enchanter all to herself. She wished to remove him from "poisonous Paris," to a less tempting ambience. They settled in Geneva, where they set up an agreeable enough salon, though Marie despised those stiff local Calvinists and they in turn were less than gracious to her.

Something more was needed, Marie felt, to bind the much courted artist-lover to her. Of course—a child. A child would float about their union like a cherub in a Titian Assumption. In December 1835, Blandine was born. Her parents still loved each other, or thought they did, and Liszt, the twenty-four-year-old father, was quite captured by the ravishing baby. Marie was not, the reality of nursing being less romantic than the idea, the swaddling clothes being rougher than her silks. The child was miscast in that idyll dreamed up by Marie, in which she would take her lover by the hand and lead him to the higher life, with Goethe and Dante and Tasso to show the way. Liszt was willing to be led, but while breathing rarefied air, he yet longed for the stuffy greenroom, the overheated concert hall, the audience that held its breath and swooned in worship. He began to absent himself, physically and spiritually. Between the spring of 1836 and the winter of 1837 he gave twenty-one concerts.

Yet Marie's spell still held; she knew how to weave it, after Geneva using Italy as the stage setting for her sorcery. If you were French and in love, you went to Italy. (If you were Italian, you went to France.) They rented a villa on the shore of Lake Como, near Bellagio, lived *"in alta solitudine,"* took picnic lunches under the olive trees, and rowed on still sunny days in still sunny waters. For a time Liszt was happy in what she called "the narrow frame of a *tête-à-tête* existence." It did not remain undisturbed for long. Another child was on the way.

Francesca Gaetana Cosima Liszt was born on December 24, 1837. She was not an entirely welcome Christmas present. With her scrawny little body and a nose of almost Pinocchian proportions, the new baby was not nearly so attractive as the fair Blandine. As soon as decently possible after her birth, Liszt went to Milan. From there he sent Marie copious love letters in the ripest Romantic style—sunset, the pale moon, and Correggio paintings included—which could not quite hide his pleasure at being again in a big city and away from family cares.

He was more than ever in a restive mood. He didn't know whether he liked or secretly disliked Cosima. All the same, he returned to Marie briefly, they moved to Venice in February, but in April he was off again, ostensibly and no doubt sincerely to help raise money for the victims of a disastrous flood in Hungary, but essentially because he needed the freedom of the vagabonding virtuoso.

While he triumphed in Vienna, Marie wrote that she was ill, she needed him. He rushed to her, he protested, "I love you with all my strength," while at the same time he told her of "the women who have thrown themselves at my head." She wept and in a bitter moment called him a "Don Juan parvenu." Nonetheless, they again lived together, and in May 1839 their son, Daniel, was born. Now Liszt, master of volatility, realized how deeply he was bound in domesticity. Three children . . . the noise they made was not very musical, not to his ears. He sank into a black depression. He didn't work, smoked incessantly, and drank twenty cups of coffee a day. They resumed their peregrinations, taking Cosima and Blandine with them, while Daniel was left in Palestrina with a nurse.

The villa in Lucca in which they spent that summer was a perfumed bower, an Arcadian resting place. To Marie it was a prison:

> My faculties are exhausted. I suffer horribly: I feel I can't live like this, that I must die soon or sink into imbecility and then what despair for him! His life would be shattered, his artistic future lost, his genius extinguished. [*Mémoires*]

His genius extinguished? She was a faulty prophet. Away from her, it was to develop superbly. Yet he, too, suffered because of this love he wanted to break away from but never could, entirely. Even in later years, when he hated her, the bond could never be cut clean. The children were but supernumeraries in the sexual drama of Liszt-d'Agoult, but there they were and they could not be got off the stage. What was he to do about them? All he wanted was to have them safely bestowed and brought up decently without his having to expend precious time in playing games with them. Marie's attitude toward them was divided between a sense of somewhat manufactured pride—the "these are my jewels" kind of assertion—and a sense of irritation, as if they were weights hanging from arms stretched out toward new adventures.

At the end of the year, Liszt announced that he had decided to go on another concert tour; this time he would travel widely, play in many concert halls.

Where would Marie and the children live during his absence? Italy she now regarded as a false paradise; it had not helped her to pinion her restless lover. Nor, as they moved here and there, had it helped her to acquire what she passionately wanted: the adulation of "an entourage of distinguished people," as Liszt put it. He meant men. She didn't want lovers, she wanted flatterers (though later she did have several affairs). She was ashamed of going back to Paris in the role of discarded mistress, yet she felt that there, at the very center of Romanticism, she could best build a private stage on which to enact the stellar role. They talked it over. They decided that she would go back, living for a time in the house of Liszt's mother, Anna, and entrusting the children to their grandmother. The children would be safe with Anna. Grandmother was delighted.

On October 19, 1839, Marie embarked from Livorno with the four-year-old Blandine and the scarcely two-year-old Cosima. Liszt had accompanied them to the ship and filled her cabin with flowers. From Genoa, where the ship stopped briefly, she wrote him:

How to leave the soil of beloved Italy without a last adieu? How to watch these two beautiful years detach themselves from my life without a regret? Oh my dear Franz!

They had not been beautiful years, not entirely, though knowing her gone, Liszt felt an upwelling of recollective love.. "Good-bye, darling Marie," he wrote, "think sometimes how much I love you and let that thought be sweet to you." Then he sighed with relief and set out on a pianistic progression which took him to Vienna, Budapest, Prague, Dresden, and Leipzig. It was six months before he turned up in Paris. By that time Marie had set herself up in a charming house—which included a Moorish salon, a drawing room lined with antique mirrors, and a Renaissance boudoir—and though she compared herself to Ariadne sighing for Theseus, she had gathered some lively celebrities around her: Eugène Sue, Sainte-Beuve, Victor Hugo, Lamartine, and even Balzac, who had drawn a mean portrait of her in his novel *Beatrix,* but who was not averse to the creations of her superb chef.

The girls were at their grandmother's, a simple, uneducated, unworldly, but warmhearted woman, who would do anything her son asked of her. For the first time they experienced what it was to be touched by love. For the first time they were truly hugged and kissed, and they kissed Anna's cheeks in return, though these felt dry to young lips. Anna was comfortable to be with—not too much "do this" and "don't do that." "Sit up straight when you eat" and "Eat everything on your plate" were almost the only instruction Anna gave Cosima. As to her mother, she and Blandine knew she was near, but they hardly ever saw her.

When Liszt met Marie again, the fire leaped from embers which he himself had thought extinguished. However hurt her vanity was, Marie still loved him. However hurt he was by her seeing him clearly, she still attracted him. He went to England and she followed him. She was unhappy there; she reproached him less for his infidelities than for his intoxication with success, which "can produce nothing but a hangover." The affair would not end. The alternation between embrace and obloquy continued for another four years—during which they saw each other less and less frequently, though they did spend three summer holidays in Nonnenwerth, an island in the Rhine. Finally, in the spring of 1844, Liszt decided he had had enough. He was in Paris and he asked to dine with her alone. He found himself confronted by a woman who told him she "hated music, having loved it for too long," and that she was weary of everything: *"In vain* seems to be the denouement of my life." It was the wrong tactic. Shortly after, Liszt wrote her: "I want neither to speak to you nor to see you, even less to write to you."

Marie was unable to accept so harsh an end. She tried a new ploy: she wanted to meet him and discuss the future of the children and she spoke solemnly of duty and maternal tenderness. Liszt refused the meeting, but declared himself willing to have Marie direct the children's education, or at least (as he wrote ironically) to have her occupy herself "with it more than in the past."

"I see no difficulty on my mother's side, she having up to now acquitted herself well, in my view, in the painful task which she accepted." As to taking the three children away from their grandmother —Daniel had joined the girls at Anna Liszt's home—no! Decidedly not.

Marie was far from tolerating this interdict placidly. And nobody asked the children where or with whom they wanted to live, even had they possessed the courage to voice a wish.

Moved in infancy from place to place, now by the shore of an Italian lake, now being trundled in the Bois de Boulogne, now at some *pension* in the mountains, with nursemaids and servants frequently changing, with a mother busy at the dressing table and at the writing desk,* with a father mostly absent and not really present when present, they were, so to speak, orphans whose parents were alive. More than thirty years later, Cosima wrote in her diary:

> Thursday, 23rd [March, 1871]. The day is occupied with preparations to receive my mother. I make order among some papers and read old letters from my father. They show me once more that I had neither mother nor father. R. [Wagner] was everything to me. He is the only one who has given me love.

In every family of two girls, one is "the Beauty," the other "the Clever One": Blandine was the beauty. Cosima admired her elder sister and agreed with the occasional visitor who remarked on Blandine's looks. Yet Cosima was not jealous of her. The two were close friends. They shared a room. They shared their "secrets." When Anna, at Liszt's request, sent Blandine to a fashionable girls' school, Cosima was so miserable and begged so tearfully that Anna enrolled her too —*"cette petite folle"*—in the same school. On Anna's name day she found a note, carefully penned and with just a few mistakes in spelling, on her pillow:

> Dear Grandmother: Whom have I to thank for life's delights? Who is it who gives me loving tender looks? I feel it and won't forget it. You are all my happiness.
>   Cosima Liszt

---

*She had begun her journal in the first years of her union with Liszt, though her writing under the pseudonym Daniel Stern dates from after their parting.

To Marie, the children were reminders of her growing older, even as she hoped that her hair would remain blond and her complexion exquisite. Although from time to time she announced that she intended to embrace what she called "the fruits of her womb," her chief interest in them was to use them as instruments of revenge and to try to take them away from the man whom she had deeply loved and who had deeply offended her. Liszt, weak, easily influenced, yet a man of kindly impulses, worried about them from time to time and then forgot; he was too taken up with his struggle to lift himself beyond his achievement as an incandescent virtuoso, to become a creator of important music. He could be no more than a father *malgré lui.* After the rupture with Marie, he avoided Paris, not returning for nine years. In 1846, Marie published her novel *Nélida,* under the name Daniel Stern. It gave an account of her life with Liszt that was nothing short of vindictive. In that year Cosima was nine years old—not old enough to understand, but old enough to sense.

When it came time for Cosima's first communion, she wrote Liszt begging him to come to the ceremony. He didn't. Such a rebuff tends to toughen a young soul, or to crumble it. Cosima did not crumble. Early she became determined in the pursuit of what she wanted. Early she showed strength. Possibly she learned perseverance from Marie. It was Marie, too, who had given her the old advice—one surely already known to the women of Mesopotamia—that a girl must make the best of her good features. Cosima was told that she was "interesting looking." Her best feature was her long blond hair, an inheritance from Marie, and Cosima soon knew its value: as a teen-ager, she spent time every morning and evening in brushing it and caressing it, and she developed a gesture of saying yes by saying no, shaking her head so that her hair flew about.

That was deliberate, a movement studied before the mirror. But to cultivate her mind was to her a natural, unselfconscious process. No one did, and no one had to, lead her. She found in books a second life, and she read helter-skelter everything she could get hold of. As a French girl growing up in the Romantic Age, it was to be expected that she should gobble up every word of *The Three Musketeers* and *The Count of Monte Cristo,* of *Notre-Dame de Paris* and *Les Misérables;* but she tackled as well Dante, and Goethe's *Faust* (in translation), and as soon as she knew enough English she plunged into Byron's poetry. George Sand's *Indiana* was her special favorite; she hid the book whenever her grandmother was around. Her father had bestowed on her an innate musicality, and even as a child she responded to music, listening with open eyes and a judicial mien. When she was about eight she took willingly to the piano and learned quickly; soon she was playing Mozart sonatas, and Weber's "Invitation to the Dance" in her father's transcription, which she found difficult "because I am not very strong"—and because it *is* difficult.

As her appetite for reading grew by what it fed on, she saw herself as a famous writer, an author making her own rules of conduct, another George Sand. Or could she become a pianist like her father? She wasn't sure; she was sure only that she would "be somebody," somebody different from those bonbon-munching girls at the boarding school. With her large blue eyes gleaming with curiosity, her exclamation point of a nose, her lips set in a "grown-up" expression, taller by inches than her contemporaries, her long, well-shaped legs ready to run, she was a decisive little girl. Grandma's friends, when they discussed her over a cup of tea, called her *"sage,"* yet there was a wild impulsiveness suppressed in her. Conscious of who her parents were, she was not free of a certain naïve arrogance, and sometimes she acted in school as if she had escaped from a columbarium for prize doves. Consequently, she had few friends, and she expended her need to love on her brother and sister. In afteryears she remembered:

> The extraordinary position created for us by our birth forged a bond between us three such as the majority of brothers and sisters can scarcely picture . . . and which I now drag about me like a heavy, cumbersome chain. I often feel as though I had been torn up by the roots. . . . [Told to Du Moulin Eckart]

2

To the young girl, Liszt was the Launcelot of the legend. Why would he not come, take her in his arms, and deliver her from that jejune boarding school, or merely by his presence lift her to importance among her schoolmates? At the age of twelve, she wrote to him: "Now that the holidays are beginning—will we see you during this time? You have too long postponed this visit which would make us so happy, but I am sure that this is not your fault and that you too cherish the desire to see us." Liszt cherished no such desire. His letters to her read like

those of a self-righteous schoolmaster: he criticized her way of expressing herself (she wrote to him mostly in French, occasionally in English), he found fault with the spelling, he admonished her to seek
"life's higher aims"—hectoring epistles without softness or warmth,
laying a distance between himself and the daughter who reminded
him of past ecstasy and present encumbrance.

Increasingly the three children turned to their mother. Marie
wanted to take Blandine to live with her; she didn't want Cosima and
Daniel. Yet soon all three began to visit the perfumed salon, at first
with Grandmother's knowledge, then so frequently that they felt they
had to keep their visits secret. Liszt of course heard about it. He was
furious. He wrote to his friend Joseph Massart, who was administering
Liszt's money:

> . . . I obviously cannot contest . . . Madame d'Agoult's right to occupy
> herself with her two daughters and to intervene in any number of
> ways. My only resource . . . is to refuse the money she can demand
> for the purpose, and that is why I asked you to get back her accounts.
> Now, it is as certain that I will refuse to give three thousand francs for
> Cosima as it is undoubted that I will send you this sum regularly for
> Blandine. In my opinion, Cosima and Daniel ought to stay with my
> mother and I hope Madame d'Agoult will agree. If . . . she tries to
> take Cosima by force, I will retaliate in full by taking the three
> children to Germany, where she will have no hold over them. [Spring
> 1845]

Marie had no intention of taking Cosima; nevertheless, she broke
out in a fury of offended motherhood, fumed, shouted—and then
sought legal advice. Could Liszt take the children away from her if
she wanted them? No, advised her lawyer, since it would be impossible for Liszt to have the children declared legitimate. Liszt's lawyer
gave him a contrary opinion: he could have them acquire Austrian
citizenship and thereby cancel any claims Marie might put forward.
The correspondence rose to a crescendo of acrimony.

Liszt to Marie:

May 2, 1845

> A year ago, Madame, I could believe that the incredible view of me
> you have conjured up and put forth in numerous letters would be a
> secret between us. I even concluded from your ardent devotion in the
> past that you would maintain with other people the same reserve I
> have imposed on myself in regard to you: now this illusion is no
> longer possible because I cannot ignore your telling all comers the
> wildest and most abusive things about me. . . .

Marie to Liszt:

> You are capable of the worst cowardice: that of threatening *from a distance* and by *virtue of legality* a mother who reclaims the fruit of her womb. . . . I see I am vanquished, Monsieur, in a hopeless struggle to which I can only invoke your heart, your reason and your conscience. But I protest before God and man, I protest before all mothers, the violence done me. . . .

She ended this protest by proclaiming: "Henceforth, Monsieur, your children have no mother."

But it was playacting. Marie was well content not to assume maternal responsibility in earnest and to exercise her blandishments on the children when it suited her. They appeared as washed and starched visitors, Cosima eyeing the books standing in red rows in Marie's library, and Marie could dismiss them when she got tired of the role of sweet benefactress for that afternoon. Anna saw no harm in these visits. Why shouldn't the children enjoy their mother's lively home and her delicious cakes?

Liszt thought the contrary. Early in 1847—that is, three years after his separation from Marie—he met and fell in love with the twenty-eight-year-old Princess Carolyne Sayn-Wittgenstein. Liszt wrote his mother that "the problem of my life is solved" by this *"très extraordinaire, mais très extraordinaire et éminente"* woman. Extraordinary she was, strong-willed, possessed of a fanatic religiosity which never prevented her from slaking her desires. Liszt and she made love in her bedroom under a ten-foot cross. She left her husband, left her large estate, whose meadows were smoothed every morning by barefooted serfs, sold everything she owned, and applied for permission to emigrate. Her husband—he was no less a personage than adjutant to the Czar—managed to stop that. Nevertheless, she set out with her little daughter, Marie, several servants, and tons of luggage. The 1848 revolution was coursing through Europe, and the Czar suddenly decided that the frontier was to be locked and bolted. A courtier galloped after Carolyne to call her back; he arrived an hour too late. Carolyne had crossed the frontier to join Liszt.

Once across, Carolyne took over the management of Liszt's life, every detail of it, the children being more than a detail. Those children: they were spending too much time with the woman who had written *Nélida* and were too much indulged by old lady Liszt. Such was Carolyne's firm opinion, and she knew the solution: they needed a stern hand; she knew such a hand—it was the very governess who had ruled her own childhood. This Madame Patersi de Fossombroni had managed to control an exceptionally wayward and reckless girl—herself—and Carolyne, though never tamed entirely, had become fond of Patersi, who was now nearing seventy and living in St. Petersburg. A better guardian could not be found, Carolyne said. The old lady, encased in her black dress with its whalebone collar, was induced to come to Weimar, where Liszt had accepted the post of court conductor and where Carolyne had joined him. Madame Patersi arrived, more dead than alive, because on the long train ride from St. Petersburg she had sat erect and immobile, declining to lean against a cushion and presumably refraining from using the train's toilet. Carolyne put her to bed and nursed her for two months. She was then ready to go to Paris. Liszt wrote to his mother:

Weimar, October 25, 1850

I would have preferred to have this letter delivered by Mme. Patersi herself. I ask you to hand over my two daughters to her care. Henceforth she is to supervise their education. I thank you with all my heart for the love which you have offered my daughters in the last months and I am sure that they as well will remain grateful for the care you have bestowed on their early youth.

Unfortunately Mme. Patersi fell ill when she arrived here and she can not come to Paris for another two weeks. Since you will be moving, her sister Mme. Saint-Mars has kindly consented to call for the children and to take them to Rue Casimir-Périer 6, Faubourg St. Germain, where they will be living from now on, remaining with her until Mme. Patersi arrives. Would you therefore please, on receipt of this letter, deliver Blandine and Cosima at once to Mme. Saint-Mars. Would you also be so kind, dear mother, as to arrange to send to the above-mentioned flat all the furniture which according to your declaration you can spare, as well as other household necessities. . . . They will need six silver sets of cutlery, glasses, dishes, table and bed linen, etc. I should have to buy all that new and therefore I would be much obliged if you could let them have whatever you yourself are not using. I have asked Mme. Patersi to visit you often with my daughters; however, she is to accompany them everywhere. . . . She alone is to decide what is to be permitted them and what forbidden. . . .

Anna was deeply hurt. Why this sudden cutting of a natural relationship? Why this peremptory removal? It was Liszt who wanted it, prompted by that impulse which made him bow before the titled. He, who had sprung from the humblest of origins, wished his daughters to be brought up as "aristocrats," and Anna was too plain for the purpose. Liszt now deemed the "fashionable" boarding school not fashionable

enough. He said that the school had had "evil effects on their education." So Blandine and Cosima were handed over to the unsmiling
governess. They were to be massaged into princesses.

Cosima at first rebelled, soon was cowed. Cosima to her father:

> I tell you frankly that I felt great pain to have to part from a
> grandmama who has shown us so much kindness. But Mme.
> Saint-Mars is good, I am now completely used to her and I quite love
> her. I am ready to feel the same toward Mme. Patersi, whom you like
> so much. . . . [1850]

She was lying. Nor was she truthful when she wrote Carolyne in-
gratiating letters. At thirteen, she had learned the use of subterfuge.
How else could she come to terms with that faraway father and the
woman who had now taken possession of him, whom Cosima had
never seen and of whom she knew little more than that she said one
prayer after another and smoked one cigar after another? As to her
anachronistic caretaker, she knew she would have to be docile and
silently follow her own bent.

Yet Madame Patersi proved to be not too bad a teacher. If her
curriculum was exacting, it did not scare Cosima in the least. She
taught Cosima history, laying much emphasis on the tales of kings and
giving credit for man's progress to "heroes" such as Peter the Great
and Napoleon. They read the "classics": Corneille, Racine, Shakespeare. "I prefer *Macbeth*. I have learned by heart the passage in which
the hero sees a dagger before him—that is the finest in the whole
piece. I prefer Shakespeare to Corneille, but I like Racine better than
either." Patersi made Cosima learn German—a language in which she
showed such proficiency that she translated one of La Fontaine's fa-
bles—and perfect her English. (A letter from Cosima to her father of
June 5, 1851, is written in good English.) Above all, Patersi taught her
how a "noble lady" must behave, how to alight from a carriage, how
to enter a drawing room, how to greet a duchess as against a commoner, how to eat without showing that she was hungry—and how not
to betray herself when she was hurt. "You must be strong—tears are
useless water." . . . "You must pray—but don't be humble. God loves
the proud." Cosima absorbed it all.

Carolyne was watching Patersi. Patersi was watching the girls. All
the same, they, and Cosima in particular, managed to slip away to
Marie. Anna lived at a great distance from the Faubourg St. Germain;
she never saw the children without their governess; and adoring
mother that she was, she now sided with her son. She disapproved of

Marie's interest: "Madame d'Agoult is quite able to find distraction without assuming any share in the education of these children." Marie naturally took a very different view: "I cannot help asking myself by what strange caprice he has imposed on his children a *chance* mother [Carolyne] instead of simply allowing their hearts to follow the natural feelings that would have led them in my direction. . . . He has brought trouble into their young minds; he has insisted on appearances and *simulations* in place of real sentiments."

For a time the girls were forbidden to mention their mother's name, while every one of Cosima's actions, every one of her gestures, was supervised. Patersi permitted her to write her father only once every two weeks, and all her letters were censored to make sure that they were bland. After her mother's death in 1876, Cosima reminisced in her diary about disobeying the strictures with her secret visits to Marie: "I cannot describe the impressions those Sundays always made on me. I can still see myself devouring with my eyes my mother's wonderful library, and when we returned to our narrow, strict, suppressed life with two seventy-year-old governesses the impression remained with us of having returned from the realms of the blessed."

It was, then, Princess Carolyne who pulled the strings, acting through her local deputy. She had leased a villa in Weimar, the Altenburg, and she lived there openly with Liszt while she hoped to persuade the Vatican to grant her a divorce. Liszt became more enamored of her the closer they moved together, an infatuation which none of his biographers has been able to explain fully, but which may have been rooted in the satisfaction a man who has known many beautiful women finds in a plain one, and one who tells him what to do. Presently Carolyne wanted the children near her—Liszt did not—obviously because she wished to control everything in and about his life.

3

It may have been the princess's idea that Liszt should go to Paris to see the children, and it was certainly the princess's wish that she go along. They journeyed to Basel, where they met Wagner. Already famous—*Rienzi* had met with considerable success, and Liszt, ardent champion of his music, had staged *Tannhäuser* and *Lohengrin* in

Weimar—Wagner was now forced to live in Zurich, having been banished from Germany in 1849 for his openly expressed revolutionary political opinions. He was supported by money borrowed from friends and by a yearly allowance granted by an admirer, Julie Ritter, the mother of Karl Ritter, an aspiring poet and composer. On Liszt's urging, Wagner went along on the excursion to Paris. There they all were on October 10, 1853—Liszt, Carolyne and her daughter, Wagner, Anna Liszt, Madame Patersi. Blandine was almost eighteen, pretty and nubile, Cosima not quite sixteen, so slender and tall as to have earned the nickname "the Stork," and Daniel, fourteen, startlingly resembling his father. It was the first time in *eight years* that Liszt had seen his children. However constricted that first greeting was, whatever uneasiness may have prevailed, whatever embarrassment over this stranger of a father Cosima may have felt, it was resolutely dispersed by Carolyne, who embraced and kissed them all, lauded them all, gave them tiny gold watches, and hoped that from now on they would all stay together. The next week, Liszt gave a "family party," to which he invited Wagner, Berlioz, and the journalist Jules Janin. Inescapably, Wagner read from his works. This time it was the text of the last act of *Götterdämmerung.* How bored the young people must have been! What could they make of this ponderous fragment? Cosima did wonder how an opera composer could possess enough skill to write his own librettos, and shortly after, she read Wagner's texts for *Lohengrin* and *Tannhäuser.* Yet at this first meeting neither Cosima nor Blandine made an impression on Wagner; he noted only "their insuperable shyness."

Carolyne's daughter, the charming "Magnolet" (Marie), remembered the occasion:

I was older than the two girls, who were still rather unpolished and looked out at the unfriendly world with timid doe eyes. The elder, Blandine, was prettier, plumper, more pleasing though in no way heaven-storming, and she was already rather pleased with herself. Poor Cosima, however, was in the worst phase of adolescence, tall and angular, sallow, with a wide mouth and long nose, the image of her father. Only her long golden hair, of unusual sheen, was beautiful. In che poor child's heart a volcano raged . . . dark stirrings of love and overweening vanity. . . . Now and then her thin lips would curl with the inborn mockery of the Parisian. . . . After a simple meal . . . Wagner read to us the end of the *Nibelungen.* The children scarcely knew enough German to understand the words. Still, even they were gripped by our emotions. . . . At that time, Wagner had no eyes for the ugly child. . . .[Marie Hohenlohe, *Erinnerungen an Richard Wagner*]

To Cosima, who had been in a fever of anticipation, the visit proved a letdown. She hardly ever saw her father alone, while Liszt dashed about in Parisian society. When the time came for his and Carolyne's departure, nothing had been decided about Cosima's future. She received a few more moralizing speeches—and then he was gone, almost as much a stranger as before. Madame Patersi decreed that Cosima was not to write her father immediately, but was to let a "seemly interval" pass before she thanked him for his visit. Then Cosima wrote so sweetish an epistle—stuffed with such treacle as "the perfect motherly goodness of the Princess," "our gratitude in bearing your name," etc.—that one can be sure it was the governess who dictated it. Liszt's reply was that she must study her music.

Shortly after, the girls were taken to a concert given by Berlioz. There they ran into Marie d'Agoult—was it by design?—who had kept herself apart while Liszt and her successor were in Paris. Marie burst into tears and cried that they must see one another again, she could no longer live without her children, they were all she had left in this world, and would they come next Tuesday? Delightedly, the girls acquiesced: certainly Marie was more fun than Carolyne. Cosima wrote her father about it, partly because he would hear of it anyway from Patersi, and partly as a trial challenge:

[Spring 1854]

Madame Patersi will have told you, my dear father, that our mother was present at Berlioz's concert last Sunday, and that she arranged with us there to fetch us on Tuesday at one o'clock and bring us back at nine. And this has actually taken place. She drove us to her house and first took us up to her study, where she left us alone for a moment, asking us to choose for ourselves something there. Over the bookcase, dear Father, we saw the bronze medallion of you, and your portrait *en face* by Ingres, which was hanging all by itself on one of the walls. Then she came back and asked whether we thought the house pretty. She made minute inquiries about the arrangement of our life, our work, social relations, and habits, and said that she found Daniel extraordinarily charming. In accordance with the wish which she expressed of becoming acquainted with Wagner's works, we took her [the piano scores of] *Lohengrin* and *The Flying Dutchman.* We could not give her *Tannhäuser* yet, as Daniel has it at school. This shall be done another time, and with it we shall take your pamphlet on the two works, in which she displayed great interest. She was extremely charming to us, full of tenderness, love, and motherly care, showing nothing but happiness and joy, without any sort of *arrière-pensée*. We talked a great deal about you, dear Papa, in the way that one can. Among other things she said that if the money she

offers us is in the least displeasing to you, she would say no more
about it, or about the Italian master whom she would like to give us,
because he is a very distinguished man, who would teach us Italian
splendidly, and whom she thinks we would find agreeable. But she
expressly insisted that she would abandon the idea unconditionally if it
did not suit you, and added that the most essential thing to her was to
see us, and that as soon as you had given your consent to this, she did
not wish to complicate matters in any way. Today she is going to see
Daniel, where we are going to join her. . . . [Quoted by Du Moulin
Eckart]

There was not much Liszt could do. Even he realized that Blandine
and Cosima were old enough to choose whom they were going to visit,
even if it *was* their mother. He fumbled and issued a few silly restric-
tions: the girls were always to be called for in a fiacre or private
carriage and she, Marie, was always to call for them herself, was under
no circumstances to send a substitute. "On the days when Mme.
Patersi will bring them to you, it goes without saying, she is not to be
treated as an ordinary governess and made to wait in an anteroom on
the lower floor, but you are to show her every consideration due her
position, her age, and her character. . . ." (Letter to Marie, September
4, 1854)

Marie had of course no intention of obeying such instructions. Her
one purpose was to bring the young people to her side—and away
from that Wittgenstein woman. She still thought Liszt's liaison with
Carolyne one of his transient infatuations and nothing like the true
union of genius and beauty of which she continued to dream.

In furthering her design, she put her wealth to work. Blandine
was of marriageable age and Cosima soon would be. She would give
each 100,000 francs as a dowry—a generous gift, but one Marie could
afford. In reply, Liszt once more mounted the family pulpit. Liszt to
Marie:

November 20, 1854

. . . I hope that my children share my view of life and would never
sacrifice, for a possible pecuniary advantage, one particle of my moral
bequest, which to them should be more precious than all worldly
goods. . . . I have detailed to you in precise numbers what I am able
to provide for their future. Up to now I could afford to pay, with the
interest on the capital I have earmarked for them, their maintenance
and education. . . . If you wish to augment Blandine's and Cosima's
dowry, I can neither prescribe the method to you nor forbid it. It goes
without saying that my daughters would never connect their pleasure
in seeing you again with a thought of personal gain, even if it were to
be a husband. . . . The word "business" which you used in your last

letter is inappropriate, since I cannot regard either your return to the children or their marriage as "business." . . .

He sent this letter through Patersi, instructing her to make Cosima and Blandine read and copy it. For them he added a postscript:

> Be convinced that it was never my intention to use you as a pretext for a quarrel with your mother. If up to now I deemed your separation from her as inevitable, and insisted on it, I was prompted solely by a high concept of my *duty*. I must admit I would have preferred it if this sense of duty had given me less trouble. Now you are to do just one thing: to wait until Mme. d'Agoult repays Mme. Patersi's visit. Under no circumstances are you to call on her prior to this visit.

It is clear that Liszt was not feeling easy about Marie's influence, especially as Cosima continued to report happily that she had been taken to the Louvre and "Mama explained all the pictures to us," or what a good time she'd had at lunch at Marie's house, or that they had gone to hear *The Barber of Seville* and Marie gave her books by a new English author, Dickens, who told such marvelous stories that she raced through them. If Liszt was uneasy, Carolyne was doubly so.

The Vatican proved intransigent; Carolyne's divorce was not granted. Liszt did not mind all that much, but Carolyne was unhappy. All the harder did she try to sever the link to his former love, all the more did she want to become the substitute mother of his children. Patersi could not do the whole task. Proximity to that siren Marie made conversion impossible. That was evident. Carolyne decided that the young people must be removed from Paris. She had no trouble persuading Liszt. But where and under whose care were they to be housed?

4

Liszt had acquired a favorite pupil: Hans von Bülow, nineteen years his junior. Liszt considered him his "legitimate heir by the grace of God and his own talent." That talent had had stony ground to traverse: Bülow's parents had insisted that he become a lawyer and he had fought them unceasingly until his extraordinary endowment proved itself in his youthful piano recitals, strong and brilliant. Then his father gave in, while his mother still protested. Their marriage became increasingly strife-torn. When Hans was still almost a child, his parents divorced and the father remarried. Hans lived in Berlin with his mother, a large-boned woman with tight braids and tight lips. "A hard soul," Du Moulin Eckart called her.

Franziska von Bülow had a ready-made answer to all life's problems and an opinion as inflexible as quartz about any man, woman, or idea within her ken. She knew it all either from the Bible or from the newspaper. She knew what was "proper." Among the things she counted as improper was the new music of Richard Wagner, for which her son displayed so fiery an enthusiasm. Liszt, however, was all right; he was a gentleman. Franziska was responsible for increasing the strain on a son who almost from the beginning was overwrought, tense, dictatorial, carrying with him the tradition of the German Junker. Perhaps Bülow was too brilliant for his own good. An intellectual, impatient with slower minds, never in perfect health and injuring what health he had by frantic work, he would wound his enemies *and* his friends with exquisite sarcasm; even his praise, as Brahms said, "smarted in the eyes like salt." Such natures, when they worship, succumb entirely, and Bülow had succumbed to Wagner's music. For that, and for his talent, Liszt loved him.

Liszt and Carolyne now conceived the plan of transferring the girls to Berlin, to Frau Bülow's care;* there they would be nearer Weimar, and there Cosima could develop her music under Hans's tutelage. Madame Patersi was getting old and feeble; she had better be replaced by a Teutonic counterpart. Frau Bülow could hardly refuse, considering how much Liszt had done for her son, and the move seemed reasonable to Liszt. The truth was that on the one hand he wanted his daughters separated from Marie, and on the other did not want to saddle himself with having them in his own house. To Berlin, then. Very likely he thought—or made himself think—that he was doing his best for his daughters. That he was ordering them to a house in which one inhabitant was a flickering personality, the other a corseted old woman—that he didn't see.

Whatever the pretended reasons, the plan amounted to little short of an abduction. When Cosima and Blandine heard the decision, they wept. Were they once more to be removed from familiar surroundings, did they once more have to face a stranger in a strange city, and were they never going to visit their mother again? Cosima even dared

*Daniel remained in Paris to pursue his studies.

Cosima at eighteen. Drawing by Friedrich Preller

to speak of the "tyrannical demands of her father." And Anna dashed off a long letter to her son, imploring him to reconsider:

September 3, 1853

I can wait no longer, but must write to you, I am so upset since hearing the latest decision about Blandine and Cosima ten days ago. The Princess told me about it with the greatest indifference, that they were to be sent to Berlin under the charge of Madame de Bülow, who is to be with them always and *gouverner* them. I could find nothing to say but that the children were too big to make another change. The Princess replied that otherwise there would never be an end to Madame d'Agoult's scribbling, as she had been very impertinent in her letters to you for some time past. But consider, dear son, to hand these children over to strangers in a strange land, where they do not know a soul, is certainly no indifferent matter for them, and I am afraid that if this happens, one or the other of them will fall ill. It would have been better if the Princess had left Madame Patersi in Poland or in Russia and not entrusted these children to a woman who was, moreover, already in her seventy-second year when they were handed over to her charge. She was already too tired. When I was in Weimar for the first time and saw her portrait, I said to the Princess: "This lady is too old for such an undertaking," but she rejoined at once: *"Ah, elle est encore bien verte"* [She is still full of vigor]; but I was sad for the children, and perhaps you may still remember that I cried a good deal. But when I got to Paris, I saw that I must resign myself, and God gave me the grace to do so. I prepared the children for their new residence and had to say a great deal that went against my feelings—and somehow we managed. They became reconciled to this old lady, who never felt any affection for them, and had been, even before she arrived here, filled with prejudice against their mother by the Princess. . . . The children are good and must be guided by love, for they have proud, sensitive hearts. Madame de Bülow seems to me to be a kindly disposed woman, but to send the children away to Prussia on account of their mother! . . . [Quoted by Du Moulin Eckart]

Their father would not listen, though before Cosima and Blandine were shipped off to the Bülows they were permitted to visit him in Weimar. Liszt was in a depressed mood and the visit was not an unqualified success. The girls tried to cheer him—they had regained some of their gaiety and they were thrilled to be with their father— but he didn't like his routine being interfered with, as it was when they interrupted his evening game of whist and when they woke him at seven in the morning; he spoke, half jestingly, half seriously, of their *"tapageocratie"* (rule by noise).

Marie d'Agoult, who was away from Paris, did not learn of the

Berlin plan until her return. She sat down at once and poured out her anger in three letters to Cosima and Blandine: "One waited until my absence before forcing you to do something which will debase you. . . . You will meet a dishonorable fate, without suspecting it. You will eat the bread of a stranger, a person who is not your father's wife and never will be. It would be better for you to seek work to maintain yourselves or even to go and beg—anything but this last disgrace." She asked Blandine, who was nearing her majority, to refuse point-blank to go to Berlin. "Don't weaken." And if they did go to Berlin, let them behave so obstreperously that whoever was in charge would be glad to get rid of them. "I'll do my part. In Heaven or Hell I belong to you and you to me. Oh, my proud children, remain proud!" (August 15, 1855)

In the haste and excitement of departure, the girls left Marie's letters lying about. Madame Patersi found them, read them—and sent them on to Liszt. He in turn was furious enough to answer the letters point by point, as if he were refuting an ultimatum sent by a hostile government. He sent his answer not to Marie but to his daughters, as if *they* had written their mother's words. To Marie's statement "You will eat the bread of a stranger . . ." he answered:

> From the day of your birth until this very day your mother did not
> worry in the slightest over the bread you ate, the place you lived in,
> etc. Though she enjoys a considerable income, she prefers to spend it
> on her own personal enjoyment. For nineteen years I and I alone
> have exclusively shouldered the task of caring for your needs and
> paying for your education. If a "stranger" were to appear to share this
> responsibility (which is not the case), then in my opinion she would be
> less of a stranger than your mother. . . . The violent outbursts of Mme.
> d'Agoult merely prove that she concocts large phrases in order to
> quiet a bad conscience. . . . I would be much obliged if, with the help
> of illumination supplied by your mother, you would explain to me in
> what way this "person" has ever betrayed you, when she tried to
> suppress you, how she has debased you. . . .

To Marie's "Oh, my proud children, remain proud," Liszt rejoined:

> This is a singularly imprudent apostrophe. . . . If you were only proud,
> you would have to blush at your mother's outbursts and ill feelings.
> Since she wishes me evil at all costs and on all occasions, and since she
> can strike at neither my position nor my conscience, she takes
> pleasure in injuring me in your affection, and in the respect and deep
> love that I hold, as the purest flame in my life, for a woman who
> ought also to be *sacred* to you on account of the devotion she has so

nobly shown me in the afflictions, sacrifices and incessantly renewed griefs of the past nine years.

After all the outbursts, Liszt's will prevailed. How could it not? He was "father." And it was the nineteenth century. Blandine and Cosima, who was not quite eighteen years old, were transplanted from soft Paris to dusty Berlin.

The change betokened a condition of which Cosima was by this time well aware. She was shunted from strange pillar to strange post. She could be neither with her father nor with her mother. She did not belong, not anywhere. To protect herself, she buckled tighter her armor of self-reliance.

CHAPTER II

The Uneasy Bridegroom

MUSIC, "MOODY FOOD of us that trade in love," served Bülow sometimes as food for trading in hostility. He loved music so intensely, it produced in him so hot a fever, that he could not condone audiences who took it casually. As pianist and conductor, he spent every particle of the force that was in him at every single concert and he demanded that his hearers spend *their* force in understanding whatever he was putting before them. *"Je travaille comme un nègre,"* he said, and expected everybody to work with him. If the communion did not satisfy him, he showed his contempt. Amy Fay, Liszt's American pupil, wrote: "His face seemed to say to his audiences, 'You're all cats and dogs and I don't care what you think of my playing.'" He would lecture his listeners condescendingly, or worse still, he would walk out in the middle of a concert. At one of his recitals he happened to espy in the front row a pianist he detested, Ferdinand Hiller. Bülow would not continue until the ingenious manager changed the position of the piano to block out the view of Hiller.*

Bülow called his concerts "Assassination Concerts." He introduced Beethoven's last five piano sonatas—then considered impossibly difficult—to the major cities of Europe, and later, in 1889, he gave a series

*Cosima recollected the incident in her diary. Hiller was a Jew and Bülow was almost as anti-Semitic as Wagner.

24

of recitals in New York, playing twenty-two of the sonatas. A Bülow program: Beethoven's Ninth Symphony; then intermission; then the Ninth Symphony repeated in its entirety, a procedure which the critic Hanslick called "baptizing the Infidels with a fire hose." When he became conductor of the Meiningen orchestra—his last regular employment—he made the musicians play from memory, his own memory being nothing short of fantastic.

This sharp little man with his sharp little beard, who could have impersonated Don Quixote—when he conducted he seemed to be fighting windmills—was avid for recognition, yet made a point of ridiculing honors and seemed to enjoy making enemies. "My unpopularity is unbounded," he wrote, and he refused a laurel wreath, saying, "I am not a vegetarian." An uncomfortable man—yet he exerted a tremendous influence on the interpretation of music, and everybody knew it.

Why was his great ability polluted by drops of acid? It is probable that he was incapable of simple and direct feeling, incapable of letting himself go, incapable of the warm naïveté which is so important an ingredient of music making. He substituted for this lack an excessive enthusiasm companioned by an excessive disdain. In Munich, he wanted the orchestra pit enlarged; when it was pointed out to him that this would cause the loss of some valuable front-row seats, he replied, "Then we'll have a few fewer *Schweinehunde* in the theater," a term of opprobrium (equivalent to "bastards") for which the journalists nearly hounded him out of town. It is certain he suffered from a deep discontent, knowing that he was a "mere" interpreter and that he was not, nor in all likelihood could ever become, a strong creative artist. He seemed an oak; he was an ivy, drawing nourishment from Berlioz, Liszt, Wagner, and in his last years from Brahms.

Bülow's relationship to Liszt was more than that of pupil to teacher: it was that of the acolyte to the priest, son to father. Now Liszt's daughters were with him, envoys of his demigod. Blandine left him indifferent: she was too independent and perhaps too pretty. He could feel more "protective" toward the younger sister, seven years younger than he. Living in the same house, though closely watched by the watery eyes of his mother, and seeing her every day, he began to be attracted by Cosima.

He mislaid his cooler judgment when, only a fortnight after he began to give Cosima lessons, he wrote to Liszt that both Cosima and Blandine, but "especially the younger one," had "reduced him to stupefaction and admiration." "They possess not only talent—but genius." Genius? That hyperbole hardly convinced Liszt, who replied: "Do not pass over any superficiality or slovenly playing." Bülow was to instruct them in their father's music: "Turn them into splendid propagandists for the Music of the Future."

Propinquity helped to move Cosima and Hans together, the approach hastened by their needs, which were similar: he needed softness and warmth, she needed the assurance of belonging somewhere and to someone. They had gifts to give each other: she opened for him the pages of Musset, Victor Hugo, and George Sand; he sounded for her the tones of German Romanticism, of Weber and Schubert, and he deepened her understanding of the Wagner of *The Flying Dutchman, Tannhäuser,* and *Lohengrin,* music she had already known. From day to day, Cosima's admiration grew for this man who treated music—including the debated "Music of the Future"—with the zeal of an evangelist. Yet her admiration sprang from her mind more than from her heart.

On October 19, 1855—some six weeks after the girls had taken up residence in Bülow's home—he conducted a conventional enough program, except that he chose for its last number the Overture and Venusberg music of *Tannhäuser.* The music was not all that new: Weimar and Dresden had heard the entire opera without ill effects and Wagner had conducted the Overture in Zurich in 1852, a performance which Mathilde Wesendonck in her old age remembered as "a revelation." Yet on that October night it seemed an evil potion to the Berliners: they hissed, whistled, stamped, and booed.

Bülow felt the insult the more keenly because Liszt had come from Weimar to attend the concert. Frustrated and exhausted, he fainted in the greenroom afterward. Liszt remained with him, while the two girls returned home with Bülow's mother. At 2 A.M. Liszt took Bülow home, leaving him at the door; everybody had gone to bed, everybody except Cosima, who had stayed up to say a word of comfort. They were alone. They talked. He told her that she had become a necessity to him; he no longer knew what to do without her. Cosima replied, "Then I will remain."

This betrothal, stammered at dawn after a turbulent night, was too insecure to be called love. Cosima, not yet eighteen and only half awakened, was prompted by pity; Hans loved her not wholly for herself but because she was her father's daughter.

He was not at all sure that he could make a satisfactory husband. Because of his self-doubt, it was not until April 20, 1856, six months later, that he formally asked her father for his daughter's hand.

Bülow to Liszt:

Berlin, April 20, 1856

Be so kind as to accept this, my confession, without a doubting smile. Believe me, it is only due to my inborn shyness and maladroitness, which has often got in my way, that I did not speak to you sooner of my love.

I feel for her more than love. The thought of moving nearer to you encloses all my dream of whatever happiness may be vouchsafed to me on this earth, you whom I regard as the principal architect and shaper of my present and future life. For me Cosima is greater than all women, not only because she bears your name but because she resembles you so closely, being in many of her characteristics a true mirror of your personality. . . . I swear to you that, however bound to her I feel myself through my love, I will never hesitate to sacrifice myself to her happiness by setting her free, were she ever to feel disappointed in me. I will regard her every wish, even her caprice, as sacred. . . .

Liszt did not hide his doubts: he was afraid, he said, of Bülow's sickly moods, his neurasthenia, his headaches. Besides, he had hoped that Cosima would marry into the nobility. (It must be said, however, that he was quite content when the following year Blandine married a handsome and dashing French advocate, Emile Ollivier, who later held an important post in the French government.)

Liszt might have opposed the marriage indefinitely had not the better side of his nature perceived how much Hans's desire for it was growing—and had not Marie d'Agoult opposed it: "Cosima, child of genius, is very like her father. . . . Circumstances have pushed her into a marriage in which, I think, there will be happiness for no one." She sensed that Cosima was not really in love with Hans; she also sensed that both Cosima and Blandine would venture much to have homes of their own and that Cosima wanted to free herself from the domination of Bülow's mother, whom she considered stupid. (She *was* stupid.) Marie wanted Cosima to become a professional pianist. Liszt thought "God forbid!" and Marie's disapproval was enough to tip the scales.

After interposing a considerable number of ifs and buts, Liszt finally consented. (In announcing the date of the wedding to Princess Carolyne, Liszt wrote, "If this is agreeable to you!") They were married in Berlin on August 18, 1857, in a Protestant church, though Cosima was a Catholic. Liszt was present at the ceremony, Marie d'Agoult was not.

A strange honeymoon followed.

They did not set out alone; Liszt accompanied the bridal couple to Weimar, their first stop. From there bride and groom went to Baden-Baden to visit Richard Pohl, a poet and a friend of Bülow's and Wagner's; they then proceeded to Lake Leman and Geneva, in company with young Karl Ritter. Karl and Bülow had gone to school together and Karl was overjoyed to be permitted to belong, however tangentially, to the Liszt-Bülow-Wagner circle. He had just married, and his bride did not look with unalloyed pleasure on Cosima and Hans descending on her, but there was not much she could do about it. Willingly or not, she fell in with the plan: they were all going to visit Wagner in Zurich.

Wagner lived on the "Green Hill" on the property of Otto Wesendonck, who had assigned a comfortable home to him, virtually as a gift. In gratitude, Wagner called the house the Asyl—the "Refuge." His wife, Minna, had joined him there. This did not prevent Wagner from falling in love with his host's wife, a passion that draped sexual attraction in a mantle of abstruse philosophy. The leavening of genius was strong within him: he had just finished sketching most of the second act of *Siegfried.* At the moment, he badly needed somebody who would listen and understand. Neither Minna—who was unsympathetic to that "impossible" mastodon of a *Ring*—nor Mathilde Wesendonck, who with all her admiration and intelligence was musically ignorant, could fill the bill. But Bülow—he would understand, he could read and "hear" this music merely by looking at the sketches, and he would help the composer comprehend his own achievement. Even before Wagner had settled in the Asyl, he pleaded that Bülow come.

Wagner to Bülow:

April 1, 1857

Dear Johannes:
If you can make yourself free for my sake, try to figure out how you can manage to visit me this summer. If Cosima came along, that would be capital. I am moving into a little house, beautifully situated and neatly furnished, open and as quiet as I could wish, with a big, pretty garden. I owe this benison to the sympathy of the family Wesendonck: they bought the house solely for my lifelong use, just for a tiny rent. There will I write the remaining two acts of *Siegfried.* If you come, I promise you a paradise during your whole stay. I want to make music with you. You have to play my new compositions: otherwise they remain strangers to me. . . . The first act of *Siegfried* turned out well (already orchestrated), better than anything I have done so far. . . . Come soon and we'll play it. . . .

On the way to Zurich, Bülow, with the typical absentmindedness of the artist, lost the trunk in which he had put all his money. Cosima was shocked: could they appear "as beggars" before the Wagners and the Wesendoncks? "Let us return to Berlin." Fortunately, after telegrams hither and yon, the trunk was found—with the money intact. The young couple presently moved to the Asyl, there to be with Wagner morning, noon, and evening, while the Ritters stayed in Zurich and came over for frequent visits. Bülow played the *Siegfried* excerpts, and played them as securely as if they were beginner's exercises— Wagner could hardly believe it—while, bent over the keyboard, he kept exclaiming, "colossal," "unique," "fit for the next century," "redemption from the world's filth." Cosima and Mathilde listened, Minna bustled about the house, serving champagne to the composer and Swiss beer to Bülow; Cosima kept silent, looking at the jumpy little man who usurped all attention, demanding to know in detail what each and every one thought about each word and note. Asked point-blank, Cosima mumbled, with the restraint that emotion had laid upon her, that her German was not adequate to express herself.

Wagner, with his passion for reading his texts aloud—he read with an actor's skill—now treated them to a recital of *Tristan and Isolde,* the manuscript of which he had given to Mathilde. Bülow borrowed the poem and copied it. Cosima took the copy; alone in her room, she read and reread it, late into the night. She said nothing either to her husband or to Wagner, but Wagner noticed that she seemed "strangely troubled" and that she treated him "rather distantly," while he treated her banteringly, as if she were a childhood friend.

During the remaining weeks of their sojourn at the Asyl, Cosima would sometimes appear with a tearstained face, only to break into overbright laughter; she would recite French doggerel, run through the fields and woods, play the piano very loud. In the evenings she watched Wagner playing whist with whatever visitors could be pressed into the game, or listened to him discoursing, often opaquely, sometimes with lucid sense, on diverse subjects—reforms of the theater, the essence of the German character, Beethoven's Ninth, the decadence of Paris, the poison injected by the Jews into the body politic—while all the time Bülow sat and squinted at the scores as if he were about to shoot arrows at the black dots. Cosima looked at the man who had created these new sounds. She still remained silent. Wagner wondered about her. He wrote to Bülow after the couple had left that "Cosima's reserve toward me really disturbs me. . . . If my manner had been too odd, if an occasional abrupt remark or a little joke offended her . . . I regret that in my trustfulness I let myself go too much. My unthinking confidence in those whom I find sympathetic has more than once led to an estrangement before now; may that of your dear young wife be of short duration." The dear young wife and her husband returned to Berlin on September 28, having spent some three weeks at the Asyl. They carried with them the copy of the *Tristan* poem. "It was far from the usual honeymoon," wrote Bülow to a friend, "but my wife is not jealous."

2

In Berlin, Bülow plunged into work, giving recitals, conducting, organizing musical activities, a serious merry-go-round which confined him in a circle in which he felt happy, or as happy as he ever managed to be. He was now the panjandrum of Berlin's musical life, and Cosima easily assumed the role of hostess and wife of a famous conductor. Franziska Bülow was exiled to an apartment of her own, which her son rarely visited. The home of Hans and Cosima became a meeting place of celebrities, among them the astronomer Giovanni Schiaparelli, discoverer of the supposed "canals" on Mars; the German revolutionary poet Georg Herwegh, whose *Gedichte eines Lebendigen* strengthened, though only briefly, Germany's liberal movement; the urbane Ferdinand Lassalle, disciple of Marx and founder of the German labor party, for whose personality Bülow conceived a great liking, despite Lassalle's being a Jew, and anti-Prussian to boot. Cosima detested him, hardly managed to be civil to him, and refused to accept his dinner invitations. She suspected that he was taking drugs—hashish—and thought he might induce Bülow to do likewise. The Berlin friend for whom Cosima felt the keenest admiration was Karl August Varnhagen, at the end of his life, but also at the height of his fame as diplomat and writer; his wife was the brilliant Rahel Levin, who in her youth had been Beethoven's friend. Varnhagen guided Cosima toward what was best in German literature and she began to translate German works into French for the *Revue Germanique.* Her translations were published anonymously; they were reasonably good.

What she wanted above all was to help turn her husband into a creative artist. By this time she knew that she was never going to become a great writer or excel as a musician. Her role, she felt, was that of co-worker. She would inspire, spur on, prompt, encourage. Even at a distance, she longed to take part in the shaping of a work of art. She jibbed at seeing Bülow spend his energy on the interpretation of other men's music, an effort which turns to a mere memory as soon as the last note has sounded. He had composed several minor works; would he have the stamina to write an opera? He was enthusiastic about the figure of Merlin, the magician of King Arthur's court, and had asked two of his literary friends to write a treatment of the story. Both attempts dissatisfied him. Now Cosima, working in secret and with great concentration, sketched a Merlin scenario, and on Christmas Day he found the manuscript, gaily wrapped, on his desk. Bülow was overcome with joy: he would set to work at once and by the spring, he promised, he would have finished the first act. Nothing came of it, as nothing came of an even more ambitious project, a treatment of the *Oresteia.* Bülow later destroyed whatever he had composed of *Merlin,* and Cosima destroyed her libretto. The *Oresteia* sketch is extant; not a note of it was composed.

It was a foregone conclusion that the climax of their second holiday, in 1858, was to be a second visit to Wagner. Like many second visits, it proved less lucky. When they arrived in late July, the Asyl was occupied by not one but *two* tenors. Wagner had invited Joseph Tichatschek, his first Tannhäuser, who unexpectedly was closely followed by the young Albert Niemann, whom the composer was considering for Tristan. Two tenors in the house: the result was that *both* refused to sing. Presently they cleared out and Cosima and Hans moved in. But on that very day they were unwilling witnesses to a scene between Wagner and Minna that astonished and shocked them. They did not then know what had preceded it.

Wagner, in the outpouring of the *Tristan* music, his whole being in a trancelike state, as if he himself had swallowed the magic potion, saw in Mathilde Wesendonck a symbol of his Isolde. She was there; to her he addressed his apostrophe, which was in truth an apostrophe to love itself. He intended to send Mathilde, at dawn on April 7, 1858, the pencil sketch of the Prelude to the first act—that tone poem which Thomas Mann has called "music beyond music"—along with an eight-page letter, which ends: "Today I will go into the garden. As soon as I see you I hope to snatch a moment alone with you! Take all my soul as a morning greeting!"

As it turned out, Minna intercepted the servant with the packet, took it, opened it, and read the letter. Read calmly, it would have been obvious that it was not much of a love letter, but rather a statement of Tristanesque resignation and abdication.* Yet Minna, suffering from heart disease, conscious of losing her beauty, conscious that her husband was turning away from her, interpreted the letter as a jealous wife would. She stormed at him in the traditional language of outraged probity, shouting that she would revenge herself on that "vile woman" and that Richard was driving her to a premature death. Wagner tried to calm her; she became the more furious and she now poured over him all the bitterness of her disappointed life, the impossibility of establishing a decent home with so wayward a husband, the insanity of writing stuff like *Tristan* instead of operas people could enjoy.

She was calmer the next day,† and it was decided that she should go for a cure to Brestenberg, a clinic recommended for heart disease. Before she left, she called on Mathilde, "warning her," as she expressed it, "against the consequences of any imprudent intimacy" with her husband, and showed her Wagner's letter. Mathilde at once told Otto all. She wasn't going to have her comfortable marriage ruined, much though she prided herself on being Wagner's "inspiration" and great though her satisfaction was that he set to music the texts of several songs she had written, the "Wesendonck Songs."

Otto and Mathilde decided that one needs to be tolerant with an artist and that they saw no reason why the Wagners should not continue to occupy the Asyl, even if Mathilde at first declared that it would be impossible for her ever to enter there. Yet however broad-minded the Wesendoncks may have been (or anxious not to lose their captive celebrity), and whatever love Mathilde may have been capable of, they could not help feeling some constraint, which reflected on the man who again removed himself from the world of day to enter the night world of his second act. Minna was away, he could compose undisturbed, and his old affection for his wife welled up. In his letters he urged her not to worry, to think of nothing but her health, to give up opium, and to rejoin him as soon as she felt better. All would be well.

*In the same spirit, Wagner wrote Mathilde on July 6: "The terrible conflicts we fought—how could they end other than in a victory over all longing and desire?" Yet it was not to be expected that Minna could see anything but the ordinary triangle in this. She didn't mind that so much, she said: "Men so often have an affair"; she minded "the mortification." She could hardly understand that Mathilde was necessary to Wagner as long as he was working on *Tristan* and that by July, or shortly after, Wagner would be inwardly beginning to separate himself from her.

†She was taking opium for her heart condition. That may have accounted for the extreme variability of her moods.

All might have been well had Minna been sensible. On July 15, Wagner brought her back from the clinic. A floral arch of welcome had been constructed over the door of the Asyl. Minna was delighted: she saw in it a sign that she was returning in triumph "over her rival," and she insisted that the arch stay up for some days. Mathilde objected to the arch—she was not quite the "angel" Wagner described her as being. Surely a woman of finer grain than Mathilde would not have made a fuss over so childish a gesture, hitting out against a woman over whom she had the advantage of looks, health, age, and wealth. Minna on her side took up the jealous litany again, accusing "my ludicrously vain husband" of behaving shabbily. It was into the midst of this situation that Cosima and Hans walked six days after Minna's return, and both Mathilde and Minna took Cosima aside and poured out their grievances. Now Wagner realized that he could not remain much longer in the Asyl.

Probably he no longer wanted to remain. All of *Tristan* had been composed, if not on paper then in his mind. For the detailed fastening of his ideas, for the exact shaping of the vocal lines and the orchestration, he needed to separate himself from both Minna and Mathilde. Yet for the moment he had to remain where he was, because not only the Bülows but other visitors crowded in: Marie d'Agoult, the pianist Karl Klindworth, the Munich conductor Franz Lachner, and Karl Tausig, a small, very young, cigar-puffing, superb pianist, who imitated Liszt, and at whose bragging Wagner smiled but whom he liked all the same. They stayed in Zurich and came over to the Asyl to keep Wagner company, entertaining one another with enthusiastic renditions of excerpts from *Rheingold* and *Walküre.* All the same, Bülow said, the atmosphere held "the sultriness before the thunderstorm." Cosima was fearful: when would the next tirade break out? Would she have to witness new excoriation? Before their departure, less than a month after they arrived, they went with Wagner to the Wesendonck house, where he bade farewell to Mathilde. Bülow was "bathed in tears, Cosima morose, silent."

In afteryears, Cosima was sure that at that time she was already in love with Wagner. That may have been the kind of fictional recollection that one constructs to shape the story of one's life. It is certain that she observed Wagner's suffering and that she pitied him. The poem of *Tristan* sounded in her mind, with its tones of love's frustration. How eloquently this man, who paid so little attention to her, expressed her own thoughts!

3

While the Bülows were staying with Wagner, they had gone to Zurich to welcome Cosima's mother. Marie came from Paris because she wanted to meet her son-in-law and he wanted to know her. He wrote: "She made an unexpectedly great impression on me. Still marvelously beautiful, aristocratic in features and bearing, white-haired . . . she possesses dignity and nobility without severity—a fine and elegant *laisser-aller. . . .*" He added: "I must not let myself think of that other one [comparing her to Carolyne] lest I break out in a rage at the parodistic caricature which now acts as shadow to his [Liszt's] light." (Letter to Richard Pohl, July 24, 1858) Bülow then returned to the Asyl while Cosima and Marie went on to Geneva to see Blandine. There they ran into Karl Ritter.

Cosima was attracted to this handsome and intellectual pupil of her husband's. She also realized that he was a deeply disturbed man. He told her that his marriage was a dismal failure,* and she must have confessed to him her own unhappiness in a union with a man whom she could respect but never love, a being stunted and self-deprecatory who told her that "having Wagner as a neighbor dwarfed him into impotence." Yes, she was as miserable as he. She no longer wanted to live. The wild streak in her broke through in Karl's presence, as another's unhappiness often pushes one's own unhappiness to the surface. They took a little boat and went rowing on the lake. Suddenly Cosima begged him to push her overboard and drown her. Karl said he would do what she asked only if he himself could follow her. No— that was too horrible! So grim a pact she would not accept. Clinging to each other and weeping, they both determined to postpone the mortal decision for three weeks. They would then examine their minds once more and act accordingly. The danger, however seriously they meant it at the moment, passed; after three weeks Cosima wrote Karl that she deplored her impulsiveness, felt ashamed, thanked him for his sympathy, and urged him to keep the incident secret. He didn't; he told Wagner.

Cosima returned to the Asyl. Their time was up; Bülow had to return to Berlin. At the hour of farewell, indeed almost at the last moment, Cosima bent down, took Wagner's hand, and covered it with

---

*Karl had experienced two homosexual affairs and thought that marriage would change him.

tears and kisses. He looked up, astonished. The sudden demonstrative-
ness of this reserved young girl made such an impression on him that
he mentioned the incident later in the diary he was writing for Mathilde Wesendonck.

It had been decided that Wagner would go to Venice to work,
sharing the expense with Karl Ritter (Karl of course paid practically
all of it), while Minna would remain at the Asyl as long as necessary,
supervising the moving and the sale of a few personal effects, then go
to Dresden to entrust herself to Dr. Pusinelli, her staunch friend. On
August 17, Minna and Richard rose at dawn. She made him some tea
and accompanied him calmly to the station to take the five o'clock
train to Venice. They walked up and down, watching a bright and
beautiful sunrise, and suddenly Minna burst into tears. "Look at me,
Richard," she implored. He would not.

Minna left the Asyl on September 2. She could not help launching
a parting shot. "Honored Lady," she wrote Mathilde. "Before my
departure, I have to tell you with a bleeding heart that you have
succeeded in separating my husband from me, after almost twenty-
two years of marriage. May this noble deed contribute to your satisfaction and happiness!"

However one wishes to interpret Wagner's involvement with Mathilde, whether the elements that fed the fire were spiritual or physical
—or, as seems probable, a mixture of both—it had been evident to that
little band of friends that a flame was burning on the Green Hill. Later,
in anger and embarrassment, Wagner denied it, even to himself, but
at the time it did blaze high and bright—and Cosima saw it. In fact,
she saw it long after it had been extinguished. It was a disturbing
memory, which she could not help summoning time and again, though
time and again it gave her pain. Not only did Cosima and Wagner
speak of it often, not only did Wagner, dictating his autobiography to
Cosima, gloss over the affair with half-truths for her assuagement, but
Cosima herself could not let the subject lie, dragging it from the
recesses of the past to discuss with her favorite daughter, Eva. It was
not usual for Cosima to refer to her lover's former loves; Mathilde,
however, remained a pang that would not leave her mind. She was
adroit enough to keep silent most of the time, only observing when she
saw Mathilde after an interval of four years that the lady had changed
from a blonde to a brunette. Many years later—Wagner was already
dead—Eva wrote down what Cosima had told her. Here are some
excerpts from that manuscript; it is Cosima speaking:

In August 1858, when Bülow and I were in Zurich, all relations between your father and Mathilde had been broken off. [Not true] He wrote in his diary: "She has betrayed me to her husband. Deception, most lofty, yet most painful." They returned their letters to each other, at the wish of Frau W., and she handed over all manuscripts to him. [Not true]

I called on Frau W. to seek clarification. While I was there your father entered by surprise. I got up to leave, he exclaimed, "Stay," and that is how I learned something of the contents of that letter. When he left, Frau W. would not shake hands with him. . . . Soon thereafter we [Cosima and Bülow] left, in despair that he would have to relinquish the Refuge. After having tried several times to change Frau W.'s mind, your father said to Minna: "Pack, Minna, that one is jealous." . . .

Over the course of years your father told me: "The need was so terribly great." "She was very lovely." "She helped me nicely in my work with daily attentions." "It was a relation incapable of being tested by trial."

When the time came for [the premier of] *Tristan* and nobody let her know about it, I took it upon myself to write to her and to invite her. She answered that she would come only on an invitation from the Meister himself. Since he obviously had no such intention, she derived some sort of consolation, however sparse, from leaving things as they were. Or so she said. I showed her answer to your father, whereupon he wrote her a short note.* Nothing else was communicated to her. Not even our wedding, later. . . .

The estrangement grew deeper, and when she heard the *Ring* here [in Bayreuth] in 1876, she said to me merely: "Ah well, Kriemhilde is now called Gutrune."

When Frau W. visited me in Munich in 1868, she asked me whether I could stand all that music. She added: "Don't you think life becomes more interesting all the time? One has plenty of compensation for a loss." I knew that she was trying to tell me that she had got over the affair.

As for her and *Tristan*—when he conceived the idea their relation was merely a charming and pleasant one. When he had finished the poem (by which time the principal musical themes existed), the relation rose to a visionary exaltation. *"Träume"* and *"Im Treibhaus"* [poems by Mathilde] were merely "illustrated"—as your father expressed it—by existing themes from *Tristan.* It is not true that the second act is inspired by *"Träume."* When it came to the publication of the five songs, compelled by necessity, your father said in a jocular tone that Mathilde W. could not quite hide her gratification at coming before the public in partnership with himself. Later he wrote to me in bitter words: "She let go what ought to have been her holiest possession. Those songs have now become valueless to me. I give them as a gift to sopranos who have lost their voice."

*The note: "Friend! Tristan is going to be wonderful. Will you come?? Your R.W. Premier May 15."

From these jottings, true and false, only one certainty emerges: to the end of her life, the one woman of whom Cosima was jealous was Mathilde Wesendonck.

4

Now Cosima was in her twenties, and it was as if Fate wished to apologize to her for a feeble marriage by bestowing on her the gift of greater beauty. The sharp features of her morning face modulated into softness, making her eyes appear an intenser blue, in vivid contrast with her tawny complexion. Though her parentage was French and Hungarian, she looked Italian, resembling one of those worldly Madonnas by Correggio. Her blond hair glistened. Bülow stood in awe of her, as he confessed in a letter to his mother: in his marital relationship he "still felt as embarrassed as when he was a bridegroom."

Between Cosima and her all-too-respectful husband stood the image of Wagner. How could she forget the scenes at the Asyl? How could she forget the fullness of that music, brought to life by a single piano? What would it sound like when the orchestra played it? Wagner's genius had become a living presence to her, even if Wagner as a man still remained a figure removed. She did not dare to think of him as other than a friend—a friend of both hers and her husband's—however often she did think of him. She was still the loyal wife, the adroit hostess, a level-headed business representative, and an untiring traveling companion. In 1859, Bülow gave concerts in Prague, then in Paris, and the enthusiasm of the French audience compensated him for the lack of it in "those beer-soaked Berliners." Marie d'Agoult entertained them, gathering a coterie of "names" at Friday night dinners composed by a chef good enough to have been previously employed by the Rothschilds. Baudelaire was a guest. His *Les Fleurs du Mal* had been published two years previously and condemned as obscene, but the author was welcome, more perhaps as the translator of Poe than as a poet in his own right. Cosima was to recall his poems later, when she heard that Baudelaire tried to express in verse the "color" of the *Lohengrin* Prelude.

The author of another scandalous book, *Madame Bovary,* though something of a recluse, also came to greet the illustrious conductor and stayed to confide to Cosima his exhausting search for the right word.

They met Turgenev and his beloved Pauline Viardot, and Cosima succumbed to Pauline's charm, as who did not? They attended a brand-new opera, Gounod's *Faust,* which they hated, and were entertained by Berlioz, whose music Bülow had championed. Berlioz was fifty-six, not in good health, and struggling vainly to have his great work, *Les Troyens,* accepted by the Paris Opéra. Cosima and Bülow saw him frequently and liked him, although he was unenthusiastic about Wagner.

Drawn into the circle of fine minds, sprinkled by the silver dust of Parisian conversation, they spent weeks during which they felt closer together, or at least weeks during which Cosima was too busy to notice emptiness. She was happy in the ambience of her childhood—better in review than it had been in reality—happy to speak French again, happy with her mother and her grandmother. Madame Patersi was still alive, but it is doubtful that Cosima visited her often.

After Paris, the Bülows returned to Berlin, and Hans devoted endless hours to fashioning the piano score of *Tristan.* "As soon as I'm finished, I'll try composing again," he wrote his mother. He didn't, not seriously. Then, in August, Cosima's brother, Daniel, came to stay with them. He had been studying jurisprudence in Vienna, had shown great talent and won several academic prizes. As a boy he had been as handsome as his father—he resembled Ingres's drawing of the young Liszt—but when Cosima saw him now she was heartsick: he was evidently ill, emaciated, and plagued by a dry, wispy cough. Soon he took to his bed. The diagnosis was obvious: consumption. Almost certainly it was a death sentence. The Bülows nursed him for the next three months, Hans spending much of what little free time he had at the invalid's bedside. Daniel lay still, hardly saying a word, but he read incessantly—*Gerusalemme Liberata, Don Quixote, Faust*—as if he didn't want to die without first harvesting as much as he could of other men's thoughts. Sometimes he wrote his father in a thin penciled scrawl, but he didn't ask Liszt to come to see him. It was Cosima he wanted, every waking moment.

Liszt did not come until the terminal days, and even then it was Carolyne who had urged him. He wrote to Carolyne on December 12, 1850: "You were right, my dear, to send me here. The doctor holds out no hope for him." The next night, at midnight, he suddenly got up and went into Daniel's room. Cosima was there, kneeling; Daniel was dead. Cosima performed the death services. She washed his body, wrapped him in a shroud and placed in his coffin a picture of Pascal, of whom they had been speaking at the last. Only Liszt, Cosima, and

Hans accompanied the coffin to the cemetery. Bülow wrote: "A sad visitor has arrived. Death. He came not in his Christian misshapen form, but as a Greek youth carrying a burnt-out torch." Cosima wrote: "Sometimes I feel my heart will burst . . . then I think that he did not love life . . . that he came only to touch it lightly. . . ."

She had to find consolation somehow; she knew that she was facing a new chapter in her own life: she was pregnant. On October 12, 1860, she gave birth to a daughter, whom she christened Daniela Senta, partly in memory of her brother, partly as a Wagnerian allusion. Why Senta? Was the intention autobiographical, likening the perturbed creature of the legend of the Flying Dutchman to herself?

Neither father nor grandfather greeted the baby with the joy with which a firstborn is normally welcomed. Liszt was in a bitter mood, his career at Weimar having met serious obstacles and his marriage to Carolyne still an uncertainty—she herself was in Rome, asking the Pope to sanction her divorce, and Liszt had a premonition that the plea was never to be granted. He was feeling old, conscious that he, the peerless Romantic hero, was now a grandfather. Nor could Bülow accept the role of father with unembarrassed ease; he wrote to Joachim Raff: "I appear to myself a little ridiculous. . . . Robert Schumann used to go to bed during a similar event, one which was not infrequent in his house, or used to storm through all the rooms howling and complaining. Well, I didn't go as far as that, but I did feel a little like a criminal. Even my piano stool seemed to have turned topsy-turvy. At the moment the piano is silent, giving way to the 'chant' [of the baby]."

Cosima was unable to nurse Daniela and that grieved her. She lost weight, looked listless, and the doctor suspected her brother's history might be repeating itself. Rest and fresh mountain air—those were the only treatments known. She was promptly packed off to Reichenhall, a famous spa in the Bavarian Alps, while her husband went to Paris to assist Wagner with the production of *Tannhäuser* in March. "I cannot abandon Wagner at this most critical moment," he wrote. "It is a question of a *coup d'état,* musically and dramatically."

The *coup* turned out to be a colossal failure, the famous scandal of the Jockey Club. The young aristocrats who were members of this club had been angered by Napoleon III's insistence that the work "by a German" be performed. They were further infuriated by being denied their wish to have the ballet in the second act. To *begin* an opera with a ballet, when they could hardly manage to arrive at curtain time, was nothing short of preposterous. So they organized a demonstration.

Armed with whistles, flageolets, and other noisemakers, they constantly interrupted the music, and the caterwauling and rowdiness got worse at each of the three performances, after which the opera was withdrawn. Baudelaire wrote: "What will Europe think of us? . . . A handful of boors maligned us all."

Wagner, with that unquenchable confidence in himself, recovered, and having at last received a political pardon, he was able to return to Germany. But first he went to Vienna to hear his *Lohengrin* for the first time in his life. Then he visited Liszt in Weimar. Liszt, immersed in his own troubles, had proved less than helpful to Wagner, refusing to come to Zurich at the time of the Asyl breakup, and the temperature of their friendship was cool just then, partly lowered by Carolyne's jealousy of Wagner's fame. Wagner thought it prudent to stoke the embers of old affection. While at Weimar, he met Blandine and her husband, Ollivier, and Blandine proposed that they all go and visit Cosima in Reichenhall.* Since Wagner had to return to Vienna, he readily fell in with the idea; he was delighted to be able to spend a few days—of course as Ollivier's guest—in that beautiful spot which lay directly on his way, and delighted to see again the young woman who had bidden him so strange a farewell in Zurich. They found Cosima not only recovered but positively blooming. She and Wagner went for walks, Cosima running ahead over the green and yellow fields and stretching her arms toward the sky. They laughed together and ate berries heaped with mountain cream. Wagner called her "that wild child," but Blandine saw in her new behavior the *"timidité d'un sauvage."* When Wagner took his leave, he met her "shyly questioning gaze."

5

Like the Dutchman of his opera, Wagner was now condemned to move from place to place, always a step ahead of pursuing creditors, from Vienna to Paris to Venice, back to Paris, to Mainz, to Karlsruhe, then to settle at Biebrich, a small village on the Rhine, where he hoped to finish his new work, *Die Meistersinger.* He was forty-nine, he had little prospect of seeing his *Tristan* produced, less prospect of solving his marital problem, and no prospect at all of crawling from under

*Robert Gutman, in his provocative book *Richard Wagner,* says that Wagner had an affair with Blandine. Evidence for this seems lacking.

his debts. Minna had come to Biebrich at the end of February 1862 in an attempt to reestablish a household, but the very next day she could not repress her recriminations, Mathilde Wesendonck still the subject of her fury. After ten days—days that Wagner described as "ten days of hell"—she departed. The attempted reconciliation had failed.

Soon after, on a brief journey to Frankfurt, Wagner met Friederike Meyer, a pretty and apparently talented actress whom he had little difficulty in persuading to relieve his loneliness. Three women were now playing a part in his troubled life: Minna as Ortrud; Friederike as Venus, though as a worldly Venus; and far away, her image fading, Mathilde as Isolde. The cast was insufficient: as usual he needed intellectual companionship, as usual he needed a sympathetic audience, and as soon as he had sketched out the Preludes to Acts I and III, he begged the Bülows to come and bear witness to what he called "my most successful masterpiece." They came, he read, he played, they were overwhelmed. After the death-dedication of *Tristan,* this creation of a smiling world of centuries ago, this comedy filled with lilacs . . . Cosima especially was exalted by it. She loved the ardent young knight, but she loved Hans Sachs—a portrait of Wagner as he saw himself—more, transferring her mounting feeling for the author to his fictional creation; there she could worship with impunity. Hans Sachs, the poet who believes in the new in art, Hans Sachs, the philosopher who regards the world and its vanity with tolerance, not with disdain, Hans Sachs the older man who can bestow affection on one as young as Eva—he seemed to the twenty-five-year-old Cosima the tutelary idol ministering to her imagination. Truth and poetry merged. She wrote of her enthusiasm, though in guarded words, to a friend, the poet and novelist Alfred Meissner:

Biebrich, July 20, 1862

. . . We are only a step or two from Wiesbaden, where we often go out of sheer idiocy, just as one goes to see disagreeable people because they live in the neighborhood. I always return in an even more misanthropical mood than that in which I started. It is a fearful sight, this accumulation of degraded women, gamblers, rope-dancers, and Jews, where one looks in vain for a respectable figure. It is the native land of disreputable people, who congregate here in the same way as the representatives of the social hierarchy: here one finds age without dignity, elegance without attractiveness, aristocracy without nobility, wealth without brilliance; everything is common, base, vulgar, ignoble, and if by chance one hears the song of a bird in the park at Wiesbaden, one asks oneself how such a pure warbler can still lift up its little voice amid this shameless masquerade.

After these remarks you will ask why I have settled down in this region. Ah, *voilà!* We are here out of friendship for Richard Wagner, who has found a nest at Biebrich, and who, like all mortals, feels the need of exchanging a word with a friendly being from time to time. He begged us to come, and we have come and rented a house for two months. . . .

Wagner's latest libretto, *Die Meistersinger—Hans Sachs—*is a masterpiece. Like Shakespeare, he has effected a union between lively comedy and the sublime. Greatness hangs like a sun over the plot, which is adorned with the most ludicrous incidents, in which humor is combined with the profoundest emotion, without losing any of its power. Hans Sachs is cast in bronze from head to foot, full of life and strength, as though Peter Vischer had wrought him.

To her father Cosima wrote in a similar vein:

Biebrich, July 1862

Die Meistersinger is to Wagner's creations what *The Winter's Tale* is to Shakespeare's other works. Wagner's imagination has made an excursion into the realm of mischievous gaiety, and by its magic has so conjured up medieval Nuremberg, with its guilds and corporations, its journeyman poets, its pedants and its knights, as to call forth in the sublimest and most noble way the laughter that does most to emancipate the spirit. Quite apart from the intellectual content and import of the work, its artistic execution may be compared with the tabernacle in the Church of St. Lorenz in Nuremberg. Like the sculptor of the tabernacle, the musician has here achieved the purest and most graceful form, with the most consummate boldness of conception, and just as, at the base of the tabernacle, Adam Kraft bears up and supports the whole structure with an expression of grave and concentrated reverence, so in *Die Meistersinger* it is the figure of Hans Sachs that dominates and directs the action with a cheerful and lovable serenity.

Bülow spent five days, eight hours a day, in making a clean copy of the poem. A heat spell made the work grueling, but he kept at it, and the more he kept at it, the lower became his estimate of his own creative ability. A work like *Die Meistersinger*—he knew that was forever beyond him. He could not even bear to read the proofs of some songs of his own which his publisher had sent him. Cosima, too, knew this: she realized clearly that her husband could never fulfill her hopes. And Bülow? He could hardly remain blind to the adoring looks Cosima bestowed on Sachs-Wagner. He seemed to be standing like a misshapen rock in the stream of admiration which was flowing between his wife and his friend. Wagner gave vent to his excitement by behaving like a schoolboy away from home—standing on his head, declaiming nonsense rhymes, and plunging into the Rhine with his dog. But as yet, all was "a silence and a secret."

When the Bülows left, Wagner accompanied them as far as Frankfurt, where a performance of Goethe's *Torquato Tasso* was to be given, with Friederike Meyer in the role of the Princess. Crossing the square, Wagner saw an empty wheelbarrow and offered to push Cosima in it to their hotel. Cosima at once said yes, but Wagner got embarrassed and nothing came of it. In later life they remembered that bit of flirtation with delight.

Suddenly there was frightening news from St. Tropez. Blandine was ill. Following the birth of her first child, she had developed puerperal fever. Ollivier had hesitated to tell Cosima, but Blandine's condition had worsened, and Ollivier begged Cosima to come. It was too late. On September 11, 1862, Blandine died. In one way her death hurt Cosima more deeply than the death of her brother, because Blandine had been closer to her. But because the tragedy had taken place far away, Cosima was spared its immediacy, the sight and sound of the closing moments. Her husband, her mother, her grandmother—indeed, everybody who had known her had loved the gay and pretty Blandine, and Cosima very much wanted to console her mother and grandmother. Or, perhaps, she wanted an opportunity to absent herself from Berlin for a while. While Liszt went to see Ollivier, Cosima went to Paris. There it was Anna, with whom she stayed, who comforted *her.* After some weeks the old lady, hobbling about on crutches, could not bear to be parted again from her only remaining grandchild, and Cosima almost let herself be persuaded to move to Paris, in the musical life of which Bülow would be welcome. Liszt sensibly pointed out to his mother that such a move was impractical:

> Poor dear Cosima would gladly have prolonged her stay with you; she clings to you with heartfelt love. On the other hand, her husband cannot do without her in the position which he occupies in Berlin and in Germany generally. It would not be a good thing for him to leave his home in Berlin before being offered an equally secure position elsewhere. Bülow has to pay particular regard to his sovereign, who has appointed him his Court Pianist and honored him with a decoration. . . . His name and antecedents place binding obligations upon him: he must maintain the bearing of a man who can be relied upon unconditionally. . . . I have explained all this to Ollivier and he will have written it to Cosima. . . . [October 1862]

So she went back, dressed in black, wan, torn by the loss of her sister, confused by unadmitted love, and anticipating that life would not become simpler in the near future, as she was once again pregnant. She had hardly been home for a fortnight, she had hardly had time to bring the house in order and get rid of a slovenly maid, when she set out with Bülow for Leipzig, where he was to play Liszt's new A-major Piano Concerto. Wagner's young friend Wendelin Weissheimer would present some of his own compositions, and Wagner would conduct the *Tannhäuser* Overture, and for the first time anywhere, the *Meistersinger* Prelude.

In Leipzig inevitably Cosima and Wagner saw each other again. This time, one glance sufficed, one word of greeting was enough to envelop them; everything around them at once seemed unimportant —even music. They cared nothing about this concert, remained untouched by Weissheimer's pedestrian efforts, uninterested in the new concerto. Only a sparse audience attended the concert on November 1, but Wagner's adherents cheered loud and long. Yet for once that virtuoso of self-importance remained unmoved by applause. He was thinking of her. Cosima seemed to him a being from another world, her sorrow "so profound that only the total absorption in our joy of meeting again helped us to bridge the abyss. . . . The rehearsal seemed like a remote shadow play, watched by laughing children."*

They had to separate immediately after, his eventual destination Vienna, where he hoped *Tristan* would be produced. He had very little money left, and practically all sources from which he could press fresh contributions had dried up. Giving concerts was the only possible stopgap, and he had come to look at conducting as the incubus which sapped his energy and prevented him from putting notes on paper. His concerts in Vienna, the first on December 26—the Empress Elisabeth attended; her lonely soul was touched by Wagner's music— the second on New Year's Day 1863, and the third on January 11 (again in the presence of Elisabeth), were artistic successes and financial disasters. Then in February he received an invitation to concertize in Russia—the wealth was there, as Berlioz and Verdi and many other musicians, including Liszt, knew—but Wagner, by this time without a gulden to his name, didn't know how he could get there. Bülow, by no means a wealthy man, came to the rescue by selling a ring the Grand Duke of Baden had given him, a gesture Wagner acknowledged by writing: "Whoever else still possesses any valuables he does not particularly care for must cheerfully sacrifice them to me. I mean it in all seriousness. . . . I shall win back and restore the stuff splendidly and gloriously." And off he went, to return from Russia in April 1863 with the tidy sum of twelve thousand marks, enough to live on decently for more than a year. Not for Wagner, though; the money fled from his pocket as fast as vanquished soldiers. He moved his furniture

Autobiography.

from Biebrich to Vienna, then got rid of most of it and refurnished his new home in the most sybaritic and expensive style: all silk draperies, overstuffed armchairs, Oriental rugs—and *three* servants.

On his way back from Russia, he stopped in Berlin to find Cosima still weak and ailing after the birth in March of her second child, whom she named Blandine.* Bülow commented: "I am now the father of two daughters. Only the third is missing for me to become King Lear."

Wagner's money was used up, and he had once again to embark on a round of concerts. Curiously enough, he managed to obtain a little money from Viennese moneylenders, who surely must have known that he represented the worst possible risk, but neither his publisher, Schott—who told him that only a prince with millions could satisfy his needs—nor the Wesendoncks would come forth to plug the unpluggable leak. By the late autumn he guessed he would once more be a fugitive from the *chasse à courre* of his creditors. After a last visit with the Wesendoncks in Zurich, he was scheduled to go to Löwenberg. He had arranged to meet Bülow when the train stopped at the Berlin station in order to ask his advice. Bülow persuaded him to interrupt his journey for a day and attend a concert Bülow was giving that night. While Bülow was rehearsing, Cosima—now fully recovered—and Wagner went for a ride in a carriage. They were alone, close together, the day sweetly autumnal, and suddenly their long restraint melted away. "We gazed into each other's eyes and suddenly an overwhelming craving for acknowledged truth compelled us to the confession, for which no words were needed, of an incalculable disaster which had befallen us"—so Wagner wrote years later. That night he stayed in Bülow's house. That night they became lovers. The date was November 28, 1863.†

---

*Du Moulin Eckart stated that Cosima nearly died because of the cruelty of Bülow's mother, who didn't summon the *sage femme* until the baby was already born. As usual, he offered no proof for the statement, nor is the fact mentioned by anybody else.

†The date itself would seem unimportant were it not for the fact that several biographers leave the reader in the dark as to the beginning of the relationship, for example C. F. Glasenapp, the "official" Bayreuth biographer, who got his information—or rather misinformation—from Cosima herself. W. A. Ellis, his British counterpart, echoes Glasenapp. Du Moulin Eckart slides over the affair without a timetable. Ernest Newman conjectures the correct date, basing it partly on the fact that a sentence was omitted from the official edition of Wagner's autobiography at the point where he speaks of their afternoon drive together. The omitted passage, restored in the privately printed version, reads: "With tears and sobs we sealed our confession to belong to each other alone." In Cosima's diaries she mentions November 28, 1863, as *the* date several times, and regards it as the turning point. Yet Geoffrey Skelton, the translator of the diaries, still gives June 1864 as the moment when "Wagner's and Cosima's love was physically consummated."

CHAPTER III

Growing Intimacy

Such was the chain of incidents that led to one of music history's great love affairs. There was something novelistic about the progress of their coming together, following the often described trajectory from indifference, even mockery, to an undeclared attraction in vain denied, to open avowal, and to consummation. Six years previously, writing to Carolyne Wittgenstein's daughter, Marie, Cosima had expressed herself ironically about Wagner's way of life. She had deplored the fate of Lamartine, who had become very poor and for whom a subscription was being raised; she said she would rather give money to him "than to Richard of Zürich":

> I have come to the conclusion that the famous bankruptcy of Wagner
> is happily covered by this modern Beatrice [Mathilde Wesendonck],
> who opens out to her poet the heavens of material tranquillity and
> easy luxury—perhaps the only heaven in which he believes!

When she first visited the Asyl, she had expected to be bored, perhaps embarrassed. "I will tell you," she wrote to Marie, "about the tragicomedies which I shall witness and of which I shall be, perhaps and alas, the confidante." But in the end, the "tragicomedies"—Wagner's conflicts with Minna, and his frustration over Mathilde—were to strike her as more tragic than comic.

Wagner's feelings toward Cosima grew even more slowly; at first he thought of her, twenty-four years younger than he, as a schoolgirl in a pinafore. Even when she came to the Asyl as a newly married lady she was only twenty, and he seemed old enough to himself when he was in a low mood (he was going on forty-four) to make the difference in years unbridgeable. When, in 1859, he and the Bülows had become sufficiently good friends for him to ask Cosima to translate *Tannhäuser* into French for the Paris production, he addressed her as "dear child." (Cosima attempted it but soon gave it up: it was "impossibly difficult.") But three years later, after Hans and Cosima visited him in Biebrich, Wagner wrote her a letter which, if one reads between its careful lines, reveals a growing attraction:

Biebrich, September 12, 1862

I looked up at your windows [of the house where she stayed in Biebrich] with real anguish recently on leaving the station. Believe me, I am childishly sensitive to affection! I felt quite lost, knowing that you were no longer up there. Only one thing calmed me: I had to say to myself—"This is not the first time!" — How often have I experienced the same forlornness and desolation! It is a strange, damp and cold feeling, the heart shrinks—"but deep in my breast's recesses glows an unseen fire!" — I have said something like this to you already!*

*This and some following excerpts are taken from the very few relics of the Wagner-Cosima correspondence that escaped destruction. In 1927, their correspondence was supposed to be still extant, locked up in an "iron cupboard" at Wahnfried, and copies of some letters were made.

In 1930, Eva Chamberlain declared that she burned the entire collection and that she did so "at the express wish of my mother and my brother." This happened shortly after Siegfried's death. His widow, the late Winifred Wagner, claimed that as the trustee of the estate, "no one other than myself . . . had the right to open the Wahnfried archives without my consent." The letters had presumably been taken by "somebody" while she, Winifred, had gone to visit Toscanini to discuss his conducting *Parsifal* in 1931. Winifred instituted legal proceedings against "person or persons unknown," knowing of course, that Eva was the "culprit." Eva, backed by the testimony of her husband, Houston Stewart Chamberlain, testified that she and Cosima had "carried out an auto-da-fé of old letters" in Wahnfried in 1909 and that this was done at Cosima's request. Presumably these letters were Cosima's letters to Wagner, while the letters burned in 1930 were Wagner's letters to Cosima. Millenkovich-Morold, writing a biography of Cosima, looked into the question; Eva answered:

Bayreuth October 4th, 1935

Most honored Herr von Millenkovich,
As I understand from your letter of October 1, I am accused by Frau Winifred Wagner of lying and of theft.
I now consider myself constrained to set forth the events to which these accusations refer:
1. My mother personally destroyed all her own letters to my father.
2. My mother personally gave me, a long time ago—she still directed the festivals at the time—*my father's letters to her.* She took them personally out

Yet even after Cosima and Wagner became lovers, other women did not totally disappear from Wagner's thoughts. Not only was he still, though vaguely, dreaming of Mathilde Wesendonck, but viewing his union with Cosima as clandestine and dangerous and not what he needed for permanence, unable to imagine that she would ever join him openly, he considered embarking on a relationship with Henriette von Bissing, a wealthy widow who promised "to produce for him a not inconsiderable sum of money which would give him independence for a longer period." This passed, largely on Henriette's wish, as she believed that "Even if I save Wagner, in the end he loves only Frau Wesendonck."

Viewed in a social context, it is obvious that Cosima and Wagner were equally unfree. Emotionally the situation was different. Before she became attracted to Wagner, Cosima's deep feelings had been unengaged. Her capacity for love lay unemployed. In that sense she *was* free. Wagner was emerging from a profound involvement and groping for new connections, however tenuous or confused. It was Cosima who, so to speak, straightened him out. It was Cosima who took the lead. It was Cosima who appeared more the wooer than the wooed. And it was Cosima who swept the others away.

What drew them together? Genius, challenge, sorrow. That a young girl should thrill to the figures of Lohengrin and Tannhäuser and the young Siegfried was predictable. That the creator of this rich, heroic music was himself a fascinating and challenging figure is attested to by

of the iron cupboard in Wahnfried at the time and bestowed them on me in a large deed box, in which she included a slip of paper with the words in her own handwriting: "Dedicated to my guardian angel."

I can produce this document. My mother then said further: "You can take a look at the letters and then destroy them."

Often in the course of the years she asked me anxiously: "You have destroyed Papa's letters to me, haven't you?" I comforted her with the assurance that I would certainly fulfill her wish. My brother was sometimes present when my mother repeated this question to me, and it was on such an occasion that he declared himself to be unconditionally in favor of my mother's wish being fulfilled. This also determined my action.

3. I also received my mother's Diaries as a personal gift from her; it took the form of a dowry at my marriage. — These, too, she removed personally from the iron cupboard with the words: "They belong to you—with you I know they are safe."

The thought of this was a comfort to her until the last days of her life.

I am prepared to swear to these facts before God at any time. I beg you, honored Herr von Millenkovich, to have this, my written statement, delivered to my sister-in-law in Wahnfried.

Eva Chamberlain-Wagner

Whatever the truth, the fact remains that most of the correspondence *was* destroyed, though somehow a few scraps remained. Nothing came of Winifred's recourse to law.

almost all who knew him. But there was something else. Herself unanchored, Cosima responded to a personality who was buffeted. His life, when she came closer to it, appeared not "embarrassing" but as insecure and as exposed as her own. She understood the unruliness of the genius, dissatisfied with the more conventional works which had brought him fame, daring to walk a new, a most difficult path, his goal far off. She wrote that she saw "the profound unhappiness written on his face," and she was not fooled when, as a safety valve, he broke into boisterousness.

A powerful physical attraction added to their spiritual concord. The composer of *Tristan,* the poet who ascribed the world's perdition to Alberich's abjuring love, was a strongly sexed man, and one may conjecture that Cosima found her first sexual fulfillment with him. If Bülow, so often self-mocking, could abandon himself at all, he could do so only to music. Wagner was a more physical person, and indeed, his whole history shows that he needed physical love. He was also a satisfying lover. Cosima's diary, which begins after they had been lovers for more than five years, indicates, if only discreetly, that her sexual relation with Wagner filled her with joy. That joy was to continue until his last illness.

Cosima knew what she wanted: she had acquired her egotism early, when she was left to her own devices, and the older she grew, the more certain she became. All the same, she did not take her adultery lightly. Even after her hopes for Bülow were dashed, even after she had fallen in love with Wagner, she tried to make the marriage function. Increasingly this became an impossible task.

Du Moulin Eckart described Bülow—and for once we may trust him, since Eckart's father, having been Bülow's pupil, knew him well —as being

> not the man who is made for marriage. His violence was often so great that, long before the entry of Wagner into the Bülow household, a Berlin doctor had said that it was marvelous that Frau Cosima could stand such a state of affairs at all. But she was too much of an artist's child not to be able to do so. She knew the violence of her own father, and was able to see beyond the indefinable exasperation that was the result of Hans's artistic production and activity; she managed to get through the most passionate scenes with a certain coolness, and even with the display of a certain humor.

Summoning not only coolness but humor, Cosima tried to placate many people whom Bülow's harshness had incensed. In fact, she continued to defend him even after she had separated from him. A letter has come to light that she wrote on June 8, 1867, a time when she had temporarily returned to Munich—for "diplomatic reasons"—and when she belonged body and soul to Wagner. A split had opened between Bülow and his long-time friend Alexander Ritter, due evidently to some derogatory remarks Bülow had made about Ritter's musicianship. She now wrote to Ritter's wife, Franziska (who was Wagner's niece):

> I consider it a duty to speak to you about the unfortunate misunderstanding which has arisen. . . . Please listen to me calmly. . . . My husband was supposed to have said that he thought little of Alexander's talent. If Alexander believes this he does Hans a great wrong. Anybody who knows Hans even a little knows how gladly he recognizes talent, be it at its most obscure or at its most evident. Wherever he is he develops the seeds and acclaims the blossoms. How could he have acted otherwise, then, to a friend whom he loves and respects as much as he does your husband?

She reminds Franziska that Bülow had put forth the possibility that Alexander join him, and that Franziska, too, become a teacher in the music school Bülow was to head. At that time the plans were vague. Now Alexander had written Bülow to ask for a decision. Bülow had not answered. Why?

> . . . He [Hans] wanted to think the matter over once more, whether the positions he could offer were really worthy of both of you. Conscientious as he is, he wished to evaluate the conditions here, his own position, the favorable and unfavorable chances with which we have to reckon. Consider as well his almost superhuman labors of the last six weeks! I hardly saw him for half an hour a day, what with partial and full orchestral rehearsals, soloists, choruses, the direction of *Lohengrin,* conferences about the Music School organization, his own pupils—nobody could have demanded that he take time out to write a letter. . . .

> Your husband knows Hans, and it was Alexander himself who told Hans that his life in Berlin had made him very irritable. His curious, sometimes harsh and offending characteristics—I admit it—must be understood in the light of his importance in the musical world and his extraordinary talents. . . . When I tell you in confidence, dear lady, that my father as well as your uncle have overlooked the peculiarities of his behavior and swallowed more than one harsh word from him— this because they know the value of a nature which cannot be estimated too highly—you will perhaps admit that your husband was too hasty in arriving at conclusions which now are difficult to change and difficult to forget. Hans's cutting and peremptory behavior is no

sign of disdain, believe me! As to the few irritated words he utters—
what are they against the many proofs of true friendship and
sympathetic respect which he has given to all his friends?

Cosima saw no way to reconcile the two men, but she hoped to
resolve later, when things calmed down, and with Franziska's help,
the "horrible dissonance." She was writing in that spirit, begging Franziska's pardon for the mistakes in her faulty German.

We get another view of what it was like for Cosima to be married
to a man "who was not made for marriage" through a letter she wrote
Bülow after she had left him. It is a long and lofty letter, an attempt
both to justify herself and to exonerate him. And it is decisive:

June 15, 1869

My dear Hans:
I learn through Richter that you have handed in your resignation and
I learn from others that you plan to quit Germany. You asked me
about the future of our children and the disposition of our possessions.
This gives me courage to send you a few words: I do so in great
timidity, begging you not to be irritated if they should arrive at an
inopportune moment. I have never been very fortunate in my
conversations with you: when I have tried to reestablish an honorable
peace between us you have answered me with irony: when I have
asked for a definite separation you have refused to listen to me. Today
I beg you to listen to me in a kindly spirit, retiring into yourself,
disregarding external considerations, and recalling what we have
suffered in common for many years. . . .

She asked him why he was throwing up his position and leaving
Munich. If the reason was to be sought in his inability to endure any
longer the "ambiguities and villainies" by which he was surrounded,
she understood fully. If the reason was that he thought he must "simu-
late and dissimulate" to smooth over the situation, he was wrong: "No
blame, no shame, can ever fall on you."

The indignant clamor will be shouted at me. First, because as a
woman the maintenance of moral order is expected of me, second
because I am a mother who appears to have sacrificed our children,
third because you are a man of honor with whom I willingly
contracted a marriage. If you reply that the shame which will be
heaped on me must necessarily engulf you too, I say that it lies within
your power to spare both of us by declaring that the persecutions to
which we have been subjected at Munich have undermined our
domestic existence to the extent that *both* of us, in perfect
agreement, have decided on a separation. . . . If I will not be spared
the most severe blame, at least we will be spared the shame.

I swear to you that I would wish you to remain in Munich (apart from considerations of your health; you do need a long vacation). I desire it because of the children: I imagine that with what you earn there you could put aside something for them. I desire it as well for your sake: you are not made for the vagabonding life and I know of no place either in Germany or abroad where you would be better off. . . .

So often have I passed in review my previous life and examined my conscience. I have not hidden from myself the wrong I did you. Your only wrong was to have married me. I can honestly say that in the seven months of our separation the only worry, the only sorrow I have felt is the thought of you. (I hope you are listening to me with enough peace of mind and goodwill to believe what I am telling you.) A hundred times I have asked myself what I could, what I must, do and I swear to you that it was never just an egotistical whim which prevented me from running to see you.

The memory of our life together from the second year of our betrothal onward has always been with me to prove to me that however sincerely I have tried to do so, I could not make you happy. Nothing that I did was right. How many times, when you were ill, have you sent me away from your bedside without my understanding why! You will remember, too, that when I was enceinte with Lulu [Daniela] I did not dare to tell you of it, as if my pregnancy had been illegitimate; I revealed it to you in a dream.

All the same, I would never have left you had I not encountered that being to whom my own attached itself so completely that detachment has become impossible for me. You will never know how I struggled, what I suffered. I am unable to describe the consternation which took hold of me when the idea of a life for the three of us proved unrealizable. It was not the humiliations which you inflicted on me which drove me away—no, I had arrived at a point where I could more easily bear pain than joy. . . .*

She went on for a good page and a half, pleading for understanding and forgiveness, arriving only at the end at the "practical" problem —the children's future and the division of their property.

It was consistent with Bülow's nature that he should answer at once, taking all the blame and regretting that he had "very badly, very ill-naturedly recompensed you for all the devotion you have lavished on me." He wants to die; he is a "bankrupt." To this Cosima replied with another long letter, tearstained and gentle, which closed with:

*The letter is in French, the language in which Cosima at that time was still more comfortable than in German. There are few corrections, suggesting that she wrote a rough copy first.

I did not think you needed me—that was my error; then I hoped that your artistic activity would fill the void created by my absence. We are poor creatures, Hans, we wander from mistake to illusion until sorrow seizes us and leads us to truth. . . . We can still communicate with each other and perhaps help each other. I no longer desire death because I greatly desire to do good. I demand that you do not seek your death, because you can be of vital help to our children. This demand confirms and summarizes all my feelings: let it close my letter.

Yet her love was more demanding than conscience or prudence. She knew Wagner's reputation regarding women. She knew that he was little short of a beggar when they first fell in love. Yet she was willing to relinquish her security as the wife of a famous conductor. She was even ready to brave the strong disapproval of her father, who had become, under Carolyne's influence, the libertine turned moralist. Nor, once she had taken the step, could she cleanse herself of the guilt; it haunted her all her life and tormented her dreams. Guilt, disapproval, scandal—they were outweighed by the drive of love and by the conviction, formed early, that she, and she alone, could set Wagner's genius on the path of creative ascendancy and accompany him on that road.

From the diary, January 8, 1869:

Dear Lulu and dear Boni, today is your father's birthday. I wish that he would pass it in a mood of forgiveness and calm. But I cannot contribute toward it. Our union was a great misunderstanding. What I felt for him nineteen years ago I still feel: sympathy with his lot, admiration for the qualities of his mind and heart, real respect for his character—and total divergence of our temperaments. Even in the first year of our marriage this confusion drove me to such desperation I wanted to die. My bewilderment caused me to make many many mistakes, yet time and again I plucked up my courage and your father had not the slightest idea of my suffering. He will not, I believe, deny me the testimony that I stood by his side in good days and bad, and that I tried to help him to the best of my strength. He would never have lost me if fate had not led the one man to me for whom I realized that I must live and die. I have not a single reproach to make to your father, though the last years were horribly difficult for me. . . . Only one choice remained, which was no choice at all. . . .

Eight years later, on February 3, 1877:

. . . I dream so much of Hans. Recently I imagined I heard him play the piano, clearly and nearby. . . .

What was it in her that attracted Wagner and continued to hold a man not known for the constancy of his affections? Her youth, her unconventional blond beauty, her devotion, her quick perception, her genuine responsiveness to music—yes, all these, but two other attributes as well. She was an extraordinarily good listener. How he loved to talk! Those long monologues of his on subjects as diverse as music and vivisection, Aeschylus and Bismarck, child-rearing and women's clothes, Buddhism and the British, Schopenhauer and press censorship—she listened to all of them with absorption, knowing instinctively when to throw into the brook a little rock which would make the water bubble still more gaily. And finally he loved her for being what he was not, an aristocrat. Her manners were gracious, his were atrocious. She had inherited from Marie the art of opposing those who opposed her by smiling at them, while Wagner harangued those who disagreed with him until they and he were exhausted. He called her "the best of diplomats." Indeed, the repertoire of her diplomacy included ruthlessness, when needed. She would stop at nothing to satisfy him.

Not lightly did Cosima turn from a talented husband to the lover who was a genius. She did not commit adultery unmindful of its cost. The last characteristic she possessed was flightiness. Then and later she was all too serious. Her choice was arrived at with painful seriousness; but it was "no choice at all."

CHAPTER IV

"I Am the King's Friend"

When the clock struck the darkest midnight hour of Wagner's fortunes, he was rescued by a *deus ex machina* with a suddenness only an inept dramatist would have invented. His rescuer was a boy, not yet nineteen, who on March 10, 1864, had been called to the throne of Bavaria. King Maximilian II had died that day at the age of fifty-two; his son Ludwig succeeded him.

The elevation turned Ludwig from a dreamy and lonely youngster with insufficient pocket money to the powerful and rich sovereign of Germany's second-largest state. Since the age of thirteen, Ludwig had thrilled to the music of *Tannhäuser* and *Lohengrin.* He knew the texts by heart, and he had read and reread Wagner's prose works without ever having met their author. The Lohengrin saga held a special fascination for him; as a boy he had signed his letters with a cross and a swan, and now he saw himself as the modern descendent of the missionary knight. He had long determined that should he ever come to power, he would turn Wagner's ideas for the regeneration of German art into reality. One month after Ludwig became Ludwig II, he said to his cabinet secretary, Franz von Pfistermeister, "Find Richard Wagner."

It took some doing; Wagner was in hiding from his creditors. The secretary sought him in Munich, in Vienna, in Basel, and finally traced him to Stuttgart. (Cosima had no idea where he was in those days; she worried about him.) The card of the "Royal Bavarian Secretary" was sent up to Wagner, who was disturbed that his whereabouts in Stuttgart had been discovered and suspected that the card was a trick thought up by a persistent creditor. He sent down word that he was not in. The hotelkeeper later told him that the man wished to see him on an important matter, and reluctantly he made an appointment for the next morning. He slept miserably that night, wondering what new troubles were in store for him.

In the morning he learned the truth: a king had called him, an adoring king willing to give him all he needed. A word had summoned him from penury to glory, from the hotel room with the locked door to the palace with the open gate. The day was May 3, 1864, and Wagner penned a tearful letter to Ludwig, speaking of "the divine reality which has entered my poor life in need of love. That life, its last poetry, its last tones, henceforth belongs to you, my young beneficent King."

The 5 P.M. train for Munich was about to start, and Pfistermeister was already seated in a compartment. Wagner arrived with his friend Weissheimer, assuming that his fare to Munich would be taken care of. No longer possessing a mark in ready money, he had paid his hotel bill with the last of his valuables, a snuffbox he had been given in Russia. Now, realizing that he had neither a ticket nor a single pfennig, he begged Weissheimer for help. Weissheimer ran to the ticket window, ran back to the train, and threw a ticket into the compartment as the train was pulling out of the station. The little incident must have given Pfistermeister something to think about.

Ludwig was deeply moved when he finally met the nervous little man with the huge head and the sparkling eyes, whose ideals he had for so long made his own. The very next day he sent Wagner a note: "I will do everything in my power to make up to you for what you have suffered. The ordinary cares of the everyday I will banish from you forever. . . . Though you did not know it, you were *the sole source of my delight* from my early youth onward—the friend who spoke to my heart. . . ."

King and composer saw each other daily for the next few months. They signed a contract giving Ludwig the rights to the productions of and income from Wagner's future works, in return for which Wagner was to receive a generous yearly subvention of four thousand gulden. The king at once gave him an additional four thousand gulden—to expunge his most pressing debts. (Wagner did not use all of that gift to pay his creditors, and he lied even to his good friend Dr. Anton Pusinelli as to the amounts he was receiving from the royal purse.) A pleasant villa (the Villa Pellet), on the nearby Starnberg Lake, near the king's own castle at Berg, was put at his disposal. There he was to think out the plan for model performances of his works—*Lohengrin* in 1864, *Tristan* in 1865, *Meistersinger* and *Tannhäuser* after that—and for the creation of a music school, along the lines of the Renaissance academy. These were halcyon days, these were noble plans, and Wagner worked with enthusiasm and sincerity. Yet not for a moment did his longing for Cosima abate. Less than a month after settling at the villa with housekeeper, valet, and dog, he wrote to Bülow:

June 1, 1864

. . . What has happened to me here is heavenly, undreamed-of, incomparably wonderful and beautiful. It is beyond understanding . . . and only to me could something like it have happened. I myself have begotten it for myself out of the depth of my longing and suffering: a Queen had to bear this son for me. . . .

Yet something was missing to complete his ecstasy. To Bülow, a week later:

June 9, 1864

What I am about to tell you and what I am going to ask you for— please don't consider it as a sudden or passing whim. Treat it as if it were an important paragraph in a last testament. I invite you, with your wife and children and maidservant, to stay with me this summer for as long as possible. This decision is the result of a long communion with myself. Hans—you find me in prosperity. My life is completely transformed, lifted by a great love and a pure will. Yet—my house is lonely and I feel this now more painfully than ever. . . . Come and populate my house, at least for a time. . . .

He assured them that a whole floor would be put at their disposal and that if they wanted privacy they would have it. But he needed them at this, the most decisive moment of his life. "So—no 'No'! I could not bear it." The letter was followed by a barrage of telegrams. They must come!

A week later, he wrote Cosima a long letter, since Bülow was apparently hesitating. He told her that they should trust his judgment when he proposed that Hans use the summer to introduce "my dear young King" to music. "He has been brought up without any music whatsoever, knows only my works, but of Beethoven and almost all other music he knows nothing." It would be excellent for Bülow's career— just consider: to be close to the King of Bavaria! "Every day he sends

Cosima about the time she joined Wagner.

to inquire whether he may count on my friend." A salary of at least 1,500 gulden would be assured Hans as the king's pianist. Besides:

Starnberg, June 16, 1864

Munich is one of the cheapest places in Germany. . . . Hans can go on his artistic travels if he wishes, need give *almost* no lessons, need not torture himself anymore, can work nicely, and—I have you *both!*

He adds a postscript: "Here we have . . . 40 marvelous Swiss cows. What milk for the children!!!"

The letter was obviously meant for Bülow's perusal. It was dishonest only to the extent that Wagner addressed Cosima with the formal form of address—*"Sie"*—while they had been using the familiar form —*"Du"*—for some time. Was he—were they both—naïve enough to try to make Bülow believe that their relationship was "formal"?

No question but that his desire for Cosima was the force that wrung these pleas from him. Yet when he desired Bülow's presence as well, he was not being untruthful or altogether underhanded. He knew full well Bülow's dedication and skill, and considered them essential if the performances of the unperformed works were to be realized and the plan of reform was not to remain a mere memorandum to the king. Aside from himself—and he was anxious to withdraw from public performance—where was Wagner to find the musician who could do justice to the interplay of voice and symphonic writing he had created, what conductor could hold for the listener the tension of so long and new and demanding a poem in sound as his *Tristan* represented? Bülow was necessary to him: he called him his second self. Besides— and quite unselfishly—Wagner knew that Bülow would be the right man to work toward the establishment of the music academy. Bülow agreed to come.

Cosima, with little Blandine and Daniela, arrived at the Villa Pellet on June 29, 1864, only a little more than six weeks after Wagner had moved there. Bülow did not arrive until July 7. By that time Wagner's union with Cosima had assumed its definitive form. The triangle was confirmed in the house by the lake. The king was left in ignorance— he had not the faintest inkling of what was happening. Did Bülow? How much did he know? And how soon?

Before answering these questions, to which Ernest Newman has devoted the punctiliousness and ingenuity of his scholarship, it is necessary to touch the salient points of Wagner's and Cosima's relationship to the king in the first palmy period.

At first, then, Wagner basked in the roseate glow of an idealistic and romantic sovereign. Ludwig's "abnormality" took nothing away from his energy and certainty of purpose. Even at an early age he knew himself to be homosexual, but no overt homosexual component influenced his love for the composer. Though one could not tell it from the girlishly rapturous language of his letters—part of which can be ascribed to the Romantic Age, Cosima's and Wagner's letters being often as fulsome—Ludwig was no fool. He was sometimes too trusting, sometimes too impractical for his task, but all the same, and at least in his youth, his mind was perceptive and he ranked head and shoulders above other German princes. He thought in terms of German unity. He was willing to spend the wealth of his throne to further for his people the art which he understood. His sick and terrible idiosyncrasies—his fear of being stared at, his mania for building castle aeries, his refusal to confer with his ministers, his Louis XIV fantasies—these were to reveal themselves later. In the beginning it was true idealism, lofty ambition.

His love for Wagner was so comprehensive that it included Cosima and Bülow. He liked Cosima especially, seeing in her an ideal wife and mother. (Ludwig hated his own mother.) He asked her help in freeing Wagner's life "of little troubles," there being no wife to grace Wagner's existence, with Minna ill and far away. Ludwig thought of them all—himself, Wagner, Cosima, and Bülow—as a "holy quartet" dedicated to the highest aims of art. In his mind the quartet was spiritual, the friendship spotless. That anything else might be involved did not occur to the young king.

In the first week of October 1864, Wagner moved to Munich. By the king's order, a splendid and all too ostentatious house and garden had been leased for him. The Bülows had returned to Berlin from the Villa Pellet to settle their affairs. By the middle of November, they—Hans, Cosima, and their two little girls—were ensconced in a house of their own in Munich and Ludwig had appointed Bülow "Royal Pianist" *(Vorspieler)*. Bülow's house was not far from Wagner's house. They were together, then, ready to begin the great tasks.

Cosima divided her life between the two houses, though not equally. She spent more and more time with Wagner, took charge of his correspondence, counseled him as to his attitude toward government officials, was frequently present when the king's representative conferred with him, occasionally was present when he had an audience with the king, made fair copies of his essays and letters, shooed away boring visitors, and saw to it that the composer of Germanic legends did not lack for French champagne.

Her husband made his bow to the Munich concert public on Cosima's birthday that year, playing at the Odeon a Bach-Liszt Prelude, the C-minor Fantasy of Mozart, and Beethoven's "Emperor" Concerto. (Lachner conducted "quite tolerably," Bülow said.) He had chosen a conservative program, he reported to his mother, so as to "shut the mouths of the croakers who were complaining in advance of an invasion by the Music of the Future." The concert was a great success. Ludwig was present and complimentary, yet Bülow felt that "his receptivity is concentrated on Wagner's music."

It was almost inevitable, with Wagner so demonstrably the king's all-absorbing concern, with the doors of the royal Residenz swinging open to him whenever he wished, that the envious Cascas of the court would begin to grumble. They called him "Lolotte" in allusion to another favorite, Lola Montez.

At first Wagner behaved circumspectly. But by the early months of 1865, his arrogance had transpired sufficiently—he had committed one or two gaffes even with the king—for the politicians and the controlled press to band together in attacking him. Their attacks, expressed first through insinuations but soon openly, included the charge that Ludwig, lost in his *Tristan* dreams, fully orchestrated, was neglecting his administrative duties; and that Wagner was exacting "frightful" sums of money from the public purse. The deeper cause of the cabal lay not in jealousy of those who were kept waiting in the anteroom, nor in Wagner's antipathetic bearing, nor in his derogation of Munich's artistic life before he had descended from the clouds, but in the discomfort the mediocre always feel when their mediocrity is challenged. At any rate, less than a year after the king had sent for Wagner, a mud-slinging article appeared in the Augsburg *Allgemeine Zeitung*, accusing Wagner of "misuse of princely favor and liberality [which] has moved the Bavarian people for months past to suppressed as well as open, and more than justified, displeasure." Wagner was playing the "ostentatious role of a modern Croesus," while his *"Genossen"* (literally "associates," but the word has a pejorative meaning, like "partners in crime") were so brazenly insulting as to speak of "Bavarian stupidity." Bülow, who had an exceptional talent for saying the wrong thing at the wrong time, rushed into print:

February 21, 1865

A Munich correspondent of the *Allgemeine Zeitung* . . . accuses the so-called "associates" of Herr Richard Wagner of the abuse of their connections with the Royal Court. As among the said "associates" I, the

A Munich caricature of Wagner, Cosima and Bülow, inscribed "After a Tristan rehearsal. Drawn from nature, 1864."

undersigned, alone have the honor to possess any such connections, I avail myself of my right to characterize the anonymous originator of this aspersion as an infamous slanderer. Hans von Bülow.

Cosima smoothed things over by writing a tactful letter to Pfistermeister, saying that her husband resented being criticized not as an artist but as a man of honor. In defending Bülow, Cosima must have known that she herself was in danger of sinking into the mud of journalistic contumely, yet she felt she had to say *something.* And she hoped that her secret, the secret of that burning love, could still be hidden. As yet the newspapers, snapping at the heels of the two "foreigners," had not touched her. With the bravery or the delusion so often indulged in by participants, she persuaded herself that her liaison would remain behind drawn blinds.

2

At this time Cosima was seven months pregnant with Wagner's child: Isolde was born on April 10, 1865. On the day of her birth, Bülow conducted the first orchestra rehearsal of *Tristan.*

The older Wagner biographies, when they discuss the Bülow-Cosima crisis at all, assert that Bülow remained ignorant of the true nature of the Wagner-Cosima relationship until he innocently opened a letter addressed to Cosima while she was away—something he never did, but which he was prompted to do in this instance, assuming that the letter contained some message that needed to be passed on. Through this alleged letter he is supposed to have learned the truth with blinding suddenness.* This is said to have happened in May 1866, more than a year after Isolde's birth.

Ernest Newman, in a chapter of his biography (Volume III, Chapter XXI, "The Triangle"), has demonstrated that this surprise denouement is not only unlikely, it is virtually impossible. Bülow could not have been unaware of the hints which by this time had appeared in

*Julius Kapp in *The Women in Wagner's Life* speaks of this letter as "an ardent love-letter from Wagner." No evidence exists that such a letter was ever written. It is in fact extremely unlikely that Wagner would be imprudent enough to send a love letter to Bülow's house, especially when he knew Cosima to be away. On the basis of the putative letter, Kapp concludes: "Thus the whole bitter truth was revealed to him [Bülow]; the stupendous lie of the last five years stared him mercilessly in the face." Curt von Westernhagen theorizes in *Wagner* that the letter was one from Ludwig, announcing his wish to abdicate. Very improbable: why would Ludwig write to Cosima before he wrote to Wagner?

the press, nor would the talk in Wagner's circle have failed to come to his ears. Peter Cornelius, the composer, who was then an intimate friend of all three, wrote frankly about the love affair both in his diary and in letters to his bride. By the end of 1865, Cornelius was certain: "There is a complete liaison between Cosima and Wagner. . . . But what about Bülow? Has he come to a high romantic understanding with Wagner to hand his wife over to him entirely? . . . The marriage between Hans and Cosima has for some time been only a sham marriage: otherwise Hans's behavior would be inexplicable." In a later letter, Cosima speaks plainly to Bülow of a *ménage à trois:* obviously he knew about the third member. And years later, Cosima stated that from June 1864 on—that is, about the time she went to visit Wagner at the Villa Pellet—she had ceased to have sexual relations with her husband. All the evidence makes it clear that Bülow was not the traditional husband deceived. He knew. He tolerated what he could not change; he did not storm, rant, accuse—except later, once—and he did more than tolerate: he continued to help Wagner in every way he could. He is to be regarded as a figure not of comedy—the ignorant bumbler who cannot see the horns on his head—but of tragedy.

As for when Bülow first learned the truth, the answer must remain conjectural, though there are indications. When he joined his family at the Villa Pellet in July 1864, he arrived—according to Wagner— "with his nerves shattered: the weather was cold and wretched all the time, the house, in consequence, dank; and he got over one sickness to fall into another." By August, Bülow's condition had so far worsened that he seemed to be paralyzed in both legs and one arm. On August 19, he suddenly left the villa and moved to the Hotel Bayrischer Hof in Munich, and on that very day Cosima left him, sick though he was, to travel to Karlsruhe, where her father was attending a music festival. Liszt had not expected her, nor did he at first understand why she had come.

Two days later, Liszt wrote Carolyne: "I do not quite grasp the position of Hans at Munich, relative to Wagner, etc." He also learned that Bülow, in spite of the honors King Ludwig proposed to shower on him, was ready to throw it all over and was talking of returning to Berlin. On August 28, Cosima was back in Munich; her father had come with her. The next day she went to Starnberg to talk to Wagner; they both returned to Munich the same day, and Wagner and Liszt went back to Starnberg the following day. Liszt was in Munich again on the thirty-first; Wagner followed him on September 2, Liszt left on the third. On the same day, Cosima and the children left for Berlin.

Why should Bülow suddenly have preferred a hotel to the well-appointed villa where he would have been well cared for? Because a doctor was more readily available in Munich? Hardly likely. Starnberg was close enough to Munich for a doctor to be summoned. Why should Cosima leave her partially paralyzed husband alone in a hotel to go and see her father? Why should Wagner almost frantically run back and forth between the Villa Pellet and Munich? Why should Liszt, who hadn't seen either his daughter or Wagner for some time and who was anxious to get back to Rome, interrupt his journey and go to Munich?

Putting the clues together, Ernest Newman believed that Bülow's "breakdown may have been the result, in part, of a frank revelation by Wagner and Cosima of the new domestic situation that had suddenly arisen," and that "the perturbed Cosima had gone to Karlsruhe, without waiting for an invitation from her father, to put him *en rapport* with the crisis . . . and to ask for his counsel and help." It is more probable that Cosima, *not* seeking counsel, simply wanted to apprise her father of her involvement. Liszt was deeply perturbed: he pitied Bülow and he foresaw an ugly scandal in which his daughter, his pupil, and his friend would be implicated. He went to Munich in an effort to "talk sense" to the three of them. Wagner observed how gray Liszt had become, how he had aged. Though Liszt was exhilarated by the excerpts from *Die Meistersinger* Wagner played for him, he left with a heavy heart. He had not succeeded in changing Cosima's or Wagner's mind.

If Bülow knew the truth early, why did he endure a painful and degrading situation? Cornelius thought that it "was a sacrifice to friendship made for his master Liszt's sake, to give the illegitimate child [Isolde] a brilliant, honorable name, and her father a profound satisfaction and ease of mind." The cause reached deeper: he would have done anything to protect, if not Wagner the man, then Wagner the creator—"all that is still ideal and worth preserving in the German spirit lives in this one head." The performance of *Tristan* had to go forward. That was more important than any man's or any woman's fate. The work destined for immortality had to be called into life. He recognized that he was performing a supreme service to art. So he held himself as erect as a dragoon, and if he saw the smirks, he pretended to ignore them and kept slaving away at music that spoke a new language, a language that he—and perhaps he alone at that early stage—knew how to teach. He was not duped. He made his decision with knowledge.

One further consideration may have prompted him: with all his idealism, he—like most artists—knew what was good for his career, and to be appointed Munich's paramount executant musician would represent a big step up the ladder. Under King Ludwig, Munich would become a more important music center than Berlin. And, at least in the beginning, he did not have to fight a hostile Berlin coterie of critics, though he did his best to create new myrmidons of disapproval.

Only once did the bitterness that lay in Bülow's heart overflow his restraint—and then he hit out against Wagner, not against Cosima. He wrote to Claire d'Agoult, Countess Charnacé (Marie d'Agoult's legitimate daughter and Cosima's half-sister), of the torments he had undergone: only one further sacrifice could be demanded of him, his life:

September 15, 1869

. . . Perhaps I would not have recoiled even from that had I observed on the part of another, as sublime in his works as incomparably abject in his actions, the smallest hint of an approach toward loyalty, the most fugitive suggestion of a sense of honesty. . . . [This] accusation, of which more than twenty years of relations with him have provided me with proof more than enough, is necessary in order to acquit another person, who formerly, as much by the superiority of her intelligence as by the loyalty, the frankness, the nobility of her character, bore such a sisterly likeness to you, Madame.

That Cosima had to hide the true state of affairs from the Munich public and press and remain ostensibly her prominent husband's prominent wife was a task to which she was equal. She was careful always to be seen with Bülow when he played or conducted; she received his visitors and ordered his domestic as well as his business arrangements; and in public she was never demonstrative with Wagner. Yet she was not able to dry up the gossip; it was too juicy. After one of the first rehearsals of *Tristan,* a caricature was published in a Munich paper: it showed a haughty Wagner promenading arm in arm with a towering Cosima, while Bülow, bowed down by the heavy score of *Tristan,* trotted timidly behind. A hint with a hammer.

More explicit denunciation was to follow. Though Wagner dismissed the attacks as vicious slander and though Cosima preserved a dignified silence—she behaved very well, indeed, by pretending to ignore it all—the two were in a nervous state. He could tolerate a good deal of invective—as he said to the musicians who warned him during a rehearsal that he was standing too near the edge of the podium, "Gentlemen, I am used to standing at the edge of the abyss"—while Cosima was still willing to play the game, much as she longed for a resolution.

Yet both of them harbored one great fear. At all costs the truth had to be hidden from one man above all, the rhapsodist of the Residenz, King Ludwig.

3

The *Tristan* project went ahead, led by Bülow. Ludwig Schnorr von Carolsfeld, the tenor whose like Wagner was never to see again, sang Tristan, his wife Malvina, Isolde. The dress rehearsal, to which Ludwig had invited some six hundred guests, made an overwhelming effect. Then came the shock. The first performance had to be postponed, Malvina having suddenly become hoarse. When, after nearly a month's delay, the premiere finally did take place, on June 10, 1865, beginning at six and lasting until eleven, with Ludwig motionless in the royal loge, it puzzled some, it infuriated a few, and it filled most with awe and wonder. Bülow noted: "It is the greatest success that a new work by Wagner has had anywhere. The Schnorrs were unbelievable; all the others quite tolerable, orchestra excellent." Schnorr wrote to Cosima:

June 12, 1865

I know full well how much is due to me, how small was my part in the success, what driving force Wagner exercised on me: yet I am proud of that evening—from that day I feel myself dedicated as an artist. I have the certainty now that I am not unworthy to have Wagner's spirit breathed into me.

Alas, the great artist died, at the age of twenty-nine, on July 21, 1865, hardly three weeks after the fourth *Tristan* performance. It was an irreparable loss for Wagner, who mourned Schnorr to the end of his days. It was as well an excuse for Wagner's adversaries to declare that the exertions of *Tristan* had killed the singer.

To add sharpness to Wagner's grief, Cosima was forced to leave him for several weeks. She had to go to Budapest with Bülow during the first week in August, to meet Liszt, whose *Saint Elisabeth* Bülow was to conduct. Wagner, exhausted and heartsick, went off to the royal hunting lodge of Hochkopf, high in the Bavarian mountains, which Ludwig had placed at his disposal for the summer. Cosima had given him a notebook bound in brown leather—the "Brown Book"—and asked him to confide his thoughts to it during her absence. Only his servant Franz and his dog kept him company. He was reading *Les Misérables,* studying the *Ramayana,* and taking up again the story of Parsifal, but much of the time he spent longing for Cosima, daydreaming about her, unable to see a way by which he could be openly united with her.

(The Brown Book, one of the important Wagnerian documents, has only recently been published in its entirety. For years it was kept locked up, accessible only to the official Bayreuth biographers and to them only in part. Its custodian, Eva Chamberlain, mutilated it, destroying a number of pages, pasting over others in an ingenuous attempt to render them illegible, and in short, making a hash of Wagner's soliloquies.

This may be a convenient place to note that the Wagnerian documents, copious though they are, have been maltreated to a considerable extent and in some instances falsified, the original culprit being Cosima. After Wagner's death, she and her Bayreuth helpers used abundant supplies of whitewash to cover the monument; she destroyed some of the Nietzsche letters (though drafts of them survive among his papers); she burned Cornelius's letters to Wagner; she excised compromising passages from Wagner's letters to Mathilde Wesendonck, etc. And Wagner dictated to her what was in itself a self-justifying and often mendacious autobiography, *Mein Leben.*

The autobiography was written for King Ludwig, who wished to know every detail of Wagner's life. "Friend Cosima does not cease to remind me to fulfill the desire of our King," Wagner wrote Ludwig shortly after the *Tristan* premiere. It was first printed in a private edition, and Wagner distributed copies of this edition to a few close friends, exacting a promise that they were never to discuss its contents. Ludwig was given one. After Wagner's death Cosima tried to recall these copies, even Ludwig's, obviously with the intention of making changes for the public edition. However, the printer Bonfantini of Basel had been so earnestly adjured to strike only eighteen copies of the book that he realized that he had something special in his possession. He therefore made an extra copy and kept it. His widow sold this copy to Mary Burrell, an indefatigable collector of Wagneriana, who set out to "tell the truth" about Wagner, and to vindicate Minna Wagner's reputation as well as that of her illegitimate daughter, Natalie. Cosima knew of this and was astute enough to keep the changes for the official edition to a bare minimum, knowing that any discrepancy between the two editions would be discovered.

A similar hugger-mugger has been played with Cosima's diaries, which she kept from 1869 to 1883. Cosima willed these to her favorite daughter, Eva, who locked them up, making available only partial glimpses and again only to the approved clan of historians. It was only after a long legal battle that the city of Bayreuth obtained the rights to publish them. That was in 1976, more than a century after Cosima first put pen to paper.)

To return to the Brown Book and specifically to the entries made during Wagner's solitude in Hochkopf—one reads them with astonishment at their immaturity. This genius, now fifty-two years old, communing with himself, sounds like a sophomore starving for his girl friend.

August 18. O Cosima! You are the soul of my life! Wholly and completely! I looked toward the flatland—seeking "home"—imagined a Munich without you. All a grave. Nothing, nothing without you. You are the soul of everything still all alive in me. — Good night! — Parzival [King Ludwig] wrote nicely. — I worked a little! — Good night, Cos!

August 19. Good morning, my soul! A gray day, rainy, cold. One needs to seek clarity and warmth within oneself.

[The score of] *Rheingold* arrived. I'll wrap it up and send it to the King in Hohenschwangau for his birthday. [Wagner had presented this manuscript to Otto Wesendonck—and had then asked him to give it back.] ... He would be happy to see me in Hohenschw. on the 25th—but I won't go. It is too strenuous for me. Really, I am in a state where I can avoid a menacing illness only by great care and rest. I'll write him today and send the score. You did remember to send him the cushion? I hope so. [Cosima had embroidered a cushion with symbols from *Holländer, Tannhäuser, Lohengrin, Siegfried,* and *Tristan,* as a birthday gift for Ludwig.] ...

Deep within myself I no longer find joy in my own work! How can I think back on the one and only time I found true artistic satisfaction, how can I remember Tristan [Schnorr] without forever renouncing joy? I shudder when I think of Tristan! And it was the only time, the only time, that I was happy. Whence now joy, whence faith? Yes, my heart, through *your* love! Surely we will succeed. I know it. But, but! Give me the tranquillity I need! Stay with me, don't go away again. Tell poor Hans frankly I can't do without you.

Two days before, Cosima had sent him a jealous letter. Three years previously, Wagner had been attracted to a pretty and intelligent girl, Mathilde Maier, twenty years younger than he. We do not know the extent of this relationship; we do know that he tried to persuade Mathilde to overcome her "bourgeois prejudices" and come and keep house for him. He repeated the suggestion when he first moved to the Starnberg Lake (some five months after Cosima and he had vowed "wholly to belong to each other"!), even promising that should Minna die, he would marry her. Mathilde declined. As his love for Cosima grew, Mathilde's image paled; he wrote her from time to time, friendly letters, nothing more, grateful and reminiscent. (Later he sent her a copy of the privately printed autobiography—then asked for it back.) Cosima knew this: it was enough to give her cause for jealousy —or for pretending jealousy.

August 18. Good morning, naughty child! What a nasty letter you wrote me yesterday! The more I read it the nastier I find it. What you are really telling me is that you are wrong to love me so much and to treat your father so badly, who is the only one who truly loves you. Very pretty! And you say all this so glibly, especially when you are away from me and with your father! And the victim is once more the unlucky M.M.! God—what am I plotting with her, what am I going to do with her, how many caresses I'll waste on her, etc. Very telling, indeed—it looks as if you wanted to provoke a "break" with me. Just continue! Well, well! . . .

I hope a sensible letter from you will arrive soon, otherwise everything is over. [This was one of the entries Eva pasted over.]

Of course they made up their quarrel in no time. Later the same day, he wrote another long entry, one that reads like the ramblings of an ill and feverish man, which in point of fact he was:

. . . As I am totally a man of art, so must I live exclusively a life of art. That means: have almost no contact with people, discuss nothing, or only jokingly, never seriously, because discussions immediately become heated and useless. If the King agrees to my proposals and my existence will be pleasantly secured and freed of worry until my death, I will only think of creating [*schaffen*], not of doing [*wirken*]. I'll establish a regular court. Hans must see to all "doing": the school, performances, etc. I'll treat with the world only through him, and essentially as a joke, worrying about nothing at all. Once a week I'll hold court: I'll receive the reports of my General and his Adjutants. What will be accomplished will please me, what won't will not grieve me. I expect nothing. Let it go! The doctor will prescribe my diet and I'll regulate my day as to derive the utmost possible benefit to my works. It will be ceremoniously arranged as in Louis XIV's Versailles, with stiff etiquette, operated by strings. If I don't feel well— it won't bother me. Only—Cosima must be with me, always, always with me. Otherwise it won't work. But we won't talk, not seriously. Then I think I'll be able to devote all my seriousness to my works. Only in them must seriousness lie—everything else is to be light and frivolous. Only Cosima will be my serious concern. And in secret—that goes without saying. But she won't show it. Only Brünnhilde and whatever all those other characters are called will show the seriousness of it all. True? Yes —that's how it will be!

But if the King can *not* do it? Then everything vice versa—then only "doing," not "creating." I'll crawl into a cubbyhole in your house. I'll run errands all day long, treat with the people, teach, make order, converse, and God knows what else. Always merry, without rancor. I will be quite poor, possess nothing, not even my manuscripts, only your letters and Parzival's. I'll give away everything, everything, keeping only my sickbed. That I'll bring with me. Hans will be earning more and I'll live off your charity, like a beggar. . . .

And you will always be there and you may talk as much as you want.

Days later, his longing intensified, he quotes from *Tristan:* "The ship —you cannot see it yet?" While working on the Parsifal story, he imagines that the door opens. His heart leaps. It is she. No, it is only the wind.

Wagner was aware that it had been Liszt who had pressed Bülow and Cosima to go with him to Budapest, thus removing her from him for five weeks. During those weeks Liszt must have attempted for the second time to dissuade his daughter from smashing her marriage. For the second time he was unsuccessful. On September 13, 1865, when Bülow and Cosima returned to Munich, her mind and her love were unchanged. "Isolde" came back, not to die but to live. The only result of Liszt's efforts was that Wagner's regard for him froze. He vents his anger in the Brown Book, predicts that Cosima will again love her father once he is away from her, while Wagner himself will learn to hate him. On September 1, 1865, he writes:

. . . This whole Catholic junk I can't stomach. [Liszt had become an *abbé* in August.] Anybody who flees into it must have much to atone for. . . . Your father repels me and if I can bear him at all, it is only because in my blind tolerance there lies more Christianity than in his whole pious fraud. . . . [Eva tried to obliterate this entry as well.]

Ten days later, Wagner's longing mounted to despair. There is a disjointed entry in the Brown Book (it survives only in incomplete form, Eva having destroyed two pages):

Your letter, dear one! Again pure madness! Madness and no end! . . . If it has to be, let it be; I submit. Perhaps you need it. Father is pleased: he wants you with him. You want it, too. Why am *I* here? . . . God knows in what state you'll return. I remember how you came back with your father a year ago! It was terrible. You sleepless, restless, weak, emaciated, miserable, tormented! . . . It will be like that again . . . and you run away from Isoldchen, for five weeks. You don't deserve such a sweet child! If you again go adventuring *I* will take the child. And you . . . [The rest of the entry is missing.]

Cosima had no wish to go "adventuring." But another separation was to divide them, unforeseen and sudden.

CHAPTER V

Love and Intrigue

Cosima, WHO HAD PREVIOUSLY EXPERIENCED only the counterfeit of love, had now attained the real thing. Wagner gave her—her, alone —all the love of which he was capable; all thoughts of Mathilde, Friederike, Henriette, vanished from his mind. "You are Elisabeth, Elsa, Isolde, Brünnhilde, and Eva, all in one," he said, and told her that "one had to arrive at a certain age before one could really learn what love was." Similarly, in her eyes he could do no wrong. Even if she was not successful in quieting those bursts of fury and hatred into which he erupted from time to time, she endured them, unshaken in the belief that he was peerless. It was true in the beginning and would be true all her life that she

> Devoutly dotes, dotes in idolatry,
> Upon this spotted and inconstant man.

Her personality smoothed itself to be aligned with his. It was inevitable that she would adopt his ideas and absorb his prejudices. She felt herself touched by the finger of fate and summoned to a task that gave meaning to her life. As Liszt said, *"C'était une mission."* She derived satisfaction in subjecting herself to him; she gave Wagner all Wagner wanted, and yet she held on to her own strong personality. (Now and then she proclaimed her thralldom rather too loudly, with the pride of purposeful humility.) Gradually her personality assumed a German shape; the French girl became a German "wife." Soon she was with him heart and soul in the mission of saving German art and derogating French culture, and before long the mission included the saving of the "German character," the race that, as everybody (except some misguided natives of France or England) knows, is superior to all other races.

Yet her doting in idolatry did not interfere with the exercise of her sharp and often practical mind. As a result she was able to introduce, at least now and then, a measure of prudence into the life of the spotted man.

Her possessiveness surrounded Wagner. She decided which friends to keep and which to slough off. Peter Cornelius wrote regretfully to his bride that Cosima had dug a moat between him and Wagner, "who remembers people only as long as he needs them." Cornelius noted: "Wagner is completely and utterly under her influence. . . . One can no longer speak with him alone." She did not like Tausig, and so she issued a "papal bull against poor Tausig" and Wagner began to ignore him. Tausig complained that "Wagner has just had the extraordinary notion of requesting me through the Delphic Oracle [Cosima] and in an extremely uncivil manner to return the original sketch of *Tristan.*" The least he should have done, Tausig thought, was to write the request himself.

Cosima opened all letters addressed to Wagner and suggested the answers. She even opened the letters from Minna, who had heard rumors of the affair and was again berating her husband for his infidelity. On October 5, 1865, he wrote her: "I have *not* read the letter just received from you. Ever since your letter last spring which so distressed me, I have determined never again to allow anything to embitter my memory of you." It was the last communication Wagner addressed to Minna; chances are it was Cosima who inspired it.

An entry in the Brown Book shows, astonishingly, that he intended to consult her even about an artistic point, namely two possible ways of treating the story of the sacred spear in *Parsifal:* "Which is better, Cos?" But she never offered a criticism. Unfortunately! Probably she was never bothered by the prolixity of Gurnemanz or the slowing of the drama interposed by King Marke's speech or the weakness of the last act of the *Holländer* (of which he himself was aware) or the length of Beckmesser's Serenade (which is usually shortened in performance). She valued to the fullest the originality and greatness of Wagner's genius, and from the first she was certain of his high place in posterity. Every note was sacred to her; to be cognizant of his achievement, she told Daniela, it was necessary to enjoy more than the "Evening Star" or "Isolde's Love Death"; it was necessary to live in his world.

As for their royal benefactor, though they were both honestly grateful to him, they lived in uneasy proximity to the throne. "The King's love is a veritable crown of thorns," Wagner confessed. Yet a week he spent with Ludwig at Hohenschwangau was one of unalloyed happiness. (Or almost unalloyed: Prince Paul von Thurn und Taxis, Ludwig's playmate, was often present.) And, from the fullness of his admiration, the young king wrote Cosima:

> Let us two take a solemn vow to do all it is in human power to do to
> preserve . . . the peace he has won, to banish care from him, to take
> upon ourselves, whenever possible, every grief of his, to love him,
> love him with all the strength that God has put into the human soul!
> Oh, I know our love for him is eternal, eternal; yet it makes me
> happy to think I have entreated a soul so true in friendship as yours
> is, honored lady, to join me in being to him all that it is possible for
> human beings to be to an adored one, a holy one. Oh, he is godlike,
> godlike! My mission is to live for him, to suffer for him, if that be
> necessary for his full salvation.

To please Ludwig, Cosima began to collect a *"Wagner Buch"* for him, gathering everything she could of her lover's early compositions, essays (though the two touched these writings up, here and there, just to be sure that they gave no offense), and personal mementos. In her zeal, Cosima could be something less than gracious. Mathilde Wesendonck wrote to Wagner: "Frau von Bülow requests me in a letter received today to send her some of your literary manuscripts which are in my possession. I have glanced through the portfolios but find it impossible to send anything—except on the assurance of your personal wish." She sent him a list of the manuscripts she had. Wagner replied that it would be best if she would return . . . *everything.*

Wagner was the kind of man of whom Goethe's words were true: he could endure anything except a series of beautiful days, Being a composer, a poet, a conductor, was not enough for his vaulting mind; his hubris convinced him that he was as well a profound philosopher and a far-seeing statesman. At Ludwig's suggestion, the king almost sharing Wagner's opinion of Wagner, he now prepared a "Political Journal" (clearly he was courting trouble!) intended to instruct the

king in how to solve such complex questions as a constitution satisfactory to the divided German states (all that was needed was to construct it out of the "best qualities" of the German race), how to oppose the threatened hegemony of Prussia, how to eradicate the influence of Jews (most dangerous), Frenchmen, and Jesuits in public life and to find salvation in the "folk." Ludwig, seeing himself summoned as a savior, quite in the Lohengrin tradition, with the new Germany cast as Elsa, warmly thanked Wagner and Cosima, who copied the journal but on reflection had sense enough to perceive its utter dilettantism.*
Not limiting himself to theory, Wagner began to make specific recommendations for the right men for ministerial posts. (Needless to mention that the "right men" were those who would support Wagner's artistic aims.) As his egocentric view of the world took in more territory, Cosima holding the magnifying lens, his demands for still more copious contributions from the king's purse grew more importunate. These demands perturbed Munich's plain citizens—though quite a few of them acknowledged his importance as a composer—and gave the ministers further ground to brand him as an unprincipled exploiter of the king's generosity, while the hardheaded politicians mocked him as an inflated fantast. Liberal minds, and there were many such in the Germany of the Romantic Era, were repelled by his war hoots against the Jews. The ground swell of hate rose to storm proportions, so that even when his recommendations were constructive, when he advocated the new music school, or called for reform of the deadly routine at the opera house, or pleaded for the construction of a new theater, he met with the scowl of suspicion or the snicker the ignorant utter over a stein of beer. Cosima, fearful of the mounting opprobrium, more sensitive to public opinion than he, nevertheless kept telling him that he was gloriously in the right, and collaborated with him on the letters and memoranda he wrote to Ludwig.

In early August 1865, Wagner petitioned the king for an outright sum of forty thousand gulden. It was not the first time he had asked for substantial sums in addition to the annual subvention granted him, only this time the sum was larger—representing about two thirds the amount annually set aside by Bavarian law for the king's personal use —and the request stated frankly that it was to be used for the payment of old debts and for maintaining himself "decently," though the petition also contained a provision that part of the money was intended

*Thirteen years later, Wagner reworked the essay and published it under the title "What Is German?"

for helping some indigent musicians, without "prejudice to my domestic economy." As before—and after—that "economy" was wildly extravagant.

It is easy to see Cosima's style in the wording of the petition. The king kept him waiting from August to October before granting it, but grant it he did, out of fear of offending Wagner. Cosima was with Wagner when the news of the grant arrived. She suggested that she herself should collect the money: it had been awarded to him by a loving friend, and by poetic justice it should be handed to him by another loving friend. She went to the treasury, accompanied by Daniela and the children's governess. There, evidently, the officials were bent on showing their resentment: they told her that they had banknotes for only half the amount; the rest she would have to take in silver coins. Cosima was quite able to deal with the situation. She sent the governess to call two taxicabs, and she and the governess calmly began to load the cabs, carrying the heavy sacks. Apparently she shamed the officials, who after a while helped her politely.*

The matter of the forty thousand gulden might have been eventually forgotten amidst other political and economic problems if Wagner had not fallen into a trap, cleverly baited for him by the politicians.

On November 26, 1865, the Munich *Volksbote* published a direct attack on him, claiming that he had cost Bavaria some 190,000 gulden in less than a year, that he had interfered with certain proposed changes in the cabinet secretariat in order to make his influence over the king even more absolute, and that his final objective was not only financial exploitation but a drive toward "democracy." The article was probably planted.

Wagner was stung into losing his temper. Cosima, who up to then had kept hers, fumed. An attack on herself she might have endured. But this disgusting dragging down of her lover's high-mindedness? Instead of keeping silent, they collaborated on a long reply, which a rival paper, the *Neueste Nachrichten,* was delighted to publish three days later. Though the article appeared anonymously, its style, turgid and vituperative, betrayed its authors. The manuscript is in Cosima's handwriting, but she probably did more than simply copy the words. At any rate, she carried the manuscript personally to the editor of the

*This famous anecdote is usually told as a move on the part of the treasury officials to stir up public resentment against Wagner. Ernest Newman pointed out that this was well-nigh impossible, there being "not the slightest suggestion of trouble so far as the public was concerned."

newspaper. The article was nothing but a raw polemic, and a singularly maladroit one, excoriating "certain people [the king's ministers] whom I have no need to mention by name, since they are the objects of universal and contemptuous indignation in Bavaria," who were viciously injuring Wagner's and the king's idealistic plans. Worse, at several points the article mentioned "the king's unshakable friendship for Wagner."* That proved to be a cardinal mistake; it was what the politicians needed. To bandy the king's name about in such envenomed circumstances was presumption not to be tolerated. The court officials, the Jesuits, the archbishop of Munich, and members of the royal family now closed ranks to warn Ludwig that if Wagner stayed on, it boded an ill eruption to the state, and to remind him that revolution was indeed a possibility in the Bavaria that had chased out Lola Montez and forced Ludwig I to abdicate.

Ludwig II weakened. He was told that he had to "choose between the love and respect of your faithful people" and the friendship of Richard Wagner. The warning was well timed. A crisis loomed. Austria under the conservative Franz Joseph and Prussia under Bismarck in his prime were quarreling. The overt cause was disagreement over who was to govern the duchies of Schleswig-Holstein; the real cause was the question who was to take the lead in a German confederation, or, to put it baldly, who was to become the overlord of the German people. Bavaria had to take sides, one way or the other, if it was not to be demoted to a second-class state, or worse. So there was Ludwig, standing between Bismarck (whom he hated) and Franz Joseph (whom he didn't like), forced to decide whose "friend" he was going to be. It was the most difficult decision he had had to make, and he needed all the "love and respect" of his people he could earn. Baron Ludwig von der Pfordten, the prime minister, felt it his "sacred duty" to speak plainly, "even at the risk of offending his sovereign." Pfordten drew up a memorandum pointing out in strong terms that "in times like these, when the very existence of states and thrones is threatened . . . action in the real world is called for." Ludwig had to get rid of this man, "who has the audacity to assert that members of the cabinet who have proved their fidelity do not enjoy the smallest respect among the Bavarian people, is himself despised by every section of the community to which alone the throne can look for support—despised not only for his democratic leanings (in which the democrats themselves do not

*The day the article was finished, Wagner told the king that he never, never once, had instigated a newspaper article!

believe) but for his ingratitude and treachery toward friends and benefactors, his overweening and vicious luxury and extravagance, and the shamelessness with which he exploits the undeserved favor of your majesty."

Still, heavy as the pressure was, Ludwig might not have yielded to it had he not begun to have some doubts, however shadowy, about Wagner the man, though nothing could swerve him from his belief in Wagner the artist. About Wagner the politician Ludwig had done some serious thinking and had found the composer's political ideas built of cardboard scenery. What was worse, Wagner had been presumptuous in deprecating Ludwig's choice of officials. It was tantamount to weighing "the worth and honor of a king . . . in a scale of common ounces." His pride injured, yet with a deep sense of personal loss, Ludwig came to a decision: Wagner was to be ordered to leave Bavaria "for six months." (Everybody knew that six months was only a polite way of saying "indeterminate.") Ludwig wrote to Pfordten: "You will realize that this has not been easy for me; but I have overcome." Cornelius later put the blame on Cosima: he was sure it was she who was responsible for the article in the *Nachrichten*.

On the evening of December 6, 1865, the king's decision was conveyed to Wagner. He was having tea with Cosima—Bülow was away—and Peter Cornelius. A visitor was announced; it was Johannes Lutz, a pallid, tiny, hand-rubbing diplomat, who was later to rise to high power and become Bavarian prime minister. He pronounced the edict of banishment in a casual, dry voice. At first Wagner thought it was a joke. Cosima almost fainted. When Wagner realized the true state of affairs, he broke out in a stream of invective, so that Lutz interrupted him with "Control yourself! I am here on an official mission." Cosima laid a restraining hand on Wagner's arm. Her eyes filled with tears. She knew what it meant: it meant another separation. Cosima, still trying to keep up appearances, could not go with him. The ugly farce had to continue.

On December 10, at six-fifteen in the morning, Wagner, looking ashen and old, left Munich. Cosima saw him off, along with three friends. She waved calmly as the train pulled out. On that cold winter morning she behaved as if her lover were going on a week's holiday. Six months would pass. But would Wagner be permitted to return? Peter Cornelius, who was present, wrote: "As his car glided from the station, it seemed as if a vision had melted away."

2

Wagner wandered to Bern, Vevey, Geneva, Lyons, then to the south of France, to seek, as he wrote Cosima, "the nest of our repose." In Marseilles he got word of Minna's death. The news was relayed to him through Cosima by Dr. Anton Pusinelli, Minna's physician and Wagner's faithful friend, who, uncertain of Wagner's whereabouts, guessed that Cosima would know. Minna died on January 25, 1866. Pusinelli telegraphed: *"Que faire?"* Wagner, though deeply moved, asked Pusinelli to arrange the funeral of his "poor, unhappy wife," because he himself was too far away to make the journey to Dresden. Cosima wept, thinking of the declension from ardor to incompatibility which that marriage had represented; she had liked Minna in the old days when they first met in Zurich.

Minna's death gave the press an occasion for an open attack on Cosima. The Augsburg *Postzeitung* reported that on the day of the funeral Cosima went to the theater, "clad in shining white, evidently to express her joy." Bülow found it necessary to answer this smear:

> Frau von Bülow, the daughter of the honorable Abbé Franz Liszt of Rome, is no public figure, being neither an actress, singer nor writer, nor in short any of those ladies whose photographs are displayed and sold in the art shops. Therefore I deem it a most unseemly transgression if any of her private actions—and as such must be considered a visit to the theater, whether or not strikingly gowned, or even on the day of the death of her nearest relative—is commented on in public print, be it in praise or censure. . . . All statements made . . . in the *Postzeitung* are lies. In the first place, we are not relatives of my honored friend Herr Richard Wagner, nor did we have any connection with his deceased wife, and in the second place, my wife did *not* go to the theater on the day of the funeral. Finally, she never wears "shining white."

It was cold comfort to Cosima that Ludwig kept assuring her that his love for Wagner still stood at full tide. "Need I tell you," he wrote to her, "what I have endured in these days and that I decided upon the step with a bleeding soul?" Longing for each other, she and Wagner communicated by telegram, resorting to pseudonyms because of their fear that the clerks would pass on the contents to the journalists. Wagner signed "Will," Cosima "Vorstel" (from Schopenhauer's *Die Welt als Wille und Vorstellung*). In January he telegraphed her:

January 20, 1866

For God's sake, dear one, no more half-measures! We have suffered enough, without wanting to torment ourselves further. In a month, God willing, we shall be tranquilly reunited, no more talking, through with Munich—final escape!

Yet it was March before Cosima plucked up her courage and went to Geneva to see Wagner. She took her daughter Blandine along. He told her that nothing, no monetary or artistic temptation, would induce him to return to Munich. He had written Ludwig to that effect: "And so, dear one, hear what I have to say: *I will not return to Munich.* Tell this to the wretched people who deceived and betrayed you." He had again taken up the composition of *Die Meistersinger* and he needed the utmost concentration to build that great fugue of the first act. But he needed Cosima's presence as well. He proposed that they look for a home in which she and Daniela and Blandine and of course his own child Isolde would join him, with Bülow always welcome when and if he wanted to come. Wagner wanted everything: Cosima, her three children, who were living in Bülow's home, and the continuation of friendship with Bülow, who would stay in Munich, retaining his eminent position, and would supervise those model performances which the king longed to hear. Like a benevolent deity, Wagner would bless these from afar but have no part in them.

In March, Wagner and Cosima set out to find a place suitable for housing the banished rajah of the Music of the Future—and his love. After a three-day search, they came upon a large villa near Lucerne. The house, isolated by a round of poplars, stood on top of a little hill, its ground reaching to the shore of Lake Vierwaldstätter. One view gave onto the lake, the other on the high Alps, with the Rigi standing like a pompous dragon (Cosima wrote), and when the clouds gathered, Valhalla seemed to be near. The name of the property was Triebschen. Cosima looked it over with a housewife's eye, approved, and then returned to Munich. Wagner almost immediately leased the villa. He had to pay the year's rent in advance, five thousand Swiss francs—a high price—and he asked the Munich Treasury to send him the rest of his stipend for 1866 at once. Instead, the king sent him the five thousand francs as a gift.

On April 15, Wagner moved to Triebschen. He was enchanted by it—except that Cosima was not there; she was where she felt she ought to be, in Munich with the children. Wagner, longing for her, read the old folk tale of Melusine, the fairy princess who consented to marry Raymond of Poitiers on condition that he not visit her on Saturday, on which day she turned into a water sprite. He did—and lost her. Wag-

ner saw himself as Raymond: "I have just finished reading Melusine
—oh, God, my heart breaks!" he wrote to Cosima. And he pleaded
with her to come back, come back as quickly as she could, to this
"charming lake where every boat is surrounded by a shining silver
circle," where she would find "heavenly peace." He was not sure of
her. Was she like Melusine? "On moonlit nights she still tends the
youngest children—and then no more is heard of her." (The original
of this letter of April 17 was destroyed, but a partial copy of it is
preserved.)

3

As Cosima noted retrospectively in her diary, the six years she spent
in Triebschen were, with all their trials, the happiest years of her life.
There she lived in total proximity to Wagner, there she saw him
complete *Die Meistersinger* and *Siegfried,* compose the *Siegfried
Idyll* and begin *Götterdämmerung;* there she became his wife; there
her son was born.

Four days after Wagner signed the lease for Triebschen, he wrote
to Bülow, inviting him, Cosima, and the three children to come and
stay with him for "as long as possible." The entire lower floor would
be put at his disposal. On May 12, Cosima and the children came. A
week later, Cosima wrote the king: "Yesterday we took up the biography once more. In the morning I copy, in the evening the Friend
dictates." Bülow was professionally detained; he arrived as soon as he
could, on June 10. There they were all together. Bülow had come,
according to Peter Cornelius, in order to "put the final decisive question to Cosima: Do you wish to belong to Wagner or to me?"

The question had to be resolved. The *ménage à trois* was proving
unworkable, the secrecy unendurable. Neither Cosima nor Wagner
could again live through an episode as nerve-racking as the one that
occurred on May 22, Wagner's birthday.

In the preceding January of that year of 1866, Ludwig, his heart
grief-stricken because of his separation from Wagner, had toyed with
the idea of abdication and even with thoughts of suicide. He wrote to
the *"Freundin"* (Cosima): "I tell you I cannot bear to live apart from
him much longer. I am suffering terribly!" As the months passed, the
wound did not cease hurting; on the contrary, with Wagner out of his

life, it was "Torture! Despair . . . If I cannot live with and for him, let death be near." On May 15, the king sent Wagner a long telegram in which he proposed that he "resign the throne and its empty splendor." The telegram was followed on the same day by an equally despairing letter containing a concrete proposal: let Wagner find a house near Berg and be with Ludwig. He, having renounced the throne—no longer king, but unswerving in love and fidelity—would never be parted from his "dear one." Cosima and her husband and the children would live in a house nearby. "While we are on this earth let us be together; the day of your death will be mine as well."

Whether these threnodies were to be taken at full or at "operatic" value, they sounded grave enough to the two people at Triebschen, who would of course lose everything should Ludwig really abdicate. Wagner answered with advice that was as sound as he could make it: Calm yourself, let six months pass; during that time do your utmost to fulfill your kingly duties; do not remain a stranger to your people. Examine closely the motives and the loyalty of your ministers; ponder carefully your decision as to the present position of Bavaria in the Austro-Prussian conflict; appear in person at the opening of the Bavarian *Landtag* (the meeting of the Diet scheduled for May 22); and only after you yourself are satisfied that you have done all that is needed to be done for your country, determine what step to take next. All this was sensible, though laced with self-interest.

Ludwig took some of this advice. He did inaugurate the Bavarian *Landtag*, though he postponed it from May 22 to May 27 (he telegraphed to Cosima: "Reception icy—press scandalous"), but when the situation worsened to the extent that a general mobilization of the armed forces had to be ordered, he withdrew to Berg and made himself inaccessible. He did give up the idea of abdication, but one benison his sorely tried spirit insisted on: he would spend Wagner's birthday, May 22, with him at Triebschen. (Hence the postponement of the *Landtag*.) There was no getting around this request; the king had to be invited by Wagner and with a show of enthusiasm. But what about Cosima? How explain her presence, installed with the children and acting as *maîtresse de maison?* The king still believed that the relationship of Wagner to Cosima was one of friendship, nothing more. They both realized that the King of Bavaria could not conceivably visit the home of a man who was living with another man's wife. The only solution was for Wagner to tell him that Cosima "happened" to be at Triebschen for a visit. Ludwig believed it.

It is almost impossible to accept Ludwig's naiveté in face of what was general knowledge and in spite of the evidence before his eyes. Yet accept it we must, his trust apparently as unquestioning as that of a child reading "Cinderella." Undoubtedly Ludwig did not *want* to think otherwise; he needed to believe that the man who was fashioning his artistic dreams was incapable of taking the wife of his most devoted friend to bed. He needed to believe that the admired Cosima was faithful to her marriage vows. It was, if only subconsciously, a purposeful blindness. In addition to a certain idealistic ingenuousness, another motif may have influenced Ludwig, again subconsciously: though no homosexual attraction of himself to Wagner can be traced, though in fact Wagner was physically the very opposite of the boys and young men to whom Ludwig was sexually drawn, he did regard Wagner as a being (as he himself wrote) "not made of mortal clay," and he felt the homosexual's aversion to the idea of his idol's "compulsive ardor" toward a woman.

Great secrecy surrounded Ludwig's little expedition. He sent Prince Paul ahead and at three o'clock in the morning of the twenty-second he dispatched a birthday telegram to Wagner as a red herring, to make believe he was still in Berg. At that hour he was galloping toward a tiny railroad station, where he caught the express train to Lindau. From there he took a boat across Lake Constance and appeared in Triebschen in time for lunch, dressed in a blue Byronic cape and a huge hat with peacock feathers. At the door he told the servant to announce that Walther von Stolzing had arrived. He was extravagantly welcomed by Wagner and Cosima.

He left two days later, happy and invigorated by his visit. But of course the news leaked out and at once furnished food for a new scandal, uglier than the preceding ones, aggravated as it was by the fear of war which was sweeping the country. How could a sovereign leave his country at such a time, even for two days? The attacks were directed against Wagner, Bülow, and this time specifically against Cosima. The newspapers pitied the "young enthusiastic King, with no weapons as yet against such wiles," and spluttered that the "devilish trio had lured him into their sty." They shouted for the removal of Cosima and Bülow from Bavaria "to cleanse the steps of the Bavarian throne of this species of greedy, self-seeking, branded adventurers." They called Cosima "Madame Hans" in allusion to the madame of a brothel: "Meanwhile the same 'Madame Hans,' who has been known to the public since last December by the descriptive title of 'the carrier pigeon,' is with her 'friend' (or what?) in Lucerne, where she was also during the visit of an exalted person," said the *Volksbote* on May 31.

Now Bülow could not keep silent; this time he *had* to speak up, to defend his wife. Yet how clumsily he went about it! He demanded a retraction from the *Volksbote* and challenged its editor to a duel. Both demands were refused. What could he do next? Go to law? That would take endless time and an award for libel would clear neither his nor Cosima's name. And how could he prove what he knew to be untrue? He left Munich to go to Triebschen and take counsel with Cosima and Wagner.

Wagner's proposal, which met with Cosima's and Bülow's entire agreement, was this: he would beg the king in the name of their friendship to write a letter to Bülow—one that Bülow would be at liberty to *publish*—stating that he (the king) had "the exactest knowledge of the noble and high-minded character of your honored wife" and that he was personally going to "investigate what is inexplicable in those criminal public calumnies, in order that, having obtained the clearest insight into this outrageous conduct, I may see that the sternest justice is done upon the evildoers." In plain words, Wagner had the colossal nerve to ask Ludwig to pronounce the lie direct. He followed this up with a telegram on June 8 to Prince Paul in which he posed an ultimatum. It read in part: "Should the only valid satisfaction, asked for by me, be refused him [Bülow], then I must share his fate and henceforth be dead even for the exalted Friend." Both the letter and the telegram conveyed their message with the subtlety of a rifle shot. The trigger was pulled only a few days after Ludwig had visited Triebschen, his soul lifted by the magnetism of Wagner's personality and the beauty of the *Meistersinger* music. At this psychologically telling moment, Wagner, in effect, said to Ludwig: Do what I ask or lose me. It was pure blackmail.

The three in Triebschen were frantic. They could hardly have believed that the proposed statement from the king would silence the newspapers. It would, however, thwart the proposal of expelling Cosima and Bülow. It would make possible giving the premiere of *Die Meistersinger* in Munich, in a performance supervised by the composer and conducted by Bülow. Nothing—not the filthiest scandal—should interfere with that. Wagner knew Ludwig could not and would not renounce so vital an artistic event.

Yet Wagner could not rest. A day after he sent the telegram, he wrote the king a letter purporting to explain how it came about that Cosima was accused of being his mistress. On December 6, 1865—Wagner wrote—when the king's messenger came to announce to him his Royal Friend's wish that he leave Munich for a while, he happened to be dining with Cosima and the children, Bülow being on a concert tour. Cosima, on hearing the news, was so upset that she could not bear to spend the night in her own house. Moreover, she wanted to console him. "I recognized her overexcited, almost visionary condition, and it put my own mind at rest to give her security in my house." Of course, his enemies concluded that

> the wife of my friend B. is my ———; that she slept four nights at my house, and paid herself for her caresses with the moneybags she had wheedled out of the Treasury, and that friend B. acquiesced in this, and moreover appropriated to his own use the gratuity intended for the orchestra. That is how the friends of the King of Bavaria are treated in his capital, Munich!

Out-and-out deceit. In perpetrating it, the sorriest role was played by Cosima. She wrote a long lying letter, dripping tears, to Ludwig, who had done nothing except be kind and affectionate to her. She spoke of her "three children, to whom it is my duty to transmit their father's honorable name"; one of the three was Wagner's, and as she sent her letter she knew herself to be pregnant with a fourth, also Wagner's. (Eva was born on February 17, 1867.)

June 7, 1866*

For the first and last time I implore you [to act] for us. I fall on my knees before my King, and in humility and distress beg for the letter to my husband, that we may not leave in shame and ignominy the country in which we have desired—perhaps I may say have done— nothing but good. My dear, exalted Friend, if you make this public statement then all is well; then we can remain here, build once more upon the ruins, bravely and full of comfort, as though nothing had happened—otherwise we must go hence, insulted and abandoned, depriving him [Wagner] of the only friends who could give him no more than their own existence, fame and repute, and who will now have to build all this up again elsewhere, in order to be able to offer him an abode. My most august Friend, you who came into our lives like a divine apparition, oh, do not consent that we, the innocent, shall be hunted out. Your royal word alone can restore our honor, which has been attacked; it can do so completely, everything will vanish before it. My dear lord, I venture to say what the hero said to the King who had conferred an honor on him: *"Sire, vous faîtes bien"*: you will do right to take us under your protection, and the people will understand it. . . . You know those mysteriously decisive hours in which the truth stands forth bright as the sun. In the name of those consecrated hours I say: Write my husband the Royal letter. . . . If there is a possibility of your gracious letter, then I will persuade my

*The letter is dated June 7, but it is probable that she did not send it till a few days later, after Bülow had arrived at Triebschen and she had a chance to discuss it with him. It is certain that Bülow knew the contents.

husband that we should return home—otherwise—how could we remain in a city in which we might be treated as malefactors? How could my husband carry on his work in a town in which the honor of his wife had been called to question? My Royal Lord, I have three children, to whom it is my duty to transmit their father's honorable name unstained. For the sake of these children, that they may not someday inveigh against my love for the Friend [Wagner], I beg you, my most exalted Friend, to write this letter.

If the letter is possible, I will gladly bear all earthly trials in return for this happiness. If it is not possible, then I herewith take my leave of our kind Friend, I kiss his Royal hand in humility and gratitude, I call down the blessing of God on his exalted head and withdraw with my noble husband, who has perhaps received his death blow, to a place where peace and respect await him, the weary and innocent one. If I could but say that our ruined lives would satisfy the demon, and that good would come of it for our King, then perhaps the deeply wounded heart of a wife and mother would once more be able to rise superior to it and attain happiness; but I do not believe it. It is not at us alone that the wicked are aiming.

This letter reveals the darkest stain in Cosima's character. It was her most abominable lie. She never mentioned it in her diary or in any of her writings: she must have been ashamed of it to the very core of her being. The kindest thing one can say about it is that a concatenation of panic and love made her write it.

4

Well, the king wrote the letter. It was published on the very day that Bavaria, having gone over to Austria's side, declared war on Prussia. Few people believed its contents—Cornelius noted that it was written "in a style too familiar for me to be able to mistake it for a moment for the work of the King's secretary"—and fewer still now concerned themselves with the fate of a "foreign" musician, a Prussian at that. The war was soon lost, but Bismarck, sagaciously opposing his sovereign, Wilhelm I, let both Austria and Bavaria off comparatively lightly. Bismarck had obtained what he wanted: a clear sign that Prussia, not Bavaria, was to be the captain of German affairs. Nor was there any doubt as to who was to be the pilot. "The Reform of Germany"— Bismarck's plan and Bismarck's phrase—had begun. In a way, the war of 1866 resembled the American Civil War, ended the year before: the agricultural and conservative South was defeated by the industrial and progressive North.

Still, Bavaria managed, after exhausting negotiations led by the skillful Ludwig von der Pfordten, to retain a measure of independence. Pfordten was the man whom Wagner and Cosima hated more passionately than any of Ludwig's ministers. Again and again Wagner had urged the king to get rid of "that Pfordten" and recommended that Prince Hohenlohe-Schillingsfürst be called to the prime minister's position; what Wagner did not know, but Ludwig did, was that the prince quite shared Bismarck's views. As to Cosima, her hatred of Pfordten dated back to a personal interview in which she asked him whether he would consider supporting a plan of letting Wagner return to Munich. He gave her a long and convoluted speech, the net of which was "No." In Pfordten's view, Wagner represented "a danger to King and State." Cosima told Ludwig that she could do nothing with this man: "his limitations are his only props, and it was with a narrow mind I had to deal today."

Yet at this time of crisis Pfordten, wrestling with Bismarck through long hours, did squeeze out concessions for Bavaria, though the Munich treasury had to pay Prussia thirty million gulden, roughly one hundred and fifty times what they had spent for the subvention of one of the world's great composers. Ludwig, shamed and humiliated, isolated himself with his Prince Paul and played at shooting off fireworks late at night. About that letter he had written for Bülow, he does not seem to have been aware that he had been tricked, or if he was, he said nothing—so strong was his need to hold high the image of the poet-composer, so certain was he that in Wagner first, but now increasingly in Cosima, he would find assuagement for his torments and his aberrations. Indeed, one senses that after the political debacle Cosima and the king drew closer to each other, though they saw each other seldom. Cosima's letters to him became more frequent, the king begging her to report everything that was happening in Triebschen, and they assumed a more informal tone. Presently, whenever Ludwig wrote to Wagner, he would follow his letter with another to Cosima, asking her how Wagner had reacted. At a certain moment he again considered giving up the throne, and Cosima wrote to him:

If only I could send you my tears, my wishes, my fears, my worries— they would carry the only possible answer to your letter of yesterday. . . . You seem to me the martyr of the crown, as the Friend is the martyr of art. The cross you bear appears to me as the highest and holiest distinction. How would I fail to understand your profound and great soul, which flows into mine and tells me what I have already divined? And yet, and yet . . . in these horrid times when faith has become barter, I have held fast my faith in a King's mission by the grace of God. I believe only in *you* as King. . . . In this hour I see only ruins. . . . I understand you, in every fiber of your being, and I know that were I in your place I would feel as you do. . . . [Yet] I have an irrevocable belief in the continuation of a Germany. It seems to me that it is now salutary to uncover what is worm-eaten and evil. That is how we must interpret a situation which really is but a prologue. I call to you, my great friend, and say, "Shoulder the heavy burden." . . . I pray to God, from whom kings receive their power and majesty, that he uplift and console you, that he send you his angel, as he did to the Redeemer on the Mount of Olives, and that you, spender of happiness, can find happiness and peace for yourself. . . . [July 21 or 22, 1866]

Cosima helped Ludwig to regain equilibrium. He remained king. Bülow's lot worsened. His bitterness deepened. He fled to Basel for a time, but when, on April 7, 1867, he received from Ludwig—at Wagner's urging—his official appointment as "Court Conductor and Director of the future Academy of Music" (Wagner himself going to Basel to bring him the news), he returned to continue his work in Munich in an atmosphere of open dislike. A certain Herr Bülow from Mecklenburg had also moved to Munich, and some rowdies, mistaking him for *the* Bülow, smashed his windows at night. "I am music-weary, future-weary, and most of all present-weary," Hans wrote to a friend. "I want to shrink, become obscure (which will go a lot faster than becoming famous), and live on as best I can under another sky."

Yet Bülow could not bear to leave undone the preparation of Wagner's new work, which he called "magnificent, unbelievably beautiful, joyful, witty," even though at least since Christmas he had known that Cosima was pregnant with a child that could not have been his. He rushed to Triebschen when Eva was born, and approached Cosima's bed, weeping. He said to her: *"Je pardonne."* She answered: *"Il ne faut pas pardonner, il faut comprendre."* Two months after Eva's birth, she insisted on joining him in Munich, if only temporarily. She wanted to show the world, *her* world, that she was still Bülow's wife and that there was truth in the mendacious letter the king had been induced to publish. But above all, she genuinely wanted to help Bülow, who was near the breaking point, to gain some sort of hold on himself. The wonder is that Bülow accepted her coming, and that she did manage to bring a measure of calm to his household. She did this so well that some members of the Wagner circle actually believed she would return permanently, that "the affair was finished."

Her attempt at a cover-up—her leaving Wagner, taking with her not only Daniela and Blandine and Isolde but even the baby Eva—was of course prompted by the continuous fear, grown more menacing after she had written the letter of the previous June, that Ludwig would discover the truth. And one must understand the danger in that discovery not only in terms of Ludwig's feelings but in terms of nineteenth-century mores. *The Scarlet Letter* had been published the previous decade, as had *Madame Bovary*, and *Anna Karenina* was to appear less than a decade later; they were expressions of unshakable social conviction. Liaisons were commonplace; adultery by a woman, committed while her marriage was still valid, was unforgivable and far more so where children were involved. In Germany, the belief in "woman's purity" had attained a special fervor, not only through Romantic poetry but through the "Addresses to the German Nation" of the philosopher Johann Gottlieb Fichte. The Germans were "destined to carry aloft the torch of civilization," and to fulfill this destiny their men must be prepared to go to the battlefield, their women must be staunch and true to their husbands. Mothers must devote themselves to their children. They must pray and guard the hearth. Wilhelm II was to express the sentiment later in *"Kinder, Kirche, Küche"* (Children, Church, Kitchen). A German woman does not—no, never—abandon her brood of *Kinder*. If she does, the weight of social ostracism will crush her. Nowhere was the double standard more "double" than in Germany.

Cosima herself believed in this code, at least until Wagner died. And Ludwig, himself a deviate, was all the more prone to demand conventional behavior in others. He could not escape the *Zeitgeist*. Moreover, as king he could not afford to condone offenders against the code. Though he sometimes protested against it, he embraced the creed of the *Bürgertum*.

What would happen to the plan of regenerating German culture along the right—that is, Wagnerian—lines and what, in practical terms, would happen to Ludwig's financial support, were he to learn the truth? In his first ecstasy, Wagner had written:

> O Cosima! We will be happier than mortals have ever been—because we three [the king included] are immortal. Death cannot dissolve our union. All the same, I hope that by living to an old age I will nullify the difference in our ages. O Cosima! Only the works remain to be created, for we cannot become happier than we are now. The spring of our three lives stands in

full blossom. The summer can but ripen the fruit! . . . Silence! We are not of this world—you, he, and I. . . . [Brown Book, November 15, 1865]

But they *were* of this world, and Cosima saw more clearly than Wagner the possibility that the king might turn summer into arid winter.

Her return to Munich plunged Wagner into misery. He wrote in the Brown Book: "Life falls away from me. . . . How weary I am." In her absence, he stopped going for walks in the Lucerne woods, as was his habit, equipped in stormy weather with a pair of giant boots which, Cosima said, made him look like his own Flying Dutchman; he stopped playing with the dogs; he forgot to feed the two peacocks, Wotan and Frigga, who strutted about the garden. Yet in his depression he began composing the sun-drenched last act of *Die Meistersinger.* Cosima, who had been following the progress of the great comedy with adoring eye and ear, had written to the king:

It is like a softly glowing musical radiance . . . one does not know whether one is listening to light or seeing sound. As the curtain falls . . . the whole of old Nuremberg is astir amid the pealing of bells, it is as though the old houses themselves were moving off in solemn procession. I think that on hearing this the heart of every German must leap with prideful joy and consciousness of his heritage. The delicacy of the musical detail is so subtle that I can only compare it with the wondrously dainty arabesques of the tabernacle in the Church of St. Sebald [correctly, the Church of St. Lawrence], which Master Adam Kraft supports with such calm confidence, just as here Master Sachs supports a far greater wealth and adornment of music and poetry.

Near the close of *Die Meistersinger,* after Walther impulsively refuses admission to the "Masters' Guild," Hans Sachs addresses an exhortatory speech to Walther and the populace. He tells them to "honor your German Masters"; then, "were the whole Holy Roman Empire to vanish into the void, you would still possess your holy German art." This speech, aside from being chauvinistic, is dramatically inept, and Wagner felt that it should be eliminated. Cosima wouldn't hear of it. She, the Frenchwoman, insisted that it remain. As a matter of fact, the Holy Roman Empire *had* vanished into the void, but Cosima, Wagner, and Ludwig believed that all that was noble and salutary in the German character remained in Bavaria, not in Prussia, its symbol the city of Nuremberg, "in Germany's center, serene in deed and work." (As Hans Sachs says; it was one of Cosima's favorite quotations.)

5

Worldly danger was to confront them from an unexpected source, a fantastical episode set in motion by the widow of Ludwig Schnorr, Malvina. She had been the Isolde to his Tristan in that incandescent first performance, and as such, and as a great artist, Wagner and Ludwig honored her. The king had granted her an annuity, on which she lived comfortably in Munich; Cosima and Wagner had recommended the grant. It was also understood that Malvina was to join the staff of the proposed music school. The two women, Malvina and Cosima, liked each other. Malvina wrote to Bülow, perhaps with romantic exaggeration, "She is as dear to me as my own soul." In November 1866, Malvina, thinking that Wagner was alone in Triebschen, decided to visit him. With him she could indulge in memories of her husband, whom she had greatly loved. Most ill-advisedly, she took along one of her pupils, a Fräulein Isidore von Reutter, an ignorant and half-unhinged young lady, who announced to Wagner and Cosima that she could communicate with the dead—"call spirits from the vasty deep"—and that the spirit of the dead Schnorr had spoken to her and told her that she was to marry King Ludwig. Wagner, who could obtain from Ludwig anything he wanted, was to act as the advocate of this project. The dead man had so commanded. Malvina had taken this seriously. And there was more to it; Malvina herself, still heartsick over her husband's death and wearing her widow's weeds with ostentation, had succumbed to a self-serving mysticism. She too, through the medium of a "magnetopath" (whatever that was), received instructions from her dead husband. She wrote to him every night and heard his answers in her sleep. He advised her that it was to be her mission, and hers alone, to guide Wagner and to help him continue his enormous artistic task. Only with her aid would Wagner be able to produce another *Tristan.*

Wagner had preserved his love for Ludwig Schnorr, "My Tristan, my faithful one," and Cosima shared it, though less sentimentally. They received the two visitors warmly. But when Malvina and Reutter began to spin their fantasies, Wagner refused to listen. Presently he sent Malvina a note saying that he would receive her again, but not that Fräulein Reutter, who had tried to impart her spiritualistic rant to Cosima as well. Cosima delivered the note to the hotel in Lucerne where the two women were staying.

Malvina, considering herself and her benevolence repudiated, veered. Whose fault was it that they were rebuffed? Why would Wagner be unwilling to let himself be guided and "redeemed"? Cosima—she was the evil influence, she was the Princess of Darkness who had led Wagner astray. "Oh, I know full well," Malvina wrote Wagner, "the unclean spirit that speaks through your words. It is not *you! Your* spirit is noble and true, your heart is great and warm! Woe to that devilish being that has put ignominious fetters upon your noble spirit. . . ."

In her fury, Malvina threatened to tell Bülow that Cosima was Wagner's "woman." This piece of non-news Cosima could accept calmly. It was a very different matter when Malvina threatened to tell "all" to the king. Ludwig might well have been impervious to information coming from so turbid a source, but Cosima and Wagner could hardly take the chance. In fact, Malvina did send Ludwig a tempestuous letter. He, however, was absent from Munich when it arrived and did not read it until weeks later. In the meantime, Wagner and Cosima acted on the classic principle that the best defense is offense: their attack consisted of telling Ludwig that *they* could well afford to ignore Malvina's calumnies, but they much feared that *his,* the king's, reputation would be besmirched by any contact with so unbalanced a woman. It was high time, Wagner suggested in a long, careful letter, that "the most intimate matters affecting the Royal Person be protected from beerhouse tattle." Malvina ought to be told to keep quiet —on pain of having her pension annulled. As to that Reutter creature, she was beneath contempt. Such women ought to be banished forthwith, without the king's deigning to pay any attention to them or granting Malvina a single interview.

The letter was written by Wagner, but it is easy to see that Cosima was its true author. It was she who took the lead in the whole Malvina affair. She implied to Ludwig that Malvina was in love with Wagner, a sex-crazed widow chasing a widower, and this infatuation had inspired her to wreck the innocent man's peace.

Cosima might have been able to make a clean breast of her predicament, to tell the king the truth at this opportune moment. If he would have accepted it at all, he would have accepted it from *her.* But by this time she was so steeped in lies that she could not find her way to the open air. That a confession would have required great courage on her part is indicated by a later note from Ludwig to Court Secretary Lorenz von Düfflipp, concerning some political articles Cosima had written:

December 13, 1867

I received your letter this evening. It is as if I had fallen from the clouds. This refined, intelligent Frau von Bülow occupies herself with scribbling for the Press! She writes these dreadful articles! Really I should not have thought the cultivated Cosima capable of a piece of knavery of this sort! But I am still more surprised that you believe the situation as regards Wagner, Frau von Bülow and Frau Schnorr is not kosher: if it should turn out that the miserable rumor is true—which I was never able to bring myself to believe—should it after all be really a case of adultery—then alas!

At first Ludwig hoped that the Schnorr-Reutter business would just go away. He didn't pay much attention to it, didn't reply to Wagner's letter, though he did meet Wagner's wishes to the extent of ordering Malvina to leave Bavaria. She would, however, continue to receive her pension; nothing was said about depriving her of that. But Malvina would not accept this verdict. She determined to remain in Munich "come what may" and to try to prove to the king that Cosima was a "conscienceless woman."

At Christmas time, Cosima hoped that she could allay her enemy's vindictiveness. She wrote Malvina:

December 25, 1866

Malvina: Today is the day of the world's redemption; it is as well my birthday. In all honesty I have examined my heart and have found there not the slightest shadow of hate, not even any rancor against the unfortunate woman who so sadly has torn us apart. Look—I know everything you have said about me. I know all your actions. I never have done you an iota of harm—and you, you have pilloried the daughter and the wife of two sublime human beings! Nor have you spared the sorely tried Friend! I believe firmly and deeply that you were ensnared and that you yourself suffered more harm than the agony you were able to inflict on me. Now you can do no more; perhaps your hatred—which seems to be justified in your eyes—is stilled. You took your vengeance for a guilt of which I have no knowledge, you have dealt the worst blow one woman can deal another. . . . I ask you: what did you want of me that I did not do and what did I do that you didn't want? Is it possible that my disbelieving the visions of Fräulein R. and my concern that she would destroy your mind, that this turned you from a friend to an enemy? . . . I tell you now in utmost seriousness: by all I have ever loved, by all I have suffered, by all I hope for my life and death, by the fate of my children, and by the memory of those I have lost—never have I lifted a finger against you! Let peace reenter your heart! We will probably never again see each other—forget the evil you have done me, as I will forget it. . . . [And so on, for a page and a half, with variations on the theme.]

Cosima von Bülow, née Liszt

Malvina's answer was a ten-page letter to Ludwig on January 12, 1867, in which she touched a spot that was beginning to trouble him sorely:

> Last summer, when he [Wagner] *dictated* to you the letter to Herr von Bülow, he made you perpetrate a piece of folly that damaged only *you*, since the relation in which W. stood toward the wife of the gentleman in question was already known to the world, and now he is the motive force in the injustice done to me, which, if a syllable of it becomes known, will cost you thousands of hearts.

Cosima and Wagner continued to fight back. On January 2, Wagner wrote Ludwig that *Bülow* was suffering agonies under Malvina's attack, which was dragging his name once more through the mire. Not alone noble Bülow; poor Cosima . . . poor Cosima could not sleep, and as she was close to a confinement—in which he, Wagner, was to take care of her, Bülow being in Basel—her health was seriously endangered. Cosima had been accosted and "provoked" by Malvina, either in the street or in the theater. This harassment must cease, I beg of you.

Malvina was not the only problem that arose between king and composer in that grim year of Bavaria's defeat. Wagner and Cosima continued to inveigh against Pfordten. The campaign of hatred made its effect: Ludwig weakened. "To continue with Pfordten is impossible," Ludwig wrote Cosima as early as October 1866. He added astonishingly: "I am now thinking of Prince Hohenlohe." Soon Bismarck received a report from Munich saying: "If one seeks the reason for the Royal displeasure that threatens the Minister, one always ends with Richard Wagner." By December, the threat became a reality: Ludwig asked Pfordten whether there was "any objection to Wagner's return in due time." Pfordten at once perceived the meaning of the maneuver and, his pent-up anger beyond control, replied: "I consider Wagner the most evil man under the sun. I can remain only if Your Majesty will renounce him forever."

Exit Pfordten. It mattered not that Ludwig's grandfather, ex-King Ludwig, had written from Rome: "I implore you not to make these changes. Hohenlohe's convictions are Prussian, not Bavarian." Ludwig let months pass before he even answered his grandfather's letter.*

---

*As a matter of fact, Hohenlohe had only one conviction: that he himself was destined for greatness. He achieved it: he became chancellor of the German Reich.

But now a reaction set in: Ludwig began to wonder. Why did Pfordten hate Wagner and Cosima to the extent that he sacrificed his position? Was there after all some substance to the newspaper reports, some basis for all those insinuations? Was Cosima playing an unworthy game with him? Why was she so bitterly opposed to Malvina's standing before him if the hysterical woman had only slanders to serve up? Could he really take Wagner's word for a thousand pounds? His—and Cosima's—violent reaction to Malvina seemed strangely excessive. Something was "not kosher." Secretly Ludwig summoned Franz, Wagner's former servant, and questioned him about Cosima, but he could get nothing out of the wily fellow. It is ironic that the curtain was drawn aside for him, at least an inch or two, by an eccentric woman who did what she did not for truth, but in envy of Cosima.

The end of the Malvina incident was anticlimactic. Ludwig did not insist on banishing her, did not withdraw her pension, yet never saw her, nor answered her letters. She lived on quietly, dying in 1904. Neither Cosima nor Wagner forgave her. Forty years later, Cosima still expressed resentment against her. Wagner, who had compared her to Schröder-Devrient, than which he knew no higher praise, and who had called her his "unforgettable Isolde," never once mentioned her name when he wrote "Recollections of Ludwig Schnorr von Carolsfeld" (1868).

There occurred no open break with the king. Ludwig still held fast to the belief that he and Wagner could carry out the plan of the music school and the new theater and eventually the performance of the complete *Ring*, and—much sooner—the first performance of *Die Meistersinger*. But gradually the king removed himself from Wagner's incantatory presence. No longer was the Friend invited to Hohenschwangau for those intimate exchanges which lasted far into the night. For about three months the king did not even write to Wagner. Silence reigned. A silence of disillusion. As for Cosima, she now appeared in a quivering light to the young *Schwärmer,* and he lost, or purposely suppressed, some of the confidence he had invested in her. Later his love for Wagner was to rise again and he was to use Cosima as a sensitive interpreter between them. Yet more and more he absented himself from the real Wagner and hardly ever met with the real Cosima, substituting for them two beings who did not exist and who belonged to the same lamplit realm as the protagonists of the operas.

6

Die Meistersinger . . . Wagner finished the composition sketch shortly after the Malvina turmoil, writing at the end of it: "7 Febr. 1867, St. Richard's Day, completed expressly for Cosima." Three major tasks remained: first, score the work for orchestra; second, persuade Bülow to take charge of the performance, a condition Wagner felt essential to its success; and third, teach the singers what was required of them in action and expression. This last task Wagner himself was to undertake, in spite of his vow never again to set foot on Munich's streets. The second task proved to be the most difficult: Bülow did not want to come back to his Munich post. He was sick and tired of being persecuted by the journalist *Schweinehunde*. Wagner had to appeal to the king and obtain extraordinary concessions for Bülow: he was to be given complete authority to reorganize the opera orchestra, to engage the singers he wanted, to hold unlimited rehearsals, etc. It was characteristic of Cosima that she fully supported Wagner in his efforts to coax Bülow to return. They both knew that if he did, Cosima would have to join him in Munich, the idyll of Triebschen would be interrupted for who knew how long, and all three of them would have to be especially careful lest a new scandal break out. Cosima was willing to accept a role that was distasteful to her, while Wagner was willing to submit himself to being parted from the woman he loved more passionately than ever, all for the sake of his art.

Bülow arrived, Cosima joined him, they rented an apartment in Munich with an extra room for Wagner. Together they acted their comedy of innocence. Cosima played her part to perfection; again she was the elegant wife and hostess of the famous conductor. With Cosima present at all rehearsals, Wagner and Bülow worked in perfect unison.* During the rehearsals, Cosima thought that if Wagner had not chosen to become a musician, he could have become the world's greatest actor—so vividly did he teach the singers movement, expression, tone color, etc.—while Bülow was undoubtedly the nonpareil of conductors.

The first performance took place on June 21, 1868, in the presence of the king. Wagner would have preferred to remain unseen, but court protocol demanded that he present himself to the king as soon as

---

*Yet once in a while Bülow's feelings broke through. At a rehearsal in his house, as he turned the pages of the *Meistersinger* manuscript, a photograph of Wagner and little Eva fell out. Bülow got up, suppressed his tears, and left the room.

Ludwig had taken his place. Ludwig insisted that Wagner stay at his side in the royal box. At the end of the first act, the audience clamored for Wagner, but he did not appear. At the end of the second act, and again after the final act, the enthusiasm of the audience rising to an ever higher pitch, Wagner, at Ludwig's urging, bowed from the box. Bülow is supposed to have said, "Horace by the side of Augustus," a quip that flew all over Germany. It was an unheard-of gesture—a commoner, a mere musician, daring to receive homage in the presence of a royal personage. One reporter wrote that he instinctively looked up at the ceiling to see if the chandelier was falling down. Cosima occupied a seat in the stalls; Ludwig did not receive her.

It was the most triumphant moment of Wagner's career so far. In spite of some opposition, several critics finding "not a trace of a tune" in the work, *Die Meistersinger* was soon taken up by the theaters of Germany, the public loved Hans Sachs, and the entire opera became a national paean.

At dawn, after the premiere, Ludwig, still under the influence of the great experience, wrote Wagner a moving letter: "To you I owe everything, everything! Hail German art! In this sign we will conquer." Surely this would have been the moment for Wagner to be open and direct with the king. Instead, he left for Triebschen two days later. Within a month Cosima joined him there. Wagner sounded the old refrain *da capo:* he wrote Ludwig that Cosima could no longer bear the calumnies to which she was exposed in Munich. She was "so profound, so rare a being" that she wished to disappear from the world. As to himself, he had long ago renounced it, his only wish was to live in retirement, his life belonging to the king alone, for whose sake he would take care of his broken health so that he might complete the great work his benefactor had assigned to him. One can almost hear the orchestral accompaniment to this *recitativo patetico.* Incidentally, he sank a pile of money into this place of renunciation, as Cornelius observed on a visit in July. He reconstructed the Triebschen villa, built "an aviary with golden pheasants and other rare birds," laid out "a few [new] acres of park and kitchen gardens," kept "some eight servants at least, and a horse and carriage."

It was Cosima who at last decided that things couldn't be left as they were. In September, she and Wagner made an excursion to Italy and on their homeward journey they were overtaken by huge floods in the Ticino valley. Walking for six hours while a thunderstorm raged unceasingly, they nearly drowned; they thought it was the end. "To look death in the face is to know the whole truth," Wagner wrote the king.

That brush with the precariousness of existence helped to firm Cosima's mind. On October 14, a few days after their return, she decided: she was going to Munich to see her husband, to tell him that from then on her life was to be joined with her lover's, and to ask for a divorce. Even then, in their communications with the king, they faced the whole truth only by insinuation; they merely *hinted* at the new development, Wagner writing of "necessary resolutions" and Cosima of "a new orientation in her life." The king did not answer: no letter from him is extant between September 14, 1868, the day Cosima and Wagner left for Italy, and February 10, 1869.

Wagner said retrospectively that Cosima had made her decision as early as July. That is quite possible. Why, then, did she suddenly force the issue, gathering her four little girls and hurrying to Munich with them to see Bülow when she had scarcely returned from an exhausting journey? The explanation is that she knew herself to be pregnant by Wagner for the third time. How could she again have taken up any kind of existence in Munich, where her condition would soon have become noticeable not only to Bülow but to his mother—who was staying with him and who had always loathed her—and finally to anyone she met on the street? She had to act.

She was fairly confident that, as usual, she could obtain what she wanted. She was mistaken.

Bülow said no—no divorce. His reasons for refusing can only be surmised. Certainly he could not have hoped to get Cosima back. He may have wanted to spare her and himself the detonation of a divorce, coming so soon after the happy day of *Die Meistersinger,* or more probably, he may have thought a divorce would make it impossible for him to stay in Munich, where he was now enjoying his work, conducting not only Wagner's music but other operas, and those with equal devotion. There is evidence for the latter reason, his work having become his "only hold on life." Bülow pointed out to Cosima that she couldn't get a divorce, being Catholic, while Wagner was a Protestant. Cosima replied, "Then I will change my religion." "That," Bülow pleaded, "will deeply offend your father. And your father is the friend to whom I owe most." But Cosima would have been willing to offend a dozen fathers. As it later turned out, Liszt did draw away from her and ceased almost all communication with Wagner. Nearly eleven years were to elapse before their old friendship could break through the clouds of his disapproval—and then it was Wagner, not Liszt, who took the initiative.

While Cosima was pleading with her husband, Wagner removed

himself from the scene by visiting his relatives in Leipzig. He was in the gayest of moods there, mimicking the people at the Munich Opera, excoriating the German theaters, making fun of the Jews, and playing excerpts from *Die Meistersinger* while he himself declaimed every part. He returned to Triebschen on November 11 and at once fell into melancholy. Life was hard, he wrote to a friend, life was bitter, and had been so since his early marriage. No one really understood him. Where would he summon enough strength to finish the *Ring?* He knew that the king was angry with him. He was living "in a desert."

Five days later, very late at night on November 16, 1868, Cosima appeared in Triebschen with Isolde and Eva. The light shone again. They embraced. She told him that she had not come for a visit; she had come to be with him for good. She was never going to leave him. She had taken the step—it was definite. Her bringing Isolde as well as Eva clearly signaled that *both* of them were Wagner's children, though Bülow continued his make-believe about his being Isolde's father.

It was now inevitable that Wagner tell the king. He thought that in a personal interview he could best "explain" or at least soften the blow. Accordingly he asked for an audience: *"De profundis clamo.* I await your sign!" The king did not answer.

Renunciation of respectability, anxiety over the king's reaction, the contumely of Munich society, the weight of guilt, separation from her two elder children, the spicy caricatures with which the newspapers kept entertaining their readers—much as they hurt her, they could not change her great resolve. The self-dramatization which often permeated her letters and her diary merely made a certainty more certain. Édouard Schuré, the French writer who was an admirer of Wagner, called Cosima "both an *intrigante* and a heroine." In her love she was completely the heroine. She wrote:

> I will gladly suffer everything, only to stand by his side. They can besmirch me even unto a far-off posterity, if only I am permitted to help him, to take him by the hand and to say to him: I follow you unto death. My only prayer is this: to die with Richard in the very same hour. My highest pride is to strip myself of everything, only to live for him. [Diary, March 15, 1869]

But even then, in the joy of being at last united with him, she could be the *intrigante*. On December 29, 1868, Wagner wrote the king a long end-of-the-year letter, thanking him for all he had done and regretting that he himself had been for quite some time "denied the light of the sun" of his life, a letter to which (as we have seen) the king did not vouchsafe an answer until February 10, 1869. In a postscript, Wagner added that he was enclosing a letter from Cosima which *had just reached him.* He was still playing the obfuscating game, concealing the fact that Cosima had been with him for the last six weeks, and that even as he wrote she was sitting beside him. Cosima duly wrote the required letter and duly misdated it December 27.

CHAPTER VI

The Diary

LIES DEVELOP a kinetic energy of their own; they roll on even after their uselessness has become evident. Bülow told everybody at the Munich Opera who wondered about Cosima's long absence from his house that she had gone to Versailles to visit her half-sister, Countess Claire de Charnacé, and he volunteered the information even to those who could not have cared less about Cosima's whereabouts. He was lying. There can be no doubt that he knew Cosima was in Triebschen. She had scarcely returned there before she began writing loving letters to Daniela, her eldest, now eight years old, and since the child was living in Bülow's house along with Blandine, it was obviously impossible for Bülow not to have seen these letters and not to have read them. Cosima wrote sometimes in French—to help Daniela become familiar with the language, she said—and sometimes in German, the contents of her letters the usual mother-to-child small talk: Eva no longer cries when she is washed with cold water; don't you and Boni (Blandine) make too much noise in front of your father's room; obey Hermine (the governess); does Boni still weep when she loses at dominoes?; "Aunt Claire," who is visiting in Triebschen, would like Daniela to come and visit her in Versailles and that will be possible someday "if you are well behaved and do your lessons," etc., etc. As to Daniela's and Blandine's two little sisters in Triebschen, Cosima reported that Loldi (Isolde) took a heaping forkful of cauliflower and called it a "Rigi," that she looked at a pine tree in the woods and thought it must be a Christmas tree for bad children because there were no lights on it, and that Eva put a lampshade on her head and danced round the room with it.

How long did Bülow think he could keep up his fiction? How long could Cosima's presence in Triebschen be hidden? About February 1869, the unhappy man seems to have suggested that Cosima join him once more in Munich just for the sake of appearances and if only for a couple of months, to which Wagner protested that were she to leave him again, however briefly, it would mean the end of him and his work. *She*, according to her diary, was willing to entertain the idea of "going to Munich to the children for two months and then to return with all four of them to Triebschen at the beginning of May," her purpose evidently being "to avoid scandal on account of the children as well as the King." Wagner would have none of it.

Bülow, thoroughly angry, now countered by declaring that Cosima's two children, *his* children, were to remain with him permanently. Their place was with their father. Superficially, his demand appeared reasonable, but in reality it was not, since it was prompted by vindictiveness and not by love for Daniela and Blandine. Bülow knew how much he hurt Cosima by separating the children from her, just as he knew he was not fit for the role of a father and played it mainly to chastise his errant wife. He spent very little time with the children, and his mother, as tight-lipped a grandmother as Zola could have invented, merely scolded and hectored them.

Meanwhile, Cosima was still keeping up her flimflam with the king. On March 29, 1869, she began a letter to him, which she continued on April 7, 8, and 9. The second part began: "Nearly two weeks have passed since the preceding lines and now I am in Triebschen." Obviously the implication was that she had just arrived, when in point of fact she had been there for almost a year, except for the time she and Wagner spent in Italy, the month she had passed in Munich, and one or two short trips to discuss the situation with Bülow or Liszt.

Was truth to be found anywhere in this web? Yes—first, foremost, and forever in the love Cosima and Wagner felt for each other. That love was purest truth. It was as unalloyed on his part as on hers. They were a Tristan and Isolde of the nineteenth century, and the grandiloquence with which they expressed their love—he more than she—

took nothing away from its truth. And second, we may find truth, though in a subjective form, in the famous diary which Cosima began on the first day of 1869 and which she kept until the day before Wagner's death. In these five thousand pages not meant for publication, she was honest with herself. She recorded her joys and griefs spontaneously, she noted down the trivialities and the big moments, helter-skelter, without giving them the shape of "literature." Some self-justification was bound to creep in, but she did not attempt to make things look pretty when they were not, nor did she mute the sounds of her conscience. Full objectivity was not to be expected from so personal a document. Nor was Cosima a skilled stylist, and she never quite managed to express herself in idiomatic German. All the same, and with all its repetitiveness, we have before us a direct and moving account of two lives linked. No, it is more than that: the diary is a document that sheds light on their century and helps us to see it clearly. Both Wagner, for all the originality of his genius, for all his revolutionary daring as artist, organizer, and publicist, and Cosima, for all her unconventionality, were children of that century. They shared the current ideas: trust the medal-bedecked uniform of the major, mistrust parliament, believe that woman must be subservient to man, know that the socialists are vicious, admire the machine, bow deeply before the king. The diary, begun in adultery, leads finally to a middle-class nineteenth-century marriage. And Cosima is before us every day.

As often as we are on her side, so often does she offend us. She was totally blind to the baseness of Wagner's character, to his lack of sympathy with and rude disregard of people who did not think or feel as he did, his condemnation of ideas that did not fit the formulas he had set up, his fulsome pronunciamentos, his conviction that he was not only a great composer but as a dramatist comparable to Shakespeare and Aeschylus. (A caricature in a Berlin magazine showed Shakespeare and Aeschylus making their humble obeisance to Wagner.) In addition, she believed him to be the kindest, sweetest, most honest, most unselfish of men, opinions with which Wagner saw no reason to disagree. How fortunate for her to live, in Milton's words, under a "total eclipse without all hope of day," and how unfortunate that Wagner implanted in her his prejudices, his xenophobia, his deafness toward contemporary French and Italian music, his hatred of Brahms, his derogation of Schumann, his foolish judgments of English poetry (of which he knew next to nothing), and above all his virulent anti-Semitism, which as a matter of fact she had acquired early, before she knew him, but which he nurtured in her so that every fourth page

of the diary contains some snide remark against the Jews.* And yet
there emerges a personality from whom it is impossible to withhold
esteem, a sensitive woman with a fine responsiveness to much in
music, poetry, literature, and the pictorial arts, a perfect companion
to a moody and demanding man, able to minister to him constantly
without turning herself into a washrag.

It was she who in June 1867—about a year after the king had visited
them in Triebschen—prevented what might have been a serious
break. Ludwig had been ardently looking forward to a performance
of *Lohengrin*. Wagner had cast Tichatschek in the title role. At the
dress rehearsal of June 8, the king looked at Tichatschek, and what he
saw shattered his illusions. The shining hero of his imagination was
impersonated by a sixty-year-old man with a flabby body, who main-
tained his equilibrium in the swan boat only by holding on to a pole
fastened to the deck for just that purpose. What Ludwig heard pleased
him no better: a tenor's tremolo, in vain disguised by overemphasis on
loud phrases and accompanied by "grimaces." Nor could Ludwig endure the primitive arm-waving of Ortrud. Wagner was imprudent
enough to tell the king that he ought not to have looked at Tichatschek
through opera glasses! No wonder that Ludwig became thoroughly
angry with Wagner and commanded that the performance be given
as soon as possible with a different cast. Wagner sulked.

Cosima now stepped in and wrote Ludwig a long letter—one of her
diplomatic masterpieces—admitting that, of course, their gracious
Friend had been quite right in his action, but wouldn't he please
consider the point of view of Wagner, who had felt that Tichatschek,
a great artist at one time, would still be able to create a perfect illusion
in word and sound? As it was, the performance took place on the
sixteenth, with Heinrich Vogl as Lohengrin and a new Ortrud, The-
rese Thoma. Bülow coached them, achieving wonders in a few days,
for which Ludwig wrote him an appreciative letter.

After the performance, Cosima urged Wagner to ask the king for a
personal interview. Wagner refused, as usual seeing himself as the
martyr. Whereupon Cosima threatened him with a "complete rupture." No doubt she didn't mean it—but the threat was enough. Wagner docilely applied for an audience and later acknowledged that she
had been right: to refuse would have brought serious consequences.
As it turned out, Wagner, summoning his repertoire of persuasion,

---

*It has been suggested that her anti-Semitism was rooted in her hatred of Princess
Carolyne Wittgenstein, whom she mistakenly thought to be Jewish, and whose domination of Liszt she disapproved of. But this is conjecture.

obtained Ludwig's pardon. No, more—it was *Ludwig* who apologized: "I kiss the hand which chastised me." All the same, a residue of resentment remained in Ludwig's mind. Cosima knew it.

On the other hand, when another disagreement between Wagner and Ludwig arose—over the premieres of *Das Rheingold* and *Die Walküre*—it was she who stubbornly fought alongside Wagner, despite the risk of Ludwig's withdrawing Wagner's subvention—or so they thought, holding too mean an opinion of Ludwig's high-mindedness—and it was she who was willing to face penury as long as she could face it with Richard. ("A garret in Paris. One room and two cubbyholes for the children. Who knows what fate has in store for us?" she wrote. Well, she was being theatrical. By then Wagner's operas were earning enough to keep him out of the garret.)

It was she who sneaked into the rehearsals of a Munich performance of *Tannhäuser,* after Bülow had ordered her to stay away, just to report to Wagner what was going on. It was she who made the expected wifely decisions about the children's schooling, the servants, the household routine, but also acted as hostess to, and intermediary with, Wagner's friends, keeping up the flow of conversation when he felt like being solitary and reclusive.

She began her diary with a noble statement of purpose:

Jan. 1 [1869]. I had intended to begin this notebook at Christmas, my 31st birthday, but I didn't get to it in Lucerne. Therefore let the first day of the New Year serve as the commencement of my report to you, my children. You are to be apprised of every hour of my life, so that you may really come to know me. If I am to die at an early age others will have little to say about me; if I am to die old I shall learn to keep silent. You, my children, will help me to fulfill my duty—yes, my duty. What is meant by that you will understand by and by, because your mother will tell you all concerning her present life. She believes she may do so.

The year 1868 marked the watershed of my existence. That year I was permitted to convert into action what had filled my being for five years. I did not seek this action, nor did I plan it—it was fate which commanded me. So that you may understand me, let me confess that until the very hour in which I recognized my true calling my life had been a jejune and ugly dream. Of that I do not want to speak—I myself don't understand it and I thrust it from me with all the force of my cleansed soul. The outer aspect [of my life] was and remained tranquil; within me lay a desert, a wasteland, until the man appeared who revealed to me that I had never lived at all. My love for him—it was a rebirth, a salvation, expunging all that was low and worthless in me. I swore to seal this love through death, through devout sacrifice, through complete dedication. . . . I called to him: "I come—and I will find my highest, holiest happiness in helping you bear

life." Thus I separated myself from my two dear elder children. I did it
—and would do it again; yet I long for you and think of you day and night.
For I love all of you equally. . . .

On that New Year's Day she describes how the two children, Eva
and "Loldchen," clad in white satin and wearing wreaths of roses,
greet "Uncle Richard." (All the children were soon to call Uncle Richard Father, then Papa.) Before lunch he reads her his essay "Judaism
in Music," and at table they discuss its import—that is, "the Jewish
influence on art, and for the first time Mendelssohn seemed a tragic
figure to me." She begs him to continue the dictation of his autobiography, "because I am superstitious, and the belief exists that what one
does on the first day of the year one continues to do." (Cosima was
very superstitious. She believed, for example, that seeing a dead horse
brought bad luck and that you must never write a letter of thirteen
pages.) Richard plays the piano for the children while they dance; then
he demonstrates a new toy, a jumping jack, to Loldi's great joy. She
writes with the gold pen he had used for the clean copy of the *Tristan*
and *Siegfried* poems. To her it is "the pen which drew the highest
work conceived by the highest spirit." She concludes:

> Be blessed, my children, the near ones and the far ones, and also the
> unknown one now slumbering in my womb. . . . All I love is now at rest,
> so I will go to sleep. To you and to him my last loving thought!

2

Happiness breathes through the first hundred pages of the diary. They
were together, living for each other and for the children: "R. is working." She sews and embroiders and listens to the passionate themes of
the last scene of *Siegfried.* A blanket of snow covers home and garden.
The children tumble about and make a lot of noise; it doesn't disturb
him in the least. Her ecstasy mounts as the weeks go by. Not that she
isn't often sad, often worried: missing Daniela and Blandine acutely,
she hopes that the separation from them is but a temporary grief—but
when will Bülow see reason? She can't explain the king's silence,
which depresses Wagner so that he is thinking of giving up the composition of the *Ring,* a possibility which so horrifies her that she argues
with him and he gets angry. She converses in her dream with her sister
and, waking, realizes with a shock that Blandine is dead: she has no

sister or brother. She is infuriated by a moralizing letter from Liszt: "How little does my father know me!" Evchen has a temper tantrum and hits her, and she takes this seriously. Pauline Viardot writes to protest against the "Judaism" essay—in addition, some fifty scathingly critical letters arrive in Triebschen—and she composes an answer because she admires that wonderful artist. Wagner sends it off as his own, but, concludes Cosima, "it is clear that she is Jewish" (she was not), being unable to understand how offensive Wagner's harangue must have seemed. She hears Hans has canceled several concerts—"I wept the whole morning." Yet her troubles are brushed away by one look, one word from him.

On the other hand, the slightest cross word from him sets her off:

> Today Richard hurt me—he who usually lays balm on my soul. He said apropos of the autobiography which I begged him to continue, "My innocent life cannot possibly fascinate you." Why did he say that? I do not know; surely he doesn't mean it. Alone, I wept without stopping. [January 17, 1869]

Men and women of that era shed tears easily. Wagner wept, Bülow wept, Ludwig wept. One evening, Liszt said to Marie d'Agoult, "Are we dining or are we weeping?" The pages of the diary were wet with Cosima's tears, yet often those tears were but a postscript to her happiness.

Their devotion never lessens. "You ought to have a god for a husband," Wagner tells her; she answers, "But I have one." "Your former wife would now be too old for you," she says to him, to which he replies that if he had stayed married to Minna he would by now have aged very much indeed. "Dear indispensability," he calls her.

As spring arrives, she seems to him more beautiful than ever. She wears a robe of pink cashmere with huge sleeves trimmed with Belgian lace, and when they go for their walks, she puts on a large hat in the Renaissance style, decorated with roses. Almost every day he tells her something endearing: "Only one thing I know: since the world began no man as old as I [he was fifty-six] has loved a woman as much as I love you." He would rather be with her than "if Shakespeare himself came to chat with me." (No doubt, if Shakespeare had come, Wagner would have given him a pointer or two.) Before him she felt humble:

> When I was ready for bed and I had said good night, R. came in again and said: "You can't know how much I love you. It is a dream that you are here

forever. I thought you had only been lent to me." I prayed. How can I ever complain when I, without merit of any kind, without a right, without any reason whatever, have found such happiness, while I see other excellent beings beset with sorrows? [October 21, 1870]

A week later he told her:

"I want to know nothing of love's tragedy, I care not two straws about the world's soul. I want to keep you and live a long time." [October 29, 1870]

He assured her that if she had not joined him, he "would not have written another note." We must doubt this protestation; surely the force of his genius was so great as to run its course against all obstacles and surely, having got as far as he did with *Siegfried,* he would have closed the *Ring* with *Götterdämmerung.* But we cannot doubt that his love for her eased the labor of creation and spurred him on.

Often in the evening Wagner read to her: the *Odyssey,* the plays of Sophocles, Goethe (their favorites being *Faust* and *The Elective Affinities*), Schiller, Ariosto, Ovid, Gibbon, Lope de Vega, Calderón, Boccaccio, Xenophon, Taine, Scott, Voltaire, Indian sagas, Norse myths, *The Arabian Nights,* E. T. A. Hoffmann, Plutarch, Plato, Schopenhauer, Lessing, Carlyle, Byron, Balzac—and Shakespeare. Over and over again Shakespeare, the only author whom Cosima considered equal to, and once in a great while perhaps even superior to, Wagner. Their favorite plays were passed in review, lovingly discussed, and taken up once more. (Of course they read Shakespeare in German translation.) Cosima loved especially both parts of *Henry IV* and *Hamlet,* Wagner all three parts of *Henry VI, Julius Caesar,* and *Macbeth.* He read to her in his "deep and thrilling voice," so that "I go to bed moved to the very core of my soul."

"In the evening we go over the scene between Hamlet and his mother, line for line, word for word, as if it were something entirely new to us." (October 12, 1874) "Nobody would believe," Wagner exclaimed, "that my wife wept over the deaths of Brutus and Cassius."

Wagner's comments on Shakespeare were worshipful, his analyses not more than the remarks of an intelligent college student, but Cosima recorded them as if they were the distillation of a great scholar's lifetime of thought.

Next to Shakespeare, she loved *Don Quixote.* "In Cervantes I feel a Germanic spirit," said Wagner. Cosima merely noted that bit of nonsense without comment. But many times when she felt low she asked him to read to her one or the other of the knight's adventures.

Their reading of the world's literature, amazingly copious considering how much he himself wrote and composed and how strenuously she was occupied in helping him, did not teach either of them to allow for diverse views. Plato's picture of the ideal state could not lessen their belief in the strong-arm hero, nor could Lessing soften their racial prejudices. Climbing a mountain of books, they remained where they were.

They did not live exclusively with high literature. Both, but Cosima especially, read trash for entertainment: sentimental romances, mystery stories, tales of adventure. They eagerly awaited every issue of the two German humorous periodicals, *Fliegende Blätter* and *Kladderadatsch.* She read the Parisian fashion magazines, and though she loathed the Munich newspapers, with good reason, she read them and aggravated herself.

3

In the first days of June, Cosima felt ill and Wagner took over the keeping of the diary, recording that her birth pains began on the night of the fifth; he was beside himself with anxiety, paced up and down in his room like any expectant father, could not sleep, listened to her screams, became frantic when he overheard the midwife exclaiming, "God in heaven!" thought the worst had happened until a servant burst in with the news: "A son is here!" At that moment, with the kind cooperation of Nature, which obviously took cognizance of the importance of the event, the sun rises above the Rigi, its rays penetrating the orange curtains of the bedroom and bathing the whole room in a glow of fire. She hears the church bells across the Lake of Lucerne; it is 4 A.M., Sunday, June 6, 1869. Wagner weeps. At six he goes to Cosima and takes her hand in his. They discuss the son's name; of course it is to be Siegfried.

Cosima is weak, suffers much pain, and it is not until the following Sunday, the thirteenth, that she takes up the diary again: "My Siegfried, crown of my life, you will prove how I love your father! Drank tea with R. To bed at 9. R. reads to me from *Don Quixote.*" Two days later, "still very weak," she summons whatever strength she has and writes a long letter to Bülow, as a "last attempt to come to an understanding."

Cosima wrote with no great hope of a positive answer, her last interview with Bülow having failed. As Bülow later told the story of this interview to Countess Charnacé, Cosima had lied to him:

September 15, 1869

When I asked her an almost indelicate question about the motives for her brusque departure [to Triebschen in November 1868]—I had begged her in vain to await the coming of Liszt in January—Cosima saw fit to reply to me with a false oath.

That falsity was evidently her answer to his question: Was she again carrying Wagner's child? More than half a year (November to June) had passed between his posing the "indelicate" question and his receiving Cosima's letter. The baby had been born. An astonishing change took place in Bülow's heart, a change from truculence to sympathy. No one could have predicted it, least of all Cosima. He understood. He understood, and his reply, kindly and consolatory in tone, shows him at his best:

June 17, 1869

I thank you that you took the initiative, and I will give you no cause to regret it. I feel too unhappy—through my own fault—to indulge in any reproaches which could wound you. During the cruel separation which you felt necessary, I came to recognize the wrong which existed on my side. I will underscore this wrong in the discussions with my mother and your father which will inevitably follow. I compensated you badly, indeed vilely, for all the sacrifices which you copiously offered me in our life together. I have poisoned your life and I have only to thank fate that the poison did not sink so deep as to make you lose the courage to endure your slavery. But alas! since you left me I have lost my hold on life. Your spirit, your heart, your friendship, your patience, your indulgence, your understanding, your encouragement, your counsel, and above all your glance, your word— they formed the essence of my life. When I lost this rich possession, the value of which I fully realized only after its loss, I broke down as man and artist. . . .

You have preferred to consecrate the treasures of your mind and heart to a higher being: far from censuring you for this step, I *approve* it. You are right. I swear to you that the only ray of light which from time to time sheds a consoling glow into my inner darkness and on my outer troubles is the thought: "Over there Cosima is happy."

He then reviews at length his reasons for resigning his posts at Munich.

Let me add that my wrestling with that giant work, *Tristan,* has literally finished me. Sunday will be the [last] public performance. For that I accept responsibility and the performance will not be a desecration—I recently wrote Wagner about it—but it will be the last time that I will stand at the head of [this] orchestra. My stay in Munich will end where it began, more *circulus fatalis* than *circulus vitiosus.*

Then, after confessing that he was too cowardly to commit suicide —"though if anybody had handed me a few drops of prussic acid I could not have resisted"—he answers her requests:

The separation from you must be complete. I must remove myself from all that is part of you and Richard Wagner, because my past life was guided solely by these two lodestars (I could add your father); I have to separate myself from you even in my *thoughts,* if that is humanly possible. Don't misunderstand: I am not proposing the éclat and unpleasantness of a divorce. If your father thinks that your union with Richard Wagner ought to receive an official sanction, I have no objection [to a divorce]. For my part I have no reason to want it, since I do not intend or wish to get married again, as you may imagine.

The children are yours. I entrust their education to your guidance. I believe that is the best that can happen to them. I agree completely with you that it would be impossible to hand them over to my old mother or to any member of my family (if I can speak of "family"). The annual bequest from your father (and from your mother) belongs to the children: those 6,000 francs should, by right and reason, be used for their education. I can contribute only the small legacy of Aunt Frege (5,000 taler), which, if I have luck, I hope to double until they reach their majority. You will be gracious enough—I earnestly implore you—to consider the furnishings [of the Munich house] as *your personal* property. When I leave here, which I hope will be on the 1st of August, I will take with me only a few belongings, indubitably mine—my clothes, books and scores. . . . You can sell what you don't want or send it to Triebschen or put it in storage as property eventually to be used by the children, as we agreed long ago.

He assures her that he will leave Munich quietly, before the opera season reopens and under the pretext of an extended leave of absence. He will give the newspaper scribblers no material for further gossip. He is uncertain as to his future plans; the one thing he must do is to get away, far away from Munich, preferably from Germany.

Well, here you have your letter, one badly written and hardly worthy of being read by the writer of the letter to which this is an answer. It is less of an answer than a testament, penned by a brain and a heart which are ill and crippled. All the same, it is not mad and contains nothing unreasonable. . . . May God protect and bless the mother of the fortunate children to whom she wishes to continue to devote herself.

Bülow's letter arrived on the nineteenth. Cosima was still very weak from Siegfried's birth and Wagner, fearing that the letter might upset her too much, kept it. But when the next day Cosima began to worry why she had not heard from Bülow, Wagner gave her the letter, saying it was "very beautiful." When she read it, Cosima was deeply agitated. "Many tears shed today." She reflected "day and night" as to what to do next. "I want to propose to him that I come to Munich with the children, to arrive at a final solution." (Diary, June 21) Nothing came of this and soon after she went to Zurich to meet "the fortunate children," Daniela and Blandine, and take them to Triebschen.

The exchange of letters in June was the last meaningful communication between Cosima and Hans. Eleven years were to pass before they saw each other again. To Wagner Bülow never addressed another word. On July 18, 1870—a little more than a year after Bülow's generous surrender—he and Cosima were divorced. Wagner married her on August 25, putting at naught the predictions of those "knowledgeable" friends who were certain that he would not bind himself to a second marriage.

The triangle was dissolved.*

There were now five young ones in the house. Wagner proved to be an utterly devoted father—it was one of the few likable traits of his character—making not the slightest distinction between his love for his own little girls and Bülow's. Siegfried—"Fidi"—was "something special," regarded as such by both Mama and Papa.

4

Cosima, daughter of parents neither of whom spurned the purple phrase or shied from impassioned pantomime, was prone to self-dramatization. It was one of the traits that endeared her to Wagner, who saw everything that happened to him in terms of theater, a large theater with a large public. When her feelings were engaged, she reacted in a highly charged language, by which she not only confirmed

*Bülow meant what he wrote to Cosima. He refused to return to Munich, despite pressing invitations from King Ludwig, and lived for a time in Italy, where he found some sort of solace. He then toured as a pianist and guest conductor and eventually, in 1880, took over the Meiningen Orchestra, considered one of Europe's best. There he espoused the cause of Brahms. He was celebrated, indeed idolized, recognized as a great force in the history of performance, but he never found inner peace, although he married a second time. He died in Cairo in 1894.

but intensified the degree of her joy or her sadness. Part of the language in her diary was in keeping with the prevalent style, but part was due to her seeing herself as a protagonist in a historical play, acting Portia to Wagner's Brutus. She suggested having a photograph taken in which she would be kneeling before him. She mentioned her guilt toward Bülow so often that one gets the impression she was nursing it, masochistically.

> The usual night thoughts. I was startled awake by the appearance of Hans in a dream. During the day I had read his letter again. I am resolved never to obscure the evil which I have committed, however unwillingly, but on the contrary to impress it deeper on my mind in order to repent and atone for it as far as I can. [June 27, 1869]

> R. guesses my unspoken sorrow about Hans; that grieves him. He recollects scenes at which he was present when Hans beat me and says he was shocked over the calm indifference with which I bore this. [July 11, 1869]

(Surely that is a figment of her imagination. Bülow was not a wife-beater.)

She records "a sad incident with Blandine":

> I am told she pretends to read aloud from a book: "Once upon a time there was a nasty mama. She left papa and married somebody else. That was very nasty. I would never do that." She reads this to two servant girls. [October 8, 1871]

Her guilt is, "in this Eden, the serpent which I carry in my bosom." When she caught Daniela in some childish lies, she took it hard:

> My eldest child punishes me. Born of my marriage with Hans, she shows how little blessed that union was. She destroys my cherished plan to bring up a fine human being as a consolation for him. [June 6, 1873]

Living at Wagner's side, she never lacked for drama in her life, and she added some of her own making. She celebrated his birthdays as if they were cosmic events. She rehearsed for days with the children to prepare surprises. Getting up at five in the morning, she decorated the staircase with a mass of flowers, placed his bust, surmounted by a laurel wreath, in the center of the salon, and dressed the girls as angels. The girls took their posts, he woke, came downstairs—one imagines a hidden orchestra could have intoned the Valhalla motif—the girls recited medieval poems they had learned by heart (poor girls!) or poems Cosima herself had written, a birdcage was opened to let its inhabitant fly away, and at half past ten there appeared the Paris Quartet, the only group that in Wagner's opinion could do justice to

Beethoven. In the course of the day they played three Beethoven quartets. At night, after a festive champagne supper and the reading of the telegrams, fireworks were shot off. Variations on this mummery involved the girls' being dressed as characters from the operas, with Cosima, holding Fidi in her arms, as Sieglinde; or a forty-five-piece military band hired by Cosima playing *Lohengrin* in the garden, while the children placed as many candles as his years on the rim of his bathtub. Birthday presents ranged from portraits of himself to silks and satins imported from Paris to be used for his dressing gowns, to the live peacock, which joined the chickens and the dogs in the garden.

In spite of Wagner's avowed wish for solitude, he could not help being sought out by admirers; he had become a celebrity, evoking both passionate denial and passionate adherence. Cosima enjoyed fame, but it made her duties as a hostess strenuous. To please Wagner, she hired more servants than they could afford—seven or eight—with the result that while they had plenty of service, they had as well plenty of servant trouble—impudence, thefts, love intrigues—with which she had to deal.* The question of a governess was especially irksome. Cosima insisted on instructing the children herself, giving them lessons in French, English, German history, piano—so much so that no self-respecting governess wanted to remain and even Wagner would be occasionally jealous of the attention she bestowed on her brood. Only when Fidi did not have a sore throat or Boni an upset stomach would she have time for guests. When there was something wrong with any of the children, she became frantic. The doctor would be summoned immediately, and if Eva's cold didn't abate overnight, Cosima called another doctor.

The cooking at Triebschen was nothing special—Cosima hardly ever mentions it in the diary—but the two meals she enjoyed were breakfast with him and "coffee time" *(Jause),* at which they entertained visitors and Wagner often ate too much pastry, regretting it afterward. Among the most fervid of those whom they entertained in 1869 were the trio of Catulle Mendès, the French novelist, essayist, and founder of the *Revue Fantaisiste;* his wife, Judith, the daughter of Théophile Gautier; and Villiers de L'Isle-Adam, the poet and novelist. Judith was at the time only nineteen and had been married two years. She was an extraordinarily gifted girl. Her knowledge of languages and the world's literature was prodigious; she had even published

*A cook who for once proved satisfactory stole money. When Cosima confronted her, the cook quit in a huff.

translations of Chinese poems. Above all, she was dazzlingly beautiful, with her Greek profile—Baudelaire called her a *"petite fille grecque"* —her cascading locks, her enticing figure. Wagner showed off to her, being his most "boyish," climbing the highest tree in the garden or swinging himself up to the second story of the house by the sills and the shutters. Cosima noted: "She is extraordinary but behaves so extravagantly that she embarrasses me—yet she is good-natured and terribly enthusiastic. She actually forces Rich. to play and sing for her from *Walküre* and *Tristan."* (July 16, 1869) The next day: "The woman talks about what I believe in, deep in my heart. The fact that she *can* talk about it makes her strange to me." Cosima sensed . . . something.

While Wagner had been in Leipzig during the Cosima crisis, he had met a young, shy, bespectacled professor of philology by the name of Friedrich Nietzsche. Hearing that this young man had an absolute passion for his music, Wagner had invited him to call on a Sunday evening. Nietzsche, all atremble, did call. Wagner played some parts of *Meistersinger;* they discovered that they shared an enthusiasm for Schopenhauer; they talked until late at night; and at the end of this first meeting Nietzsche was invited to Triebschen. In February 1869, Nietzsche was appointed to a Special Chair for Classical Philology at the University of Basel. On May 17, he came to Triebschen. In the next few days it became apparent to Cosima that Nietzsche—looking (in spite of an enormous mustache) so young that she could hardly imagine him as the occupant of a "special chair"—was having a good influence on Wagner. In fact, Nietzsche was to visit Triebschen no fewer than thirty-three times and was to remain for many years Wagner's and Cosima's best friend. On Wagner's birthday, he wrote that "the best and most exalted moments" of his life were "connected with the name of Wagner." The younger man was as proud and self-centered as the older; all the same, he was willing to be guided in an exploration of music in its diverse forms, Wagner's music stirring in him the exhilarating storm that blew on Zarathustra's mountain. Conversely, Wagner found much that nourished his own ideas in the younger man's researches into Greek tragedy and his thoughts on "The Dionysian Outlook," an essay which Nietzsche read to Wagner and Cosima in July 1870.

Du Moulin Eckart would have it that Cosima did not like Nietzsche as well as did her husband: "She had not found it as easy as the Meister to feel at one with his nature, repelled by much that was doctrinaire in him." Cosima's diary contradicts this view* and so do her letters; they were in truth the best of friends, though her mothering him must occasionally have irritated the genius certain of his power. And she admired his ideas. He was drawn to her and was regarded by her as a member of the inner circle, a distinction that was marked by her giving him all kinds of little errands to do for her in Basel, oblivious of the fact that he might be occupied with more important tasks. Perhaps Du Moulin's purpose in reading dislike into this relationship was to prepare an explanation for Nietzsche's eventual apostasy. But Nietzsche did not decry Wagner until much later, until *Parsifal,* when they met again in Sorrento. At that time, Nietzsche, mocking its Christian hero and "Christian decadence," was building a new world for himself, "philosophizing with a hammer." His famous philippic *The Case of Wagner* was not published until 1888, after Wagner's death, and in it he did hit out against Cosima as well. To great artists, he wrote, "adoring women are their ruin."

> . . . In many cases of womanly love, and perhaps precisely in the most famous, love is merely a more refined parasitism, a creeping into the being of a strange soul, sometimes even of a strange body, and ah! at what expense always to the "host"!

At Christmas 1870, Nietzsche sent Cosima the sketch of a work he was planning, "The Origin of the Tragic Idea," which he was later to develop into *The Birth of Tragedy out of the Spirit of Music.* She found the sketch "of highest value, remarkable in the depth and largeness of his views," and she took "a special pleasure in finding here R.'s ideas developed." (December 26, 1870) And at the beginning of April, Nietzsche came from Lugano to read them *The Birth of Tragedy* in its finished form. Again Cosima praised it: "One sees here a highly gifted man permeated by R.'s thought." He left Triebschen after a week, having delighted the children with the gift of a tame snake. When the book was published, with a dedication to Wagner, Wagner wrote Nietzsche:

> I have never read anything more beautiful than your book. It is marvelous. . . . I told Cosima: After her you are next, then nobody for a long distance, then Lenbach, who has painted a touchingly true portrait of myself. . . .

Cosima wrote:

---

*The diary mentions his name more than 250 times!

Oh, how beautiful your book is, how beautiful and how profound, how profound and how brave! Here you have summoned spirits which I thought would obey only the command of our Meister. . . .

Whatever the modern judgment of Nietzsche's theory, postulating the distinction between the Dionysian and the Apollonian sources of art, it is certain that Cosima was deeply impressed by it. She recognized his genius as he recognized her understanding and was grateful for it. She was at one with him in refusing to believe in democracy, which Nietzsche called the "Judeo-Christian mania for counting noses," and she applied his concept of the "Superman" to Wagner (wrongly, since Nietzsche wrote that the "Superman is a destroyer and not a builder"—and Wagner was one of the great builders). She felt intuitively that behind Nietzsche's grandiose pronouncements—saying that his writings were "the supreme literary achievement of all time"—he hid self-penance. And she knew what terrible pain racked his body. Only after he turned from Wagner did she turn from him, calling *Zarathustra* a "spasm of impotence," explicable only by disease. He, in turn, writing the aphorisms of *Human, All Too Human,* attacked her. He did not mention her by name, but all knowledgeable readers knew who was meant when he wrote of the woman beside the genius as "the sacrificial animal":

It is by no means uncommon for a woman to conceive the ambition to offer herself for this sacrifice, and the man can then feel well contented —assuming, that is, that he is enough of an egoist to consent to the presence of such a voluntary deflector of lightning, storm and rain in his vicinity.

Cosima, reading this, told her friend Marie von Schleinitz, "I know that it represents the victory of evil."

Nietzsche's hatred was the obverse of Nietzsche's love. In the Triebschen days he was more than half in love with her; she was the woman he treasured for years, however cautiously. In November 1871, he even composed a piano duet entitled "Echo of a New Year's Eve," which he dedicated to her, and he became very excited over this little effort. Later, in the dark days of his derangement in early 1889, his feeling rose to the surface. He addressed her as "Princess Ariadne, my beloved," in a disjointed letter in which he imagined himself as having lived through many incarnations, of having been "Buddha, Alexander, Caesar, Lord Bakon [*sic*] who wrote Shakespeare. . . . Of late I was Voltaire and Napoleon, and perhaps Richard Wagner too." He was coming as Dionysus to liberate her.

5

By the time Nietzsche first came to Triebschen, Hans Richter had been living there for nearly three years. He was a young Hungarian musician, twenty-three years old when he arrived, whom Wagner decided to employ as a copyist. Being a fervent admirer of the composer, he accepted the offer with alacrity and was at once set to work copying the score of *Meistersinger*. Richter was awed by the size of the Triebschen establishment, noting in his diary that it consisted of "Wagner, Baroness Bülow and the children, Lulu, Boni, Loldi [Eva was not born until the following February]; the housekeeper Vreneli; her niece Marie; the children's governess; Agnes, the nursemaid; Marie, the cook; Steffen, the valet; the boots Jost, and myself. In addition two peacocks, two cats, one horse; friends Russ and Koss [dogs]; also a lot of mice." Cosima liked Richter because he was respectful and willing, joking with the children, taking the dogs for their walk, and going shopping for her in Lucerne. Wagner liked him very much because he recognized Richter's exceptional musical talent. Richter himself was happy because "nowhere else could I have learned what I can here, under the eyes of this genius." Another reason for Richter's contentment was the fact that Cosima offered him as much to eat and drink as he wanted: he was a mighty trencherman. Wagner immediately began to prepare him as "his" conductor and it was he who conducted the first *Ring* at Bayreuth, though not entirely to Cosima's and Wagner's satisfaction. She thought him too "foursquare." Bernard Shaw and Debussy admired him.

Richter heard the table conversation as often as any man, both then and later. He heard Wagner discuss a multitude of subjects with Cosima. Tempo, rhythm, phrasing of Beethoven's symphonies were analyzed illuminatingly. Wagner was one of the first who fully valued Beethoven's last quartets. He had a specially warm spot for Weber, with the result that Cosima elected *Der Freischütz* one of her favorites. Rossini was a genius, his *Barber* a masterpiece. Mendelssohn was an imitator of the great, "as the Jews usually are." Verdi? Cosima and he heard the *Requiem* in Vienna. Cosima's comment: "Best not to speak of it." Cosima's evaluation of the world's composers ran something like this: Wagner first and foremost, then Beethoven and Bach on an equal plane, followed by Mozart and Weber.

On subjects other than music Wagner could be foolish, and the more foolish, the more dogmatically were his opinions issued. Did he think the new French fashions in women's clothes were "indecent" and that a man would be repelled by their "showing too much"? Very well; Cosima wore full black silk dresses, varying this for evening parties with white robes trimmed with lace, or a royal-blue gown with a long train. No décolletage. The French: they were second in being guilty of the world's evils, coming closely after the Jews. French poetry was only blown-up prose: "all he hates is expressed in that language, everything trivial, low gossip." And this Frenchwoman, who loved the language, enthusiastically agreed with him in hoping for the destruction of France during the Franco-Prussian War. She swallowed whole the war propaganda: the French were unspeakably cruel, they killed the wounded, a fourteen-year-old boy gouged out the eyes of a physician; but the German soldiers—ah, the German soldiers, they behaved like gentlemen. He told her that the burning of Paris would serve as a "symbol of liberation from evil."

> There are rumors of an armistice, which give us no pleasure. R. wants the bombardment [of Paris]. [November 4, 1870]

> One hears that only Metz is to be leveled. R. is much displeased. "All that mess—and only Metz." [February 27, 1871]

In full agreement, she quotes him:

> "That the Communists wanted to burn all of Paris is the only grandiose idea they thought up. I detest them because of their pretension at governing, their deceit, their pedantic organization with its lace trimmings. A Frenchman doesn't know any better. But that they [the Communists] feel so great a disgust for Parisian civilization as to think of a conflagration I find grandiose. The trouble is that the Germans can't conceive doing without this civilization. I felt this when I wrote 'The Art Work of the Future.' I saw nothing being created in Germany, as I saw the source of all evil threatening to engulf us. Thus I designed a new world for myself." [June 17, 1871]

In 1870, riding the wave of German nationalism, he wrote a farce, "Eine Kapitulation," making fun of the suffering in Paris (where Cosima's mother was living). Even the Germans thought this piece of trash unfunny; Cosima thought it marvelously witty.

The French were not the only subject on which he vented his anger. She understood the roots of that anger as being implanted in his bitter early struggles, in the difficulty of constructing the world he had designed for himself, in the complexity of the new musical language he had perfected, the grammar of which had first to be learned by the listener. He knew much, but what he did *not* know made him suspicious and angry. She bent lovingly with the storm of that anger. Discussing the English language, which she spoke with pleasure, he said that it was not a real language at all: "A German can only regard it as a dialect." Shelley is "no poet," he decided. They read the great scene between Henry IV and the Prince and "are staggered, and we marvel." Then: "Yesterday we compared the English text with the German. The German seemed to us much more noble." Surely his opinion, not hers. But she does not disagree. He thinks America "unproductive. . . . One sees that culture has no connection with huge dimensions and a fine railroad system." Later Cosima reports that "R. receives many inquiries from the Americans and counts on them to fill the theater [Bayreuth]. Not very complimentary to the Germans."

In time, Cosima became more "German" than Wagner. He was able to say to her that a German is motivated "only by greed and twopence worth of lust" or that "We are repulsive. I may say so, because *j'en suis,*" while she in the letters to her children and friends sounds the *Deutschland über Alles* motif time and again.

Yet, as in her great love she adopted idea after idea from him, nevertheless she remained what she was, or rather she developed into more than she had been—being odalisque and schoolteacher, a reader of Dante and a housekeeper who saw to it that the laundry was properly done, a mind who could discuss philosophy with Nietzsche, a pianist of sufficient skill to play four hands with Wagner or Richter, a lover of animals and nature (as he was), who could distinguish the birds by their warbling. Sexually she was most satisfactory to him, as he to her. She is not explicit about this, but every so often she mentions in the diary "an intimate hour." The ugly little man who suffered from erysipelas, who wore a badly fitting truss for his hernia, who snuffed tobacco—one reason why he doused himself with perfume—who when crossed was so irascible that he drummed with his fists on the furniture, yet exercised so great a fascination on women that they had come to him even when he had been penniless and unknown. Except for one brief affair—and even then—his love for Cosima remained constant. Similarly, Cosima was never amorously attracted to another man, though even years after Wagner's death she was still considered a desirable woman.

She was religious, and although because of him she had formally become a Protestant, she went to confession, sent her children to church, and prayed. Every time something troubled her, she prayed: she frequently mentions in the diary her pleas to God, and almost always these pleas are wet with her tears. Once, as she left for church,

Wagner told her, "Give my best to your Savior, though from the very beginning He has created an awful lot of confusion." He himself was strongly attracted to Buddhism and its "larger view of the world. The Christian dogma leans on the Jewish religion and that is its misfortune." He discussed with her a music drama based on Indian mythology, but when he turned to *Parsifal* he allowed that he could find in Christianity sufficient inspiration for his purpose. It was she who vivified this interest. However, when Cosima was very old, she gave the conductor Weingartner a hint that she perceived the imbalance between the *Parsifal* poem, a simulacrum only of true piety, a pinchbeck faith mixed with sex, and the vision and glory of the music. What happens musically on Good Friday goes beyond the walls of any church.

Her interest in the pictorial arts was greater than Wagner's, though he accompanied her willingly on her excursions to churches and museums and enjoyed what he saw. She loved the Italians best—among them she found "light and clear air." And her appreciation was thoughtful; she did not gush. Her favorite of favorites was Titian's *Tribute Money*. The contrast of Christ's pale young face and that of the swarthy Pharisee touched her heart: "It is like music." She had little use for French artists, such as Watteau or Ingres or Delacroix, and no understanding whatever of the aims of the Impressionists. She thought Makart, that color-splashing Rodomonte of a painter of nudes with clothes on, a "bold artist of original concepts," but so did most people of her generation. She gave Wagner books on art and prints as gifts; he delighted in them. Of course he saw the pictorial arts in relation to his own work. Looking at a Dürer, he said to Cosima: "There is a man with whom I could get along." Neither he nor she had much use for Rubens—"that disciple of the Jesuits"—whose women they found of a "vulgar, lazy sensuousness." In the Sistine Chapel, "R. finds the Jewish element predominant . . . fanaticism, mourning, hate." Cosima found this bit of art analysis worth recording.

6

Their extremely rare disagreements were due either to his extravagance—"I am afraid, but say nothing," she noted—or to her opinion that he was too lenient with the children. They are so careless that they break their drinking cups; Cosima makes them drink from tin mugs. Wagner countermands her. "I concede, but am inwardly sad about it." The girl who had suffered the rigors of Madame Patersi was strict with her own children, sitting at the head of a long table and supervising their studies. The four girls went to school,* but for Fidi a special tutor was hired. Once when Blandine and Daniela behaved especially badly, fighting with Eva and infuriating Cosima, Wagner slapped them. Immediately he was beside himself with regret. He had no right, he cried, to hit a child. Physical punishment was hardly ever again resorted to, and this was exceptional in a century that believed in not sparing the rod. We have seen one example of Daniela's and Blandine's indulging in childish lies and of Cosima's brooding over it. Wagner tried to reassure her: "I ought not to take it so seriously, there is no virtue in youth." He urged her to be lenient. (November 27, 1871) Cosima couldn't see it his way and was all for stern measures. "The children were taken to task. I wept with them, I prayed, I got them to the point that they themselves asked to be punished." (December 3, 1871)

Wagner was scheduled to leave Triebschen on December 9 for some conferences in Munich and Bayreuth, then go to Mannheim, where he was to conduct a concert. Before he left, he pleaded with Cosima; the plan had been for her to join him in Mannheim and bring Daniela along. But she had changed her mind: Daniela was to be left home as a punishment. Wagner thought this cruel. At the last moment, he and Cosima had argued about it. They parted not on the best of terms. Wagner fretted during the voyage and as soon as the train halted in Zurich (about two hours after leaving Lucerne), he sent Cosima a telegram and a long letter:

> . . . How was I to understand you, O wonderful one, at our parting?
> You seemed to be quite averse to me and to avoid my touch! . . .
> Then I ran after you to receive a final embrace from you: this you
> refused me. . . .
>
> Have my blessing as you have my love, my wife, my dear glorious
> wife! Kiss all the children for me, all who wept for me! Be kind and
> be hopeful even about that which fills you with darkest care. . . . Have
> confidence, and gentleness will then no longer seem weakness!

The next day he wrote from Munich:

---

*In addition, they were tutored by a governess, from time to time.

. . . Be loving toward me and forgive me always! Are the children up? Has Fidi wet his bed again? You know that we have a son? A "son"? And good, good daughters of whom one at last, at last also looks like her mother! Kiss them all from me, that they were nourished in your womb! I love you surely as none other has been loved before. Blessed, beloved, marvelous one! Farewell, sleep well, be peacefully divine, as always when you are in your heart's home!

He could not let the subject rest. The next day:

[Munich] December 11, 1871

But now, my dear, listen to my plea. Bring Lulu with you to Mannheim. I have said all I have to say to you about it: now I can only beg you. Look for a moment beyond the horizon of those cares which fill you with such anxiety; there is another side to the matter. However, I didn't want to enlarge dogmatically on the subject, but only to ask you, and tell you that I know exactly what we will do at Christmas, so as to achieve your purpose and, at the same time, not ruin the evening which is so dear to us all. You will put their presents concealed in the gallery and the small ones will be called down alone: *then* the elder ones; they will then be earnestly asked by you or me what they think about the meaning of their punishment (this if you wish in front of the others): they should then say whether they think themselves worthy of the festival of Christmas; there are presents for them outside—whether they think they should be given them. I expect this to make a good and lasting impression, and let mercy be shown in the end. But above all do not let the important step for Lulu's development pass—don't prevent her from going to Mannheim. I beg this of you from my heart!*

Yet, curiously, Cosima remained implacable. "Great sorrow that I am not taking Lulu with me [to Mannheim]. God grant that this decision will drive untruthfulness from her heart forever." (December 15, 1871) More probably, the decision drove resentment deeper into the heart of the eleven-year-old girl.

One more serious disagreement did exist. It centered on Liszt. The diary reveals Cosima's own ambivalence toward her father. In the recesses of her heart she never forgave him, either for his distant attitude toward her as a child or for his efforts to make her remain with Bülow. The scar of that wound had not closed entirely. It was Cosima —not Wagner—who wrote that she doubted that her father would have done much to help them if the king had not rescued Wagner. In 1868, when it had become evident that Cosima wanted a divorce

*These excerpts are taken from the very few Wagner-Cosima letters that have escaped destruction. They were published by Manfred Eger.

above all things, Liszt opposed it. In July 1870, when she obtained the divorce, Bülow's friend Karl Klindworth was visiting Triebschen, and Cosima, in a flood of tears, asked him to plead with Bülow to forgive her for all the wrongs she had done him. She added (as Klindworth wrote to Bülow) that "she will never see her father again, as she is incensed over the scant sympathy he has shown." Around that time, she would not even write to him; her friend Marie von Schleinitz had to implore her to respect Liszt's "dignity" and make the first move in resuming communication with him. This she did, not warmly, as Marie suggested, but "in measured tones."

But—and this was a persistent "but"—if she harbored anger against her father, she also loved him. A part of her love consisted of the filial devotion which she regarded as natural and which she expected from her own children. A larger part sprang from Liszt's personal attributes, his enthusiasm for Wagner's music, his generosity, his handsomeness, which as he got older became magisterial, and the esteem the world offered to his genius. A still larger part was due to Cosima's realization that Liszt, in spite of his successes, did not know contentment. As she wrote to Ludwig:

> Even as a child I *knew* that my father suffered—the father whom I was accustomed to seeing only in the splendor and intoxication of triumph: I *knew* it, and I suffered with him, secretly and silently, like a child, but without end.

The conductor Felix Mottl recalled that once in Bayreuth he and Cosima were lingering over their after-dinner coffee. Wagner and Liszt had left the table. Suddenly Wagner returned in a foul temper. "That old faker," he said, "insists on playing me his latest Ave Maria. I really can't stand it." Cosima reproved him: "How can you let yourself say such things? Haven't you always had the highest opinion of Father? Didn't you say recently that he had inaugurated a new epoch in art?" "Yes," answered Wagner. "In fingering."*

Wagner only half understood the fluctuation of Cosima's feeling. Of course he *did* admire Liszt's artistry and in his early career he acknowledged the gratitude he owed Liszt—both humanely and artistically—though with Wagner, gratitude lasted as long as a soap bubble. Yet the moment Cosima showed a sign of love for her father, Wagner became jealous. When Liszt came to see them in Bayreuth on October 15, 1872, it was his first visit there and he tried to smooth away previous differences. However, something, some foolish impulse, com-

*Albert Gutmann, *Aus dem Wiener Musikleben.*

pelled him to hint his belief that "they both had Bülow on their conscience." Cosima attempted to talk the subject out with him:

> Long conversation with father. Princess Wittgenstein tortures him on account of us. He should shun Wagner's influence, artistically and morally, not see me again. His honor demands it because we committed a moral murder on Hans, etc. I am heartsick that my father is being thus nagged —he is weary and plagued. Especially that terrible woman in Rome. The only thing she knows is to make trouble. He doesn't want to renounce me or us. The conversation with father detained me for a long time. Unfortunately R. feels hurt that I left him alone for so long. . . . The whole day a certain coolness separated us. [October 17, 1872]

In July of that year Wagner had finished the orchestral sketch of *Götterdämmerung.* He wrote: "The End. All to please Cosel. July 22, 1872. R.W." It took another two years for him to finish the full score, on November 21, 1874. This is what happened on that "thrice holy, memorable day":

> Thrice holy, memorable day! Around noon R. asked me to come up and bring the newspapers. Because yesterday he complained how strenuously he was working and that he would be unable to finish before Sunday, I concluded that he was too tired to continue working. Shyly I evaded putting my question to him. Instead, and to divert him, I threw on his desk a letter from father which had just arrived; he wrote about our trip to Budapest in friendly words. Noon sounded. I see R. reading the letter. He wants explanations. I tell him how I propose to answer the letter and I purposely avoid stealing a glance at the score [lying on the desk]. I don't want to offend him. He *is* offended and shows me that the work is completed. Bitterly he says to me: "When you get a letter from your father you cease your concern with me." I suppress my hurt. But when afterward he repeats the accusation, I burst into tears and I am still weeping as I am writing this. I have been robbed of my greatest joy, and surely not through my own fault! "That a woman may become all-knowing." [Quotation from Brünnhilde's Immolation] Because I devoted my life and suffering to this work, did I not earn the right to celebrate its completion with joy? . . . That suffering, to whom can I confess it, to whom admit it? To R. I must keep silent. To this page I entrust it and to my Siegfried . . . let him understand this: no anger, no hatred, but infinite pity for that poorest of all creatures, a human being. . . . [November 21, 1874]

She was so shaken that it was almost two weeks before she managed to write again in her diary.

Less than three months before Wagner's death, they had a tiff, Wagner declaring that Liszt's latest compositions seemed to show traces of madness. Cosima objected violently. Wagner jumped out of bed and shouted, "You think you are virtue incarnate."

Liszt, for his part, was never quite reconciled to her marrying Wagner. He sent her a monthly stipend, always addressing it to "Baroness Bülow." That irritated her.

After Wagner's death, father and daughter drew somewhat closer together. Yet when Liszt died in Bayreuth in 1886, Cosima saw no reason to cancel any of the performances. Her father's demise could not interfere with her husband's works. But in the last year of her life she told Eva, "I miss him. He told me *'J'ai fait ce que j'ai pu.'* I miss him as a personality."

7

To please Wagner she learned to play whist, a game he played with great concentration and frequently, and at which he hated to lose. He grumbled when he held bad cards; wasn't it the duty of the Goddess of Fortune to deal aces and kings to the creator of the *Ring?* Though the Hungarian proverb says, "Play cards with your husband: you'll find out what kind of a man he is," Cosima did *not* find out. She even included modesty in the anthology of his virtues:

> R. lacks not only the instinct of vanity, but every bit of understanding for it. Curious that in his dreams he had nothing but visions of vanity! [March 25, 1873]

And she records the following incident about this "modest man":
They are reading the *Oresteia.* He declares: "I deem this the most perfect work in every aspect—religious, philosophic, poetic, artistic. One might mention Shakespeare's historical plays in the same breath, but he had no Athenian state, no Areopagus on which to lean." Cosima: "I consider only the *Ring* to be its equivalent." Wagner: "It [the *Ring*] is independent of time, something conceived by one man, only to be botched immediately, as has happened with new-founded religions." (July 24, 1880)

The most valuable token of his love, the work that in a sense makes her immortal, was the gift he offered her for her thirty-third birthday. Some mysterious goings on had preceded the day: Wagner was frequently absent in Lucerne and Richter for some reason had practiced the trumpet around the house so enthusiastically that Cosima felt the quiet of Triebschen seriously interfered with. Not until later did she find out what this was all about: Wagner was secretly rehearsing a small orchestra which Richter had got together in Zurich and in which Richter himself was to play the trumpet part. Early in the morning of December 25, 1870, the players took their places on the staircase leading to the upper floor, Wagner raised his baton, and for the first time the enchanting strains were heard of the wonderful little work he had composed especially for Cosima. The children and an astonished Nietzsche were present. Cosima in the diary:

Of this day, my children, I can really tell you nothing, nothing of my emotions, nothing of my exaltation, nothing, nothing. I will simply relate the bare dry facts. When I woke I heard a sound, swelling ever more, until I could no longer believe I was dreaming. Music sounded, and what music! When it stopped, R. came to me with the five children and handed me the score of the "Symphonic Birthday Greetings." I dissolved in tears. Everybody wept. R. had placed his orchestra on the staircase—he has sanctified our Triebschen forever. The "Triebschen Idyll"—that's the name of the work. . . . After breakfast the orchestra returned, playing the Idyll again. . . . We were all overcome. Then Lohengrin's bridal march, the Septet of Beethoven, and at the end once again the piece I could not hear often enough. Now I understand R's secret doings, and the good Richter's trumpet (he blew the Siegfried motif magnificently and had learned to play the trumpet especially for the occasion). I used to admonish him for it. "Let me die" [Tristan], I called to R. He answered, "It would be easier to die for me than to live for me." [December 25, 1870]

He promised that the *Siegfried Idyll,* as they called it later, was to belong to her alone, never to be published. Some time after, when the dressing gowns, the French perfumes, the eight servants, the elaborate pieces of furniture, had once again sharpened the need for immediate cash, over and above the king's subvention and Wagner's now substantial income from his works, he sold the *Idyll.* Cosima mourned —"The secret treasure becomes everybody's property"—yet she hoped the world would enjoy it sufficiently to compensate her for her loss.

And so she kept on recording her love from day to day:

Carlyle writes how little we know of great men, how shadowy they appear to posterity, and that made me think of these Diaries, where I have tried to pass on to the children R.'s nature as clearly as I could. For that reason, and ignoring modesty, I write down everything he says about me. . . . Yet —I feel it—the attempt is unsuccessful. The sound of his voice, his accent, movement, glance—how shall I reproduce these? But perhaps it is better than nothing and so I continue my bungling. [March 21, 1873]

CHAPTER VII

———◆———

"J'en Ai Assez"

Having leafed through Cosima's diary, we can take up again the story of her life, beginning in the summer of 1869, after Siegfried was born, when Bülow suddenly consented to a divorce and decided to quit Munich. In that year Cosima, serving as ambassadress and envoy plenipotentiary of the genius with the bad digestion, the tumid character, and the mind that wanted to embrace all knowledge, not only was unable to prevent the most serious break with Ludwig but was the indirect cause of it.

Das Rheingold had been finished by the spring of 1864. It had slumbered unperformed, since both the king and Wagner had first agreed that the *Ring* was to be given as a unit and in a theater especially to be built for it. The plan for the theater came to nothing, stymied by procrastination on the part of the ministers, who felt that the money could be put to better use, as well as by confusions created by Wagner himself. But Ludwig was not to be denied a view, if only a partial one, of the great work for which he was longing. He appealed to Wagner to grant what the king legally and ethically possessed already, having bought the rights to the *Ring* when the agreement with Wagner was signed. Wagner, however, angry over the failure of the theater plan and always at his worst when he was in any way thwarted, had even toyed with the idea of appealing to Bismarck to help him carry out his ambition—in other words, he seriously considered turning from Bavaria to Prussia, a bald piece of treachery against his benefactor. Cosima had dissuaded him. From Bismarck and Berlin and that pusillanimous Prussian king, she pointed out, Wagner could not expect the understanding he needed, nor the generosity. Disloyalty bothered Cosima hardly more than it bothered Wagner; she was convinced, however, that his bread would continue to be more thickly buttered in Bavaria, both financially and artistically.

Very well; he would stay with Ludwig and the comfortable subvention, but *Rheingold,* no. It was *not* to be performed in Munich. The reasons he gave were, first, that he still felt that the *Ring* must be brought to the stage sequentially in a performance supervised by himself, and second, that *Rheingold,* with its extraordinary problems of staging, would be botched in the Munich Opera House, if squeezed between performances of *La Juive* and *The Barber of Seville.* Had not the purpose of Ludwig's support been "to preserve these noble [Wagner's adjective] works from the profane contact of our opera houses"? Dresden had asked for *Walküre,* but he, Wagner, had refused; he was now implying that Ludwig's Munich Opera House was no better than the Dresden institution.

Whatever justice his arguments contained—and it was obvious that the *Rheingold* performance would be most carefully prepared and in no way "routine"—the underlying truth had a different ring. He wanted no part of Munich or its theater just then because Cosima was being treated by the press and the society of that city as a veritable criminal. How could she again expose herself in that den of journalist jackals? To name but one instance, the Munich correspondent of the Augsburg *Allgemeine Zeitung* published in September 1869 a long article congratulating the management of the opera house for "recognizing the true character" of this musical autocrat—

who, with the unconcern of genius, has carried his poetic morals into the sphere of real life and staged a Wagner-Tristan Cosima-Isolde vis-à-vis Bülow-Marke.

This was plain writing and it demanded that "so important an art institution as the Munich Court Theater should not be any longer the arena for unrestrained license."

In short, Wagner vetoed the production for more than artistic reasons; he considered his presence indispensable—and he had a point there. But then why would he not go to Munich? Simply because he felt he could not be there *with* Cosima and he wouldn't dream of being there *without* Cosima. Very likely, unconscious motives spurred his stubbornness. The love-hate he felt for Ludwig, the knowledge of his dependence on the king, the resentment that prompts one hardly ever to forgive one's benefactor, his power complex—these were strong enough for Wagner to play a dangerous game. Of course, he thought he would win.

So Wagner strides in his house in Triebschen, clad in a "Flemish painter's costume—a black velvet coat, black satin knee breeches, black silk stockings, a light blue satin cravat tied in many folds, showing his fine linen and lace shirt, and a painter's beret on his head,"* and curses all the people in Munich who have "conspired" against him. Only he is in the right. Only he is acting from pure motives. Nietzsche is with him and agrees that Cosima must be protected. Cosima can hardly sleep; she is beset with fears. What is the king going to do? Wagner reads her an Indian proverb: "You can reach the ends of the earth, you can reach the summit of the mountain, but you cannot reach the thoughts of a king." With all her heart she would like to reestablish peace, under all conditions but one. She suggests that Wagner go to Munich *without* her, take over the rehearsals, and please the king. He refuses. He refuses flatly. As to her going to Munich with him, as a publicized adultress—that is the one thing she cannot face, especially since the press has stepped up its "morality" campaign with renewed gusto. She notes with shame that the leading Munich newspaper calls her "Cosima fan tutte."

Wagner appealed to the king in letter after letter, but received scarcely any answer. Ludwig had perceived the truth behind the casuistry: if any doubt remained in his mind about the nature of the Cosima-Wagner relationship, it was dispelled by Bülow, who gave him a frank statement of the reasons for resigning. Aside from the opposition he, Bülow, had met from some disaffected members of the orchestra and the smears in the newspapers, he was suffering from

> the joylessness of my private life. It has received a heavy blow
> through the definitive separation from my wife, who prefers to devote
> herself to the loftier consideration of the creator of immortal
> masterpieces in Your Majesty's service. [Letter to the king, June 25,
> 1869]

Let Wagner storm in whatever key he wished, protesting that he was trying to save *Rheingold* from a wretched performance and that he was doing so prompted solely by altruistic motives. Ludwig now

*Nietzsche's sister, Elisabeth.

felt that the facts were capable of a very different interpretation. At any rate, he, the king, wished to hear the work. That he now saw Cosima in a murky light—and that he saw Wagner's opposition as connected with her—made him all the more insistent.

Richter had been given the post of musical director in Bülow's place, Wagner himself having urged the appointment of the talented young man. The king ordered the performance to proceed—and to proceed under Richter's direction. Wagner's musical wishes, which Richter knew, were to be carefully observed; but his refusal to come to Munich and help with the realization of an event that Ludwig had set his heart on was to be ignored. Rehearsals went on for almost two months. After the dress rehearsal on August 27, 1869, at which Ludwig was present, Richter reported to Triebschen certain technical defects which had not been solved. Now Wagner, in whom the pressure of anger had mounted to explosive force, lost whatever little perspective he still had. He told Richter and the baritone Betz, who was to sing Wotan, to *resign.* This they did at once, and Wagner was sure that this latest move signaled the end of the projected performance. *He* had played his trump card. *He* had given everybody, including those people at the Munich Opera, a taste of his power. His works were to be performed on his terms, or not at all.

It appeared that he was very much mistaken. The king, far from conceding, acted. How dared this man who owed him everything defy him? What kind of impertinence was this? *"J'en ai assez!"* He retired to the mountains, leaving instructions with Cabinet Secretary Düfflipp:

August 30, 1869

The behavior of Wagner and the theater rabble is absolutely criminal and impudent: it is an open revolt against My orders, and this I will not tolerate. Under no circumstance is Richter to conduct, and he is to be dismissed forthwith. The theater people will obey My orders, not Wagner's whims. In many of the papers it is stated that it was *I* who canceled the performance. I saw this coming. It is easy enough to spread false rumors, and it is My will that they give the true story and do everything in their power to make the performance possible; for if these dreadful intrigues of Wagner's succeed, then the whole crowd will get steadily more brazen and more shameless and finally completely beyond control. Therefore this evil must be torn out by the roots; Richter must go, and Betz and the others brought to heel. Never before have I met with such impertinence. I repeat how satisfied I am with the way you are handling the situation. . . . *Vivat* Düfflipp! *Pereat* the theater rabble! With kindest regards and all best wishes to yourself, but with curses on that vulgar and impudent pack. . . .

The performance was to take place with a new conductor and a new Wotan, as soon as possible.

Wagner now realized—that is, on August 31, when he received a telegram from the king *insisting* that the performance take place—that he had lost and that he had better go to Munich, the city he swore he would never enter again, and save what could be saved, be it of the performance itself or the king's favor. Cosima, noting that "a break with the King is a possibility," agreed that he must go at once, and go alone. She didn't know how near she came to guessing the truth; on that very day at 12:15 P.M., the king sent a telegram to Düfflipp: "If W. dares offer any more opposition, his allowance is to be taken from him forever, and not another work of his is to be produced on the Munich stage."*

Wagner could do nothing with the performance at the eleventh hour—he was even refused a special rehearsal for which he asked—and he was back in Triebschen the next day, on September 2, vanquished, crestfallen. He gave Cosima a very lopsided report of the situation. Cosima's diary:

> Sept. 2 . . . At 4 o'clock fright and joy: R. announces his return this evening. With the 4 children and the 2 dogs to fetch him. *Rheingold* impossible; the reappearance of Richter on the conductor's podium would be the signal for the resumption of the old hunt against us and the King; besides, the staging of the work is so abominable that the machinist is demanding three months to put it right. . . .

Nothing of the kind. They get a new conductor (Franz Wüllner) and a new Wotan (August Kindermann) and start rehearsing afresh. The scenic shortcomings will be corrected. Full speed ahead.

Cosima suffers. She hears Wagner pace his room, weeping. The man who has created the hero "who knows no fear" weeps. Cosima: "My heart is heavy though I take all the news calmly." . . . "How can I comfort him? I can only weep with him." He tells her that he is sick with grief, "not so much over the betrayal of his work as over the behavior of the King." Cosima counsels: no doubt he is in the right. Absolutely; he has acted properly. But for the greater good, for the future of his achievement, "he *must* keep silent. His works belong to the King. If the King chooses to use them as a toy, R. has to let him have his way." (September 10, 1869)

He promises to follow her advice. In the morning he shocks her by telling her that he has sent off a letter to the newly appointed conductor, Franz Wüllner. She has read the letter and recognized it for what

---

*The telegram was sent when Ludwig's anger was at its height; it is doubtful that he would ever have carried out the threat.

it is, a piece of ill-tempered vituperation. "I would have preferred had he not sent it. Yet it made him feel better. To have to bear something quietly grates on him." (September 11)* Richter has now returned to Triebschen, and with his help she prepares a full statement of Wagner's side of the story, to be signed and sent off by Wagner. It is printed in the *Allgemeine Zeitung.* Few are convinced; most deem the article merely verbal juggling by a singularly ungrateful man. Cosima, as furious as Wagner and pitying his defeat, yet advises patience. Be careful, be wary! She urges him not to communicate with the king or anybody else in Munich. Let time pass.

The *Rheingold* premiere took place on September 22, less than three weeks after the originally scheduled date. A flock of musical and social celebrities converged on Munich to be present, including Liszt, Saint-Saëns, Joachim, Pasdeloup, Hanslick from Vienna, Chorley from London, Turgenev with Pauline Viardot from Paris. The performance showed flaws but was not nearly as bad as Wagner had predicted it would be. In fact, the machinist Carl Brandt proved so able that Wagner was later to find him indispensable in Bayreuth. The scenic problems, the Rhine Maidens swimming,† Alberich turning himself into a toad, etc., were not altogether solved—but have they been to this day? Cosima reluctantly noted: "The A.A.Z. reports a succès d'estime." Wagner was still playing Achilles in his tent, with Cosima as his Briseis. They talked far into the night:

> Should he relinquish his subvention without saying a word? Or should he think only of completing the *Nibelungen* and let *bataille* be *bataille?* I tell him he must do what he most profoundly feels like doing, regardless of the consequences. . . . Deep melancholy! He says if I were not here it would be the end of him!! Today was my name day, he gave me flowers and father sent a telegram from Rome! I can only keep silent. [Diary, September 27]

She knew perfectly well what he felt like doing! They discussed emigrating to America. The Theater of his imagination is a temple, she said, the theater of today a stall at a country fair; he speaks the language of the priest: how could a peddler—or a king—understand him? Not a word from the Residenz.

*A draft of this letter is extant. Newman says that it is written in Wagner's "best Billingsgate style." But Newman does not seem to be sure that it was actually sent. Cosima's diary proves that it was.

†The *Bayrische Vaterland,* a conservative journal, described the Rhine Maiden scene as "an aquarium of whores. The underwater females are stark naked; the poor wretches were not permitted even the scantiest of undergarments." This was, of course, a lie. But that scene has always been a stage director's headache.

2

About a month later, on October 25, Wagner came down to breakfast all smiles, holding in his hand a letter from the king. Ludwig had broken the long silence; he has suffered too greatly, he has been too lonely in his aerie, not to try to bridge the abyss that has opened between them. His desire to hear *Rheingold* had been so strong as to outweigh all other considerations, even its creator's wishes. But he still loves Wagner, whose work is the only relief he can obtain from the task of governing, a task abhorrent to him, and whose friendship is the only nourishment that gives him the strength to live on. "Your ideals are my ideals. . . . No human being is capable of hurting me, but when you are angry with me you deal me a death blow." . . . "To serve you is the mission of my life." . . . "What is the dazzling possession of a throne in comparison with a friendly letter from you?" Thus Ludwig wrote between October and Christmas 1869. He sent the usual Christmas gifts—and with them, significantly, the assurance that he still loved Cosima. He included a fond word for the children. "Oh, how I envy you, able as you are to live in the ideal, in dear, beautiful Triebschen!"

Cosima smiled again. "Outside thick snow, inside much joy." She began to plan the celebration of Richard's next birthday. She had a new dress sent from Milan. "R. loves it when I wear a new dress." The children came down with heavy colds and she nursed them, sacrificing much of her sleep for several nights. Wagner showed her a huge gun. "With this gun I will kill myself if you don't take care of yourself." They laughed.

Yet shortly after the first of the year, Ludwig reopened a sore subject. He wanted *Die Walküre,* and as soon as possible. A production was even then being planned. "Do not deprive me," Ludwig wrote, "of the very air of my existence by forbidding me the production of your works . . . which are indispensable to me in this horrible world of my duties." Behind the supplicating tone Cosima and Wagner heard the rumble of command.

What to do? Cosima pointed out that the Nibelungen are in truth his livelihood, that "he owes his existence to them," and therefore one has to be thankful to God that they have to do with a man like the king, even if he "has a quirk in his brain and insists on seeing and having those things, without in the least encompassing the noble thoughts

connected with them." In plain words: Give in. Wagner had been
ready with the Talmudic answer:

> "He cannot kill my work. . . . Only I can kill it if I break with him and
> do not finish the work. If he spoils [the creations] now it won't matter in
> the long run, once they are given according to my ideas. They still owe
> me such performances of *Tannhäuser* and *Lohengrin.* The great perfor-
> mances demand a [higher] level of culture. If we do not reach that level,
> the most perfect performance in Munich isn't going to help. All is up to
> fate. Yet it is difficult to answer his rapturous assurances."

The correspondence with the king continued, Wagner writing with
increasing frequency. Cosima reviewed these letters carefully: "I ask
him to change a few sentences which may be wounding. He will do
it." He did it.

Peace was established once more—Wagner needing the king even
more than the king needed Wagner—the path to it smoothed by
Cosima. She was able to maintain this peace, even when Wagner laid
down conditions for his collaboration on *Die Walküre* project which
were not only brazen but totally impractical—such as that he alone
was to make all artistic decisions, that Perfall, the intendant of the
opera house, was to be given a "leave of absence," that the opera
house was to be closed for six weeks, four of them for rehearsals, that
all personnel was to be chosen by himself and placed at his sole disposal for the duration, and more—all designed to delay the production
until he could be married to Cosima and she could appear with him
in Munich. Divorce proceedings have been started, but "the law is
creeping." When she told him that for the time being she could not
bear to go to Munich even for so consequential an event as the premiere of *Die Walküre,* he answered, "Then—under no consideration!"
(January 13, 1870) and continued pleading with Ludwig, even writing
him an imploring poem. He called it *"Le dernier cri."*

Here, too, he was defeated. Preparations for the performance went
on apace without his cooperation. Looking around for a conductor
stronger than Wüllner, the opera house authorities offered the opportunity to Hermann Levi, a conductor who had already made a considerable reputation for himself in Karlsruhe. He wrote to Wagner for
advice. (According to Cosima, Wagner "esteemed him because he
called himself plain Levi, as in the Bible, not Löwe, Lewy, etc.")
Wagner answered at once, but the style of the letter suggests that it
was Cosima who actually composed the answer, as she now did with
most of Wagner's letters:

Lucerne, April 27, 1870

Your very frank question deserves an equally frank answer. The
reason why they in Munich turned to you lies in the hope finally to
find a conductor who would bring my work to life without my
personal help. So far they have not succeeded, as all the most able
conductors, friendly to my cause, have refused. If they fail with you
they will have to search some more. Since the attitude of the Munich
court intendant has for the last two years made it impossible for me to
establish any relationship with them, it goes without saying that I will
not dream of concerning myself with the performance of any work of
mine for which preparations have already begun. Such preparations
could only have been initiated by me if my cooperation were to make
sense. My noble benefactor, the King of Bavaria, now wishes to
witness a performance of *Die Walküre,* in spite of these foul
circumstances. That wish would ordinarily be most flattering to me: I
honor it as a sign of his gracious disposition toward my work and I am
forever conscious that without this grace and the countless benefits he
has bestowed on me I would perhaps today be shipwrecked, noticed
by nobody, least of all by the German people and their theater
managers. Therefore I am moved to declare: if His Majesty insists on
his wish, I will not object to the performance, whatever the
conditions, though I know all too well and to my sorrow that this, one
of my most difficult and problematic works, will meet strong
resistance, be badly judged, and make a totally unclear effect. . . .

I regret that I am forced to tell you what I have told Munich: I do not
object to your conducting my work, provided that the whole affair
remains between you and the Munich intendant, without recourse to
myself in any way whatever.

I take this opportunity to express to you my pleasure over the good
things I heard about your direction of my *Meistersinger* in Karlsruhe,
specifically the higher praise accorded your performance than to the
one in Dresden. I need not assure you how beneficent it is for me to
be able to greet a conductor of true talent in a German opera house!

P.S. I unseal this letter to tell you that I gladly permit you to publish
it, if you think it might help to elucidate the affair.

Levi wrote on the letter: "That I do not intend to do, at least for the
time being. L."

He refused to conduct. The king proving adamant in his demand
that the performance take place, Düfflipp sent a pleading letter to
Bülow: *Please* come, lend a helping hand, serve the king, serve art.
Bülow refused. They got Wüllner.

Wagner sank into gloom. It was not injured vanity alone that caused
the gloom. And later history proved that he had no objection to the
staging of separate parts of the *Ring*. That objection now was but a

cover for the reason that underlay all other considerations: Cosima had to be protected.

Cosima tried her best to cheer the man who told her, "If I did not feel fire for art and warmth for love, I would now be dead." In the evenings she summoned to her aid the plays he liked: Aristophanes' *The Frogs,* Kleist's *Kätchen von Heilbronn,* Goethe's *Faust,* Shakespeare's *As You Like It* and *The Merchant of Venice,* with Wagner enacting the principal roles in the silence of Triebschen. She marshaled the children to divert him. They succeeded somewhat: he romped with the girls while Fidi was given a ride on the back of Grane, a docile little horse the king had sent as a birthday present. They went to Lucerne for an orgy of chocolate. He taught Blandine and Daniela a few melodies on the piano until Cosima took over for more systematic instruction. He cut the children's toenails, told them a simplified version of the Nibelung saga, read them *Robinson Crusoe.* But presently he thought again of Munich and the king and returned to his room.

The closer the date of the premiere, the more nervous he became, so that finally Cosima instructed the valet to deliver all letters with a Munich postmark to her, and she suppressed the reports about the progress of the rehearsals (twenty-five of them), including an article in the A.A.Z. about the dress rehearsal. (She tore the page from the newspaper.) The premiere took place on June 26, 1870; it was an immense, indeed a spectacular, success, setting at naught Wagner's conviction that the public would not understand the "problematic" *Walküre.* The public understood and was overwhelmed by the greatness of the work. "We didn't refer in a single word to last night's performance," Cosima noted on the twenty-seventh, though they got some amusement from a telegram sent by an unknown admirer with the strange name of Napoleon Komolatsch: "Unending jubilation at the end of first act." Nietzsche did not attend the performance, out of friendship for Wagner. Liszt did, "with a cavalcade of acquaintances." Wagner's comment: "How different your father is when he faces the piano—and when he faces life."

Yet with all his anger against Liszt or Wüllner or Ludwig, he kept silent. And silently he continued to construct the arch of his epos, *Götterdämmerung.* That he was able to work was Cosima's doing. On her part, she, too, came to terms with the situation. "Yesterday I wanted very much to write Herr Wüllner to point out to him the extent of his misdeed. Today I find it more sensible and dignified to remain silent." (June 30, 1870)

Seventeen days later, on July 17, France, provoked by Bismarck, declared war on Prussia. The proclamation was written by Ollivier, Cosima's brother-in-law. Wagner's French friends, who had been traveling in Germany, gathered in Triebschen before returning home: Catulle Mendès and Judith Gautier, de l'Isle-Adam, Saint-Saëns, Duparc. Political conversation grew tense among them, but thanks no doubt to Cosima's skill as a hostess, it was deflected to artistic discussion and Saint-Saëns accompanied Wagner on the piano in excerpts from the *Ring.*

With a heavy heart, Ludwig had to turn from his preoccupation with the production of Wagner's works. Graver issues had to be decided. Was Bavaria, allied to Prussia by treaty, going to honor its obligation, was it to join the war against France? The Bavarian parliament was sharply divided, one bloc recommending "armed neutrality," the other shouting, "To arms!" Ludwig, who feared crowds as he would a forest fire, suddenly decided to show himself to "feel the mood" of his people. On July 17, he appeared on the balcony of the Residenz; he was greeted by an enthusiastic tumult. Moved and delighted, he kept reappearing and waving gaily to the crowd. His counselors told him that were Bavaria to remain neutral, it might outlive a French victory—never a Prussian one. Yet how he hated this war, as he had always hated all wars! From eleven o'clock that night until three o'clock in the morning, Ludwig conferred with the prime minister, asking him again and again, "Is there no way, no way at all, to avoid war?" At 5 A.M., he made up his mind. He issued the declaration of war in the language of the country with which he was about to do battle: *"J'ordonne la mobilisation, informez-en le Ministre de la Guerre."*

Cosima noted on that same day of July 17, 1870: "How hateful the French nation appears!"

CHAPTER VIII

Cosima Changes

Between the premiere of *Das Rheingold* and that of *Die Walküre*, Wagner had come to a decision which he kept secret from the king. It goes without saying that Cosima knew about it. Once *Götterdämmerung* was finished, he wanted to perform the entire *Ring* under his own musical and dramatic supervision and as a unit, an event that would partake of the nature of a German festival, and for which he would gather and train the best Germany had to offer in the way of singers, musicians, machinists, and scene painters. The "failure" of Munich convinced him that he would have to look elsewhere for a theater in which he could realize the soaringly ambitious undertaking. He knew full well that by this action he was breaking faith with the king. Those Medici plans they had formed together, the project of turning Munich into a modern Florence and there to nurture all the arts, but especially music and drama; those noble endeavors by which Ludwig and Wagner as equal partners would lift stolid Germans to the firmament: what would happen to them? Let them be nullified—as long as Wagner could accomplish what his brain and heart longed for, the realization of the *Ring* in its totality, with equal attention to its musical, dramatic, pictorial, and philosophical aspects, the last being to Wagner as important as the first. For this he needed a place, a theater, and an organization entirely under his jurisdiction.

As to the place: on March 5, 1870, Cosima and he were discussing —for the fiftieth time—the ideal location for a performance of the *Ring.* He had just played some excerpts from *Walküre,* and Cosima suggested that he "look up in the Encyclopedia the article on Baireuth [*sic*], the place which R. mentioned as his possible choice; we are pleased to read about a magnificient old opera house there." Cosima then asked a Lucerne book dealer to obtain books about Bayreuth; these were duly delivered in October. She and Richard were both aware that a great change in their lives would soon have to be faced, that they would have to descend from Triebschen, the refuge that they loved so dearly. "How strange is my fate," Cosima noted, "that it is forever shadowed by a menacing cloud"; while he asked, "How do you think it is going to end between the King and myself?" (March 21, 1870) The next day, she received a letter from Düfflipp, making various suggestions about the *Walküre* performance in Munich. "What a pity!" Wagner was going to answer the king directly, sketched out a letter, then decided not to send it.* Cosima herself answered the king: they would not, they could not change their minds about Munich.

Neither admitted to the other how nervous each of them was, yet despite their fears they savored moments of happiness, as when Fidi distinctly said "Papa," or when Wagner finished the scene of the oath in the second act of *Götterdämmerung* and found it good, or when Nietzsche came to visit, or when Germany was victorious. On January 28, 1871, some six months after the beginning of the war, Paris capitulated. Cosima was beside herself with excitement when she got the news. "I spring up electrified. Is it really true? It *is* true. Jakob [their new servant] brought the news from town, quite phlegmatically, in the real Swiss manner." (January 28, 1871) Wilhelm I was proclaimed emperor of Germany in Versailles. Cosima: "I expect much from the new Empire."

But her hosannas of victory could not altogether silence her insecurity—or Wagner's How would Ludwig react to the Bayreuth plan? Not for a moment did they deceive themselves about the gravity of the decision, knowing that they must renounce tranquillity for the sake of "The Work." Cosima urged Wagner on: he must not weaken.

Yet it was months before he found the strength to disclose his plan to the king—and then only in vague terms. On March 1, 1871—more than nine months after the *Walküre* premiere—he wrote Ludwig:

*The letter is lost, but the sketch is extant. It is not written in Wagner's usual style of addressing the king. Probably Cosima composed it.

"My purpose is—provided the plan succeeds—to bring into being a German national project, the direction of which must of course be entirely entrusted into my hands." Ludwig wrote to Düfflipp: "I greatly dislike Wagner's plan." That letter was written on April 19, three days after Wagner and Cosima left to inspect Bayreuth.

Cosima saw Bayreuth first at five o'clock in the afternoon and thought it lovely, but that night she got an awful fright: Richard had chills and fever. "Is this a warning by Fate?" she wondered. She sent for a doctor in the middle of the night, and the following dialogue ensued:

> DOCTOR: Well, the strange things that can happen to one! Who could have prophesied that this very night I was going to make the acquaintance of Richard Wagner? You are *the* Richard Wagner, the very special R. Wagner?
>
> WAGNER: You mean the one who has written pretty things? Yes, I am he.

The three of them laughed, the doctor ordered him to stay in bed; the next day he was well again and they went to see the eighteenth-century theater. Charming though it was, festooned with gilded traceries and flying angels, it was entirely unsuitable for their purpose. Cosima: "We will have to build: so much the better." Where would they live? They drove all over town. "Nothing is quite suitable. So we must build our house as well."

Bayreuth was the choice. Why did Wagner choose it? First, because it was situated in the very heartland of Germany, medieval Franconia, a region of old courts and castles where the Minnesingers sang the songs that formed the beginnings of German lyric poetry. Second, because it was part of Bavaria, lying in Ludwig's realm, and therefore Ludwig might eventually approve. Third, because it was difficult to get to; one had to make an effort to reach it. Wagner wanted the public to make a pilgrimage. Fourth, because it was not a spa or a tourist center, but a small backward town capable of, and perhaps grateful for, development. Cosima liked it for a fifth reason: woods and fields were nearby, offering playgrounds for the children; so-called Franconian Switzerland was not far away, verdant goals for picnics and excursions.

In Bayreuth, Wagner was soon to find enthusiastic supporters to help him: first and foremost, the banker Friedrich Feustel, who turned out to be a model of efficiency and remained a lifelong friend; and second, the mayor of the city, Theodor Muncker. Spurred by these two remarkably idealistic men, and anticipating a flow of marks soon to rain on the city, the local government decided to offer Wagner a site for the theater as a gift. Both Muncker and Feustel liked Cosima very much, and vice versa. She acted as her husband's representative and did so, according to Muncker, "with persuasion which was both charming and clever."

On January 8, 1872, Feustel and Muncker showed up unexpectedly in Triebschen. They had to tell Wagner that the owner of a part of the proposed site of the theater refused to sell. Wagner flew into a violent temper, swore that he would give up Bayreuth, forbade his two visitors, who had come proposing a different site, to mention the project. With this the two men departed. But before they left Lucerne, they decided to turn back, their decision undoubtedly influenced by Cosima. A new conference took place, in which Cosima convinced Wagner that the second site was better than the first. (So it was.)

Almost immediately, the numerous admirers of Wagner's music burst into lively enthusiasm. A festival theater for the new German Reich, destined to perform the works of Germany's greatest living composer—it was an exhilarating idea.

But presently—and soon—Wagner and Cosima learned the difference between orotund enthusiasm and the shelling out of cash. In spite of the fine speeches, in spite of such phrases as: Bayreuth will prove "that the German, now feared, will from this time on have to be reckoned with in his public art," or that the Theater will reinforce "the political strength of the nation, hitherto kept hidden" (a self-serving pronouncement which few people—except Cosima—took seriously), in spite of good work by the "Patrons" and the newly formed "Richard Wagner Verein" (some of whose members contributed merely because they hoped to get free tickets for the first performance), not nearly enough money was coming in to finance the plan. What Philistines "his" Germans were! "Once more," he told Cosima, "we will attempt something with the German fatherland, with Bayreuth; if it doesn't succeed, then farewell to the North, to art, to cold weather; we shall wander to Italy and forget everything." It was Cosima who kept up his spirits, telling him that he must and would succeed. From the first moment, she never wavered.

In the spring, he decided to undertake a concert tour. He hated to do it, but he did it to raise funds. In early May 1871, the tour brought him to Berlin, where he was honored by a banquet to which the leading scientists, statesmen, and writers were invited, and he called on Bismarck, the architect of the new Reich, who wove compliments around him but declined to interest himself in any "artistic schemes"; he had worries enough. Besides, why should Prussia concern itself with what he considered a Bavarian affair? The Berlin concert, in which Wagner conducted Beethoven's Fifth and excerpts from his own works, was attended by Kaiser Wilhelm and his queen. Wagner, tired and irritated, delegated the social duties to Cosima, who easily did the honors with George King of Hannover, or Countess Liechtenstein, or Baroness Pourtalès, using, more determinedly than before, the pronoun "we." "We will save German art—we are building for the nation—but *you* must contribute." So closely did she identify herself with the undertaking that she sometimes gave the impression of having been coauthor. To him only did she remain humble. Preaching the gospel according to Saint Cosima, she made as many enemies as she gained friends; as many drew away as were attracted. The dream of Bayreuth changed her; she now regarded herself not only as the companion to a genius but as a member of a national institution. Even more, she began to see herself as immortal, a *vates sacra* of a new art.

They got a jolt when they received a letter from Düfflipp containing a severe message from the king; Ludwig had not even deigned to write Wagner directly.

> The King wants us to know that he has been informed that the Theater undertaking will cost much more than 900,000 thaler and that the many festival performances will cause the Bayreuth citizens much expense. Second, that the Bayreuth newspapers were talking of the luxury of our house [projected, but not yet built] which made an unpleasant impression on the King. Third, that the King wants *Siegfried,* since he acquired it by purchase. [Diary, March 26, 1872]

This piece of news upset Cosima so much that a few words following the above entry became illegible. She begged Richard to return the lots on which the house was to be built, and which Ludwig had given him as a gift. As to *Siegfried,* tell the king that the score is not completed. (This was a bald lie; it had been completed a year earlier, in February 1871.)

> So we are once more delivered to the old misery! Long consultation with R. He will ask the people in Bayreuth for an explanation: should their reply be lukewarm he will abandon the whole project. We cannot succeed if the King himself is against us. R. would probably have to relinquish his salary, and we'll have to manage as best we can.

The replies from Feustel and the mayor, far from being lukewarm, were enthusiastic, urging Wagner to proceed. Thus, in the early months of 1872, he had to undertake several journeys, conferring with architects, builders, lawyers, moneyed patrons, etc. Wherever he went, he felt that "when I was at home, I was in a better place," and he longed for Cosima, expressing his love in letter after letter:

> Sleep well, my wonderful, only one! I am always, and always will be, *with you*. [Berlin, January 26, 1872]

> I have my little sedative drink before me and hope for a peaceful night. And whom do I have to thank for this? For all good things only you, my noble wife! [Berlin, January 27]

> I love you beyond all thoughts and feelings, my glorious one! [Bayreuth, February 1]

> Ah! Kiss the children and love, love, love me! I breathe in you and feel great strength in you, with you! I want to work wonders and I can do so, but only for you! [Bayreuth, April 24]

Cosima contemplated with a heavy heart giving up Triebschen and bidding good-bye to the quiet of lake and mountain. Farewell to the place of peace, where she had fulfilled her love! Nietzsche was with her in April 1872. He sat among crates and boxes, while Cosima, unable to pay much attention to him, hastily tried to catch up on her correspondence and to make some sort of order among the mass of papers and letters in the library. "Whereto are we wandering, what is in store for us, where is our home?" she worried. Again: "Splendid sunset, alpenglow, trees in blossom, the cuckoo calls, the cowbells sound, a blackbird calls, melancholy good-bye! Wonderful moonlight above the water, shining stillness around me—how different all will be from now on!" But it was to be; *he* wanted it; and king or no king, she thought he could arouse a sufficient number of idealistic compatriots to proceed with the building.

On April 29, Cosima, with the five children, two servants, and the dog Russ, left Triebschen in a downpour. Lulu was coughing, Loldi fell into a puddle, the steamship crossed the Zurich lake in a storm, she was overwhelmed by a mass of hand luggage which had to be examined at the frontier; and it was not until four-thirty the next day that they arrived in Bayreuth. Wagner was at the station, happy and smiling, calling her "his life force." They repaired to the pleasant Hotel Fantaisie on the outskirts of Bayreuth. Wagner had filled their rooms with flowers.

On May 22, Wagner's birthday, the cornerstone laying of the theater took place. It was raining mercilessly, without a moment's letup. All the same, hundreds of men and women had come and stood re-

Cosima and Wagner in Vienna, 1872.

spectfully in the empty lot. A congratulatory telegram from the king was sealed in a time capsule. (That telegram was just an act of courtesy.) The mud covered everybody's shoes and the open-air ceremony had to be curtailed, but there was time enough for Wagner to strike the stone with three hammer blows and to say, "Be blessed, my stone, stand long, hold firm!" He turned away to hide his tears.

Nietzsche was there. Years later, he wrote: "When on that May day of 1872 the cornerstone had been placed on the hill of Bayreuth while the rain poured down and the heavens darkened, Wagner rode back to the city with a few of us. He was silent and his glance, which it would be difficult to describe, was turned inward. On that day began the sixtieth year of his life. All that had gone before was a prologue to this moment."

That day, Cosima got a foretaste of what most of her life was going to be like from then on: after sitting with the children on the stage of the Margravian Opera House,* watching her husband conduct the Ninth Symphony, she presided at a huge banquet, lengthened by the usual long speeches. The next day, she acted as hostess to a stream of callers, being patient with all of them because—who knew?—they might become financial supporters; the day after, she was present at a morning conference with the excellent Carl Brandt, creator of stage miracles, then got ready for "many visitors, including a British journalist." She assumed these responsibilities with the utmost willingness, in addition to taking dictation on the autobiography and helping to plan the house in which they were going to live. Yet the difficulties of these variegated tasks, along with her realization that more troubles were in store, rendered the harsh part of her personality harsher.

The difficulties multiplied, the pressure increased. Just then, trouble between her husband and her father became more pronounced. Cosima thought she could heal the estrangement—which Liszt had expressed by refusing to come to the cornerstone ceremony in spite of Wagner's urgent invitation—if they were to visit him in Weimar. At first Wagner refused, but by and by he said, "All right, one has to be diplomatic," and wrote Liszt a "diplomatic" letter asking if their visit would be welcome. It was, and they went.

Liszt was happy to see them, but he avoided any real intimacy with his daughter by surrounding himself with people, for lunch, for dinner, for the evening. Cosima grieved to see him influenced not only by Carolyne Wittgenstein (who was in Rome) but by his latest friend,

*Bülow wrote, taking her to task for letting the children sit on the stage!

the young Baroness Olga Meyendorff (very much present in Weimar), who was now determinedly guiding his life. "I am terribly moved by the spiritual weariness of Father; in the evening he hardly spoke, while I kept chatting about this and that. . . . At night I wept when I envisioned the tragedy of his life," she wrote in the diary (September 3, 1872). Liszt did play for them—Beethoven's G-major Concerto, some Chopin Preludes, and unfortunately his own "Mephisto Waltz," which Wagner detested, and in the train going home Wagner broke into a tantrum of jealousy.

In November, Wagner and Cosima embarked on an exploratory trip to sixteen German cities, sometimes staying only overnight, to investigate what singers could be regarded as promising material for the festival. It was a discouraging journey. He was feted with torchlight parades, serenades, laurel wreaths, banquets—but the performances he heard were of deplorably low quality, the singers almost invariably stepping up to the footlights and bouncing the high notes at the audience with whatever athleticism they could muster, the conductors almost invariably acting as timid accompanists. Wagner often fled the opera house after the first act, covering his ears with his hands.

They heard a performance of *Die Meistersinger* in Bremen. On entering the theater, Wagner was received by a flourish from the orchestra and the tumultuous acclamation of the audience. Cosima:

> The conductor has really done everything possible with a small orchestra in which there are some good musicians. But the staging is, once again, abominable. The worst is that Herr Schott [the publisher] thought it fit to send the parts from Mannheim which were prepared by Herr Lachner [the Munich conductor], who makes cuts even in *Freischütz*. Therefore the third act unrecognizable and boring. . . . R. reminds me with tears in his eyes of the time in which he created the work. When future generations will find exhilaration in this music, may they remember the tears which nurtured these smiles! [December 8, 1872]

Cosima, though she enjoyed the acclaim, was acutely lonesome for the children and she couldn't wait to get home. When they did, she was not pleased with the children's looks. Boni and Eva looked "peaked" and Fidi seemed overwrought and pale. Other cares awaited her: she was shocked by the mounting expense of the house that was being built; she heard that the king was incommunicado, giving orders to his ministers only through his groom, that he decorated his hunting lodges with elaborate Louis XIV decorations, spending fortunes on them, and that he loathed Prussia and the new Germany. Not a good omen! Worst of all, on December 18—three days after their return—Wagner felt pains in his chest. She summoned the doctor, who ordered rest. She knew that the cares of Bayreuth, the enormity of the task he had prescribed for himself, were the forces clutching at his heart. How could he stop now?

2

He had to go on. Donors defaulted on their promises and at best not enough money was coming in to pay the builders and workmen at the theater, let alone hold out the promise that the festival could become a reality.

With a sad heart, Cosima made her final entry for the year:

> . . . R. very unwell, goes early to bed. I stay awake to look through the housekeeping accounts, deplore the heavy expenditures! Prepared and sorted the children's clothes. R. gets up again. Complains! Worry is making him ill. I can well believe it; what lies ahead for him and how will he summon the strength to meet it? . . .

> It is nearly midnight as I write this. Heavily this year is ending and heavy lies the year ahead of us. . . . But we cannot choose, we cannot wish, we must take what comes. . . . [December 31, 1872]

It was she who worried more about finances than he. She was frantic because "R. is embroiled in an undertaking before the money pledges are signed." She said nothing to him lest her doubts add to his malaise, which in turn he tried to hide from her. Now as before she imbibed every sentence he uttered, as he discoursed on Beethoven's Seventh, on Beaumarchais, on Carlyle, whom they were reading together; and she duly recorded such pearls of his wisdom as "Would it not be possible that . . . once the Germans will have formed a nation, the German language would become similar to the Sanskrit of India, that is the language of culture, while English would serve as Prakrit, the language of the people?"

She had been home barely a month when Feustel pleaded that Wagner undertake another concert tour to stimulate the cause by personal appearances and to quicken the sluggish flow of money. Once again and most reluctantly, they set out to various cities, subjected themselves to patronizing words from assorted counts, princes, barons, and celebrities, once again they swallowed bad food at boring banquets, once again he labored at rehearsals and swung the baton, all of which failed to bring in sufficient money. As he was conducting "Wotan's Farewell" in Berlin, he looked around and saw Cosima sitting in a box. So moved was he by a sudden realization that she was with him to love him, to give him courage, that his beat nearly went astray. She told him that he looked as young as his son—"his hair has suddenly turned quite black again"—and that he could afford to "await the triumph of his cause."

For his sixtieth birthday she determined to make especially elaborate preparations. She enlisted the cooperation of a number of Bayreuth friends, and consequently the Bayreuth papers published reports of the coming event. Unchecked, Cosima managed to have special copies printed with all references to him deleted. These he read, having no inkling of what was being planned. At seven-thirty in the morning of May 22, a group of musicians and choristers she had summoned from Würzburg, who were hidden in a neighbor's garden, awakened Wagner with the *"Wach auf"* chorus from *Die Meistersinger.* Then the children appeared, dressed in their Sunday best, each reciting a toast and bearing a gift. (Fidi brought a poodle.) In the evening, she told him, a few friends had arranged a ceremony of at most a half hour's duration at the old opera house, to which they must go so as not to disappoint his well-wishers. When he entered, he found the theater full, the audience in festive dress. An orchestra began to play an overture. Who composed this? he asked Cosima, who did not reply. He was baffled: it was certainly not by Beethoven, nor by Bellini. It must be by Hermann Zumpe, a contemporary composer he knew. Suddenly recognition came: it was his own Concert Overture which he had composed in 1831, forty-two years before. He had forgotten it, Cosima had found it. The overture was followed by various tributes, the final one being an elaborate poem to a musical accompaniment arranged by Peter Cornelius and recited by Franziska Ritter. Then everybody repaired to the Anker, the famous local restaurant.

Yet the celebration could make them forget their troubles only for a day in May. Though Wagner gave the king a roseate report—the great theater was slowly rising, Cosima and he hoped soon to move into their own home, which the king's liberality had provided for them, the Bayreuth population was enthusiastic, the project was benevolently regarded by the whole artistic world, etc.—by the summer he had to face some cold arithmetic: of the approximately 400,000 thaler required, only about 130,000, less than a third, had been raised. In August he had to confess the state of affairs to Ludwig, to tell him that the rich nobility of Germany harbored no German spirit in their hearts, preferring to spend their money on "Jewish or Jesuit projects," and that the only salvation of the great undertaking lay in the king's guaranteeing the required sum, so that a loan could be raised. The guarantee would be a mere formality, of course: Wagner was certain that the performances would bring in more than enough to cover it. Of course!

Cosima was not hopeful; she kept hearing strange things about Ludwig. Recently he had ordered dinner for twelve, entered, greeted the empty chairs, and eaten all alone. He would enter and leave by the window, never through the door. He was occupying himself with fantastic building plans. Neuschwanstein (begun in 1869) was to have an artificial grotto, dedicated to the Venus of *Tannhäuser,* which would contain a cascade and a moon lit by electric light; while Linderhof (begun in 1870) was to be a riot of lapis, malachite, porcelain, and gold, with a *"Tischlein deck' dich"* ("Table, bring dinner") which could be raised through the floor and made to disappear again, imitating the fairy tale. "What can we expect—and how soon?" Cosima wrote, and wondered whether she should pledge whatever money she might inherit from her parents. If the children were no consideration, how gladly she would do it! Wagner was all too occupied with appeals and conferences to do his real work. For weeks he had not touched the score of *Götterdämmerung,* and once, when he did, he broke the gold pen he treasured. An evil sign, Cosima thought, while she fought with the architect, the masons, and the other workmen: "they are always drunk." When would the king answer? And what?

Wagner was far from well. His leg pained him and he had to give up the walks he enjoyed so greatly. He believed he would die before the festival. What could he do? He cited Charles V's remedy for gout, "Much patience and a little screaming," and applied it to their current situation. When, in spite of "patience," he sank into a black mood, Cosima still managed to appear cheerful, confiding her fears only to her diary. Then Wagner had to tell the patrons that the festival must be postponed, at least to 1875. The king's answer had arrived: negative. The king wanted to make it "absolutely clear" that Wagner "cannot count on any moral or pecuniary assistance."

On October 21, 1873, the patrons and delegates were invited to Bayreuth to discuss the situation. An "Appeal to the German Nation," written by Nietzsche and edited by Cosima, was read to the few who attended, while the rain came down in torrents. It was decided that the "Appeal" should not be sent, because its tone was too reprimanding. Moreover, the time was not propitious; a financial panic which had begun in Vienna in May had spread to other European cities. Times were hard. Feustel, however, was not discouraged; he theorized that the king merely wanted to be urged and suggested that he and Wagner go to Munich for a personal appeal. Wagner consented, without a shred of hope. "The house desolate and empty," Cosima notes, and on the very day they leave, writes Wagner *two* letters (November 20, 1873). Wagner returned, having failed to see the king.

Cosima received an anonymous essay in the mail, obviously intended for her. Its title: "What Is Fraud?" Another post brought a brochure about "Insanity." "I cannot imagine," she comments sadly, "where people get all that venom." She and Wagner regularly run over to the future home in process of construction, which they now call "Anger Hall" *(Angersheim)*, "because we are always finding something that has gone wrong or been overlooked." Yet not for an hour did she lose sight of the great objective. On Christmas Day, though dressed in her best satin, she asked him to take her to inspect the theater. Unmindful of her finery, she climbed over the planks to reach the stage. "Grandiose impression. Like an Assyrian edifice the whole rises up unrestrained. . . ."

But shortly after, a fear she could not define overcame her: when the theater had existed only as an idea, she thought of it merely as another building. Now, beholding the giant scaffolding, it seemed to her a grave—"a pyramid grave."

And yet there was still not enough money to finish it. The king awarded Wagner a high decoration, the Order of Maximilian, but he sent no money. Wagner's pleasure in the decoration turned to fury when he learned that the same honor had been bestowed on Brahms, "that silly youngster." He wanted to send it back, but by and by he calmed down.

3

At the beginning of 1874, the festival seemed doomed. Though Wagner, unable to sleep one night, consulted Cosima at four o'clock in the morning as to what to do next and they decided once more to telegraph to Düfflipp asking for a definite yes or no from the king (the "No" arrived within hours), and though he made one or two last-stand appeals—to the Grand Duke of Baden and to Martin Delbrück (Prussian minister and Bismarck's right hand), he did these things merely "not to leave anything undone," and both he and Cosima realized that the appeals would be in vain. Cosima said, "How comforting it is to be deserted by everybody"—forgetting all the devoted workers in the cause—and he answered, "That is the only dignified state to be in." Like the student who fails the exam, he disclaimed any responsibility. Henceforth he wanted "nothing to do with the outside world" and would concentrate on writing philosophic and aesthetic treatises, a martyr to German materialism. His martyrdom would be enacted within the walls of his new house, which was almost ready and for which he at once ordered expensive draperies and rugs, all on credit; Cosima was unable to stop him.

Luxury in adversity—that was his way of keeping going, while Cosima comforted herself by holding on to the conviction that help would come sooner or later and that "idealism is not extinct in the German people." And she knew better than anybody that Wagner's hermit attitude was a pose and that he sobbed when he confronted the possibility—at the moment, the probability—of the theater's remaining "a fragment and a ruin." As usual, they found some deflection from sad thoughts in reading. Her eyes were bothering her, so he read to her: *Richard III,* selections from the *Upanishads,* and to make her laugh, *Lysistrata,* which last, however, he broke off, deeming it too indecent for her ears! Too bad; she had enjoyed it.

Early in the morning of January 27, 1874, Cosima had gone to talk again to the workmen at the house. When she returned, Wagner met her at the doorstep and handed her a letter from the king. "I don't want to read it," he said. "You read it and tell me what's in it." Cosima opened it and at once perceived that it was "most friendly." Ludwig wrote (January 25): "No! No and again no! It can't end this way: help must be given! Our plan must not be shipwrecked!" He had hesitated to give the guarantee only because the state of his own finances was precarious, even to the extent of delaying his personal building plans. But now he had decided that, whatever the consequences, he would underwrite the loan. "My enthusiasm for your divine, incomparable works [is] so deeply implanted in my soul that it would be madness to believe in any decline of my ardor for you and your great undertaking."

They could not quite believe this change in their fortune, but it soon became clear that Ludwig meant to keep his promise. Once again he had changed his mind, a change prompted not by weakness but by the strength of his admiration for the artist, by his comprehension of the benison he could bestow on posterity. For the sake of that prospect he could forgive the lies.

Late that night, Cosima remained sitting alone, grateful, joyful, hopeful. She looked at the winter moon. "I cannot take my leave of the soft rays and the great stillness." Soon that moon would shine on the theater on the hill.

Yet Cosima's happiness had a way of not remaining as peaceful as the moon. The next evening, when she bade Daniela and Blandine good night, she made some joking remark to them. After which she heard Daniela mumble something. "What did Daniela say?" she asked Blandine. The younger girl told her: her sister had said, "What a bore!" Cosima was terribly disturbed. There it was again—her guilt, the covered "sin" pushing to the fore, her fear that because of her, Bülow's children would turn out badly. She made a mountain of grief out of a molehill of childish impudence. "This I must bear," she wrote in the diary. . . . "I keep still, forcing my soul to be calm. . . . I resolve not to spoil the joy R. needs so badly and I hold back my tears. I pray." (January 29, 1874)

Cosima's lack of lightness, an essential ingredient in a child's up-bringing, as well as her all too demonstrative preference for Fidi, rendered the problem of the two older children more acute. Both Daniela and Blandine showed signs of rebellion, defying her and quarreling with the other three children. Was it any wonder? They had been treated as though they were impervious to the chaos and tensions they'd been exposed to. At that age especially (Daniela was fourteen in 1874 and Blandine eleven), they might have bitterly resented Cosima—and even hated her. Moreover, both girls had inherited from their father a nervous sensibility, a defensive truculence.

How was Cosima to handle the situation? After much hesitation and no little heartbreak, she decided it would be salutary to send them to a boarding school; and after consulting three or four of her female friends, she settled on the Luisenstift, a school near Dresden. She went there to look it over:

> Preparations for my departure tomorrow. R. laments it, making more difficult what is already difficult for me! But I must do it and this notebook ends with its account of the fulfillment of a maternal duty. From September 16, 1873, to October 16, 1874—what distress it contains, what suffering, how little pleasure from the world outside—yet an ever more profound peace for the soul, found in the confines of our home! Blessed be Richard! Blessed be the children! For myself I pray for forgiveness. . . .
> [October 16, 1874]

She liked the school, and though she hated to separate herself from her two eldest children, she decided to send them there. (Wagner, too, hated to see them go.) Having come to this decision, she returned to Bayreuth in a week. Wagner had written her every day and while she was gone he had refused to see anybody.

Yet the Luisenstift could not give the girls what they needed. Daniela, especially, long remained obdurate. As the eldest, born of a father she hardly knew, as an infant pulled from one home to the other, she looked to her mother for security, however disobediently she often comported herself. She needed tolerant understanding. She didn't get it. What she got was sermons, and oily sermons at that.

> Do not fail, my child, to pray to God for your father [Bülow]: ask Our Lord to exorcise your bad traits, your nasty instincts. . . . Your first duty is to love your father more than anybody in the world; prepare yourself so that you may assist him in life's struggle. To fulfill this duty and earn this happiness, you, my child, must renounce all vulgarity, all vanity. . . . [May 19, 1876. From a letter written in French]

> As to my severity and what you call my harshness, you know their cause very well—the fear of your way of behaving has imposed that severity on me. . . . [June 1876]

> Your conduct here showed much goodwill. I was very glad. It only remains now for you to understand—or to learn—the need to be neat, diligent, and self-reliant. In this respect you seem to be on the wrong path, which grieves me for your sake. The luxury you observed in our house is not of my doing and will disappear with the life of your father Richard. I wish you could have seen the pride with which my sister and I used to ignore external possessions. We were elegant in tone, sentiment, language, and totally indifferent toward what we did not have. As a young girl I never had a servant, I made my own bed and cleaned my room, I washed my own fine underwear, I fixed my own hair (even for balls), and all the while we frequented the best society. When I married your father I had but one maid and yet had to entertain important and rich people. Remember this, my child, and be diligent, orderly and frugal. . . . [September 11, 1876. In German]

4

Düfflipp privately informed Cosima that "The winds blowing from Hohenshwangau are more favorable than before." Wagner took two days to discuss with Cosima his reply to Ludwig. On February 3 he sent it off, a long and lofty thanks: "O my gracious King! Let your glance sweep over all German sovereigns and you will realize that you, and you only, are the one from whom the German spirit can still derive hope." Cosima, too, wrote to the king and sent—as one does to a benevolent uncle—photographs of the children, specially taken for the occasion:

Bayreuth, February 21, 1874

. . . If in the past years, so pregnant with trials, I felt that I had to keep silent, today I must speak. Speech flows from me with the force of nature, as I am unable to restrain the cascade of gratitude within me. May I hope that our Kingly Lord will be kind enough to understand the reasons why I kept silent before and now must speak? May I count on your acceptance of my poor words, they being the only thing I can offer? Your kind wish to have our pictures fills me with hope and faith. Here, noble protector, here are the portraits of those whom you have unceasingly cared for and who love you forever. Who can express all your benevolence has meant to us?

The letter is obviously a laborious piece of carving. No matter. . . . The festival was saved.

But only a few days after the miraculous turn of events, Cosima again thought it might be in jeopardy. She read an advertisement by an autograph dealer that he possessed "highly interesting" letters, nineteen in all, of Wagner and Minna, and she instantly suspected that they referred to the Malvina Schnorr episode. She was sure that if they were to be published, they would "deal a blow to the granting of the credit" for Bayreuth. Consulting a lawyer, she was advised that nothing could be done—except to buy the letters. The dealer wanted one hundred thaler, a considerable sum which they could ill spare at the moment. But they bought them—and the letters proved to be innocuous, much to Cosima's chagrin.

On the eighteenth of April, the new house was ready. They moved, lock, stock, and barrels of books. Wagner pompously called the new house Wahnfried, and had a little verse engraved over its portal. *Wahn* is impossible to translate by a single word: in the Wagnerian sense it means "vain illusion" or even "madness," as he used it in the "Wahn Monologue" of *Die Meistersinger*. The meaning of the dedicatory verse is: "Here where I found peace from my illusions, 'Wahnfried,' let me dub this house." He found no such peace.

Yet in the first year at least, his restless spirit found some happiness, thanks to Cosima's ministrations. The very first day, the children formed a solemn deputation, with Eva as the speaker, to thank her for their being "so beautifully installed." Fidi had his own little room and felt very important. A few days later, they played charades with Cosima. At coffee time they sang a little round which Wagner had composed for her, "Cos in May," and the *"Freude"* melody from the Ninth Symphony, which they sang often, crawling under the piano, with Wagner accompanying them.

Cosima worked so hard to bring the house into order that she fell asleep as Wagner read to her. It was freezing, the roof leaked, the pipes were faulty, and not until five days after moving in could the children take their first baths, which they did with much splashing. Protected from household annoyances, Wagner took up again the second act of *Götterdämmerung,* and completed it at the end of June.

That Wahnfried would be a grandiose dwelling was to be expected: it lacked nothing in grandiosity! The ground-floor "music room" rose two stories high, with a gallery running round it. Below the gallery, a frieze displayed paintings inspired by the *Ring.* The walls were Pompeian red. Six marble statues, a gift from Ludwig, stood before them, representing characters from Wagner's works, from *The Dutchman* to *Siegfried.* Two doors right and left led to the dining room and Cosima's "little sitting room." The center door, flanked by busts of Wagner and Cosima, opened into the *Saal* (the Hall), which was forty-two feet long and twenty-eight feet wide, with a bay window. It was the focal point of the house, and Wagner said it "contained all his possessions," chief among them a library comprising most of the works of European literature, in specially fine bindings, and eventually filling twelve large bookcases. On small tables were displayed bound scores and prints and folios. Wagner's desk faced a portrait of Schopenhauer. A grand piano stood near the center. The heavy draperies, the profusion of rugs and throws, gave the *Saal* the aura of a Near Eastern divan. No draft disturbed the composer of the storm that whips around Brünnhilde's mountaintop. Over the door that led to the music room a cloth of yellow damask was spread; Cosima had given it to Wagner in Naples for his birthday and Wagner called it "Isolde's sail." The ceiling of the *Saal* was coffered and each section bore a painting showing the insignia of a town that had formed a Wagner society: that was Cosima's idea. The walls were crowded up and down with paintings: Ludwig, Wagner's mother, his stepfather, Geyer, his uncle Adolf, Schiller, Goethe, Beethoven, Liszt, Marie d'Agoult. Later, Wagner's portraits by Lenbach and two portraits of Cosima were added. (Shakespeare's was absent.)* And because Wagner disliked the exterior of the

*The *Saal,* with the adjoining rooms, was hit by a bomb on April 5, 1945, but the façade of the house somehow remained undamaged.

house as being "too bare," Cosima ordered a graffito covering one whole wall. Wagner described it to the king:

> The center is occupied by Germanic Myth: since we wanted to have characteristic physiognomies, we resolved to use the features of the late Ludwig Schnorr; from either side Wotan's ravens fly toward it and it proclaims the legend imparted to it to two female figures, one of which, whose features resemble those of Schröder-Devrient, represents Ancient Tragedy, while the other represents Music, with the head and figure of Cosima; a small boy, clad as Siegfried and with my son's head, holds her hand, gazing up at his mother Music with an expression of mettlesome joy. [October 1874]

This work of art—if that was what it was—was typical of the house: overstuffed, self-important, second-rate nineteenth-century. They loved it. So did most of their visitors.

We have a description of life at Wahnfried thanks to one Susanne Weinert, whom Cosima hired as a governess in July 1875 and who remained in the household until April 1876, when Cosima dismissed her, giving as her reason that she wanted an English governess for the children. Susanne kept an informal journal during her stay, which, though its writer was no mental giant, contains some pertinent observations:*

> The front door opens into a small vestibule from which a staircase leads to a wide, bright room, the *Kindersalon.* There is a solemn quiet in the house; even the noise of footsteps is stifled by the soft carpets. The *Kindersalon* serves also as a schoolroom where, sitting at a long table, she [Susanne] would give lessons. Immediately adjacent to the *Kindersalon* is Cosima's boudoir and the so-called *Denkzimmer* (room for meditation). The furniture of the boudoir is "miraculously cozy. . . . Its doors are draped with heavy curtains." . . . The *Denkzimmer* is "particularly cozy in the evening. . . . The gaslight spreads its bright glow over the medium-sized quadrangular room and the red velvet of the *causeusen* (pillows). . . ."

> On August 5, 1875, a reception took place in Villa Wahnfried. "Members of society in Bayreuth, Liszt, and Richard Wagner's collaborators were present." . . . The governess admired the colorful picture, "the ladies in elegant robes—one of them in a heavy green satin robe—the gentlemen in evening dress or in uniform" (*"die vornehme Welt in Wahrheit und*

---

*Mrs. Willoughby Burrell obtained this journal and appended to it a note: "Ludicrous Journal of an innocent idiot Governess at Wahnfried, Bayreuth, unconsciously [*sic*] describes the inhabitants to the very Life—all their pomposity, imprudence, and impecuniosity." Mrs. Burrell, hating Wagner and Cosima as she did, went a bit far: Susanne was no "idiot." . . . The famous Burrell collection was described and annotated by John N. Burk in *Letters of Richard Wagner* (New York, 1950). The quotations used here are taken from this book (Chapter XXVII) by permission.

Dichtung"—the nobility of fact and fiction). . . . "Sitting on a sofa and hidden by an arrangement of flowers," the Fräulein and the children observed the party. The children, particularly Daniela, were less impressed by the pompous show and ridiculed the affectation, the gestures, and the dresses of the guests. . . .

The manners of the children toward their parents showed a certain ceremonial respect. "Whenever Cosima entered the room, the children approached her and kissed her hand. . . ." When Richard and Cosima visited the classroom, the children—and the governess too—rose. . . .

The parents participated in the children's games. "They played hide-and-seek with them; Richard Wagner swung them around in a circle." Wagner particularly liked to play with Siegfried. "When the boy attempted to turn a somersault or a wheel, he helped him. . . . He laid him flat on the floor," or "Wagner himself lay down, pretending to be Siegfried's riding horse, whereupon Siegfried climbed all over his father." Whenever Wagner's time permitted it, Siegfried was in his study playing around his father's chair. "Often Siegfried climbed on Cosima's knees, kissing her vehemently."

On New Year's Day they melted lead and threw it into cold water, the lead then forming shapes from which the future was prophesied:

Richard's piece was interpreted as a butterfly, whereupon he said almost solemnly, "Look, children, the symbol of immortality!" Cosima's piece turned into a little ball, usually interpreted as money. She remarked, "That is not so bad: to have money." "Wagner himself was dressed in his Meistersinger costume on this occasion." Another custom was observed: throwing the shoe backward over one's head. "If the tip of the shoe points toward the inside of the house, the owner will remain there during the following year; if it points to the exit, he will leave. . . . Frau Cosima threw her azure satin shoe, Richard Wagner his black velvet shoe, and both pointed to the inside; several other shoes flew through the air."

As for Susanne's employer:

Her "vivid and large eyes and her spiritual [*durchgeistigtes*], rather pale face reveal at once a woman with a great mind and a worthy companion of the great Master." Repeatedly she mentions Cosima's "beautiful light-brown hair, which was arranged in heavy braids down to her neck. . . . The poise of her head and the graceful way in which she walks made a most dignified impression."

Susanne mentions her "magnificent silk dresses," including several morning gowns, one of them of white satin trimmed with black velvet, which was converted from a former evening dress:

Dressed in this gown, Cosima "walks through the rooms like a fairy in a fairy tale." At the performance of *Lohengrin* in Vienna, she wore a "magnificent satin robe with an imposing train." When the Wagners had invitations in Vienna, "Cosima put on her most lovely clothes; a light-purple satin robe floated around her slim figure, pearls adorned her beautiful hair, neck, and arms."

5

The theater itself, its technical equipment, the scenery, the costumes, the cost of bringing the artists to Bayreuth, the orchestra, the living needs for almost two hundred people—all these denuded the budget as fast as the biblical locust cropped the Egyptian fields. Added to these "public" costs were unforeseen private costs for Villa Wahnfried. Cosima:

> Nothing but unpleasant news. The architect spoiled the service rooms, the decorators did their work ineptly, and ever-rising expenses! [June 11, 1874]

> More bills coming in. I remark to R. how curious it is that I, who really never lacked means, should be in a constant state of worry, while he, who has suffered so much from lack of money, never worries. [June 16, 1874]

> My small savings have been used up. They were insufficient. The cost of living is very high. [September 23, 1874]

Yet, thanks to Wagner's renewed energy and Cosima's excellent management, both private and public work progressed; that is to say, Wagner finished the composition of *Götterdämmerung;** at Wahnfried, in what they called the "Nibelung Chancellery," a little group of devoted men were copying the parts, correcting proofs, etc.; and on the hill, the stage and the sunken orchestra pit were being completed. The "Chancellery" was multinational, consisting of a German (Hermann Zumpe), a Hungarian (Anton Seidl, later a famous conductor), a Greek (Demetrius Lalas), and a Russian (Josef Rubinstein). Wagner could lay his xenophobia aside when it served his purpose, although Cosima then and for some time after made many an ugly remark about young Rubinstein, and it was only in Wagner's last year or so that she accepted him.

He would have staggered but for her. How heavy the load was! He had to pursue the wearying search for interpreters who were to abjure

---

*On the last page, Wagner wrote: "Completed in Wahnfried, November 21, 1874. Nothing more to be said."

the habits of a lifetime and, despite considering themselves "stars," would have to learn like beginners to endow words as well as notes with meaning. He had to imbue Richter and the orchestra with his ideas of melodic continuity. Both he and Cosima had to concern themselves with a hundred mundane details, such as the intricate rehearsal schedules, the housing and feeding of participants and audience, the corrections in the theater building, the experiments with the new stage machinery (not forgetting the special difficulty Brünnhilde's horse was sure to create), the problem of seating the royal visitors who were expected to attend, and—most difficult of all—the problem of Ludwig. The king would neither keep company with his fellow sovereigns nor attend any public performance, and he asked for *three* private performances of the complete *Ring,* at intervals and times he, Ludwig, would specify, so that he could immerse himself undisturbed and unseen in "the artistic delight to which I am looking forward so ardently" and for which he had had to wait many an arid year. Cosima's tasks included the supervision of the scenery, in the creation of which disputes broke out between the designer and the painter; decisions about the costumes—because Wagner had utmost confidence in her taste, she concerned herself with every detail, from Wotan's hat to Waltraute's shoe; assigning tickets for the first performances (more people wanted to come than the theater could hold); entertaining singers, musicians, machinist, ballet master, friends, patrons, publishers, Bayreuth officials, etc. She worked from morn to midnight. For her birthday that year Wagner gave her a magnificent string of pearls. The jeweler had to wait a long time for his money.

The Tetralogy, which it had taken twenty-six years to create, was still short of being realized. More money had to be raised. Wagner, sensing that further appeals to Ludwig at this time would be overplaying his hand, and dangerously so, decided to undertake another concert tour. Cosima asked Nietzsche's sister Elisabeth to take charge of the children while she accompanied her husband. Early in February 1875, Elisabeth arrived at Wahnfried, and observed how exhausted Wagner was, his nerves rubbed raw. He hit out against the stupidity of the tenors, the prancing of the sopranos, the indifference of his compatriots; sometimes, though rarely, he vented his weariness in outbursts against Cosima, even against Cosima, who crept past him and refrained from replying when he told her, "I wish all this nonsense were over and I could begin to work on my *Parsifal.*" Elisabeth commented: "To be the wife of a genius is a hard task."

The activities of 1875 fell into three groups, in each of which Cosima played her part: (1) the spring concert tour (March to May); (2) the first full rehearsals for orchestras and singers in Bayreuth (July 1 to August 13); (3) performances of *Tannhäuser* and *Lohengrin* in Vienna, freshly staged under Wagner's direction (November 1 to December 13).

The first stop of the spring tour was Vienna. Richter was supposed to have come from Budapest to rehearse the Vienna orchestra preliminary to Wagner's coming. But he had married, gone on a short honeymoon, could obtain no further leave from his post in Hungary, and thus neglected the Vienna concert. Cosima spoke of his "unbelievable carelessness": for the first rehearsal the tuba players were not notified, at the second it appeared that the harp parts had not been written out. Still, after the additional labor thrown on Wagner, he managed to give superb performances of excerpts and scenes from his own works. The enthusiasm of a celebrity-studded audience, Cosima recorded, seemed endless, and a heap of laurel wreaths was handed up to him, bearing ribbons inscribed: "To the Savior of German Art," "The Master of Humor," "The Renewer of the Old Sagas," "The Reformer," etc. Two days later, the painter Makart, idol of Vienna, gave a soiree in Wagner's and Cosima's honor in his Arabian Nights studio. Present were Liszt, many musicians, and the cream of Viennese aristocracy, up to the Andrássys and Prince Liechtenstein and Metternich's son. Cosima was far from impervious to the compliments paid her by these titled well-wishers; they confirmed in her a conviction that she belonged to the aristocracy, if not by birth, surely by association. Too often she would permit herself the disdainful smile.

The next stop was Budapest, where Richter conducted a truncated version of *The Flying Dutchman,* an unsatisfactory performance—"I am astonished at this Wagnerian *par excellence,"* was Cosima's comment—and Wagner and Liszt performed Beethoven's "Emperor" Concerto. "We are completely benumbed by my father's playing . . . an incomparable impression. Matchless magic—this is not a 'performance,' it is the essence of the music." (March 9) The tour continued to five other cities, and by May Wagner had raised some forty thousand gulden for Bayreuth. He had worked with incredible energy, but still the possibility of failure sat on him like an incubus in the night. Indeed, had it not been for Cosima morally and the marvelous Feustel practically, he might well have broken down. He was near it.

When rehearsals for the *Ring* began, in July 1875, he took new heart. It was in the main a devoted group of artists that he had gathered in that out-of-the-way spot, each of them conscious that he or she was to take part in an event which, as Levi wrote his father, "will produce a complete turnabout in our artistic life." Wagner felt happy among them. Only the tenor, the moody, nervous Albert Niemann, gave him trouble. Niemann rightly considered himself Germany's premier tenor and he chafed over the fact that Wagner would not entrust the part of Siegfried to him, but only the role of Siegmund. At one rehearsal, Niemann played fast and loose with the tempo and Wagner had to stop him several times. Niemann, realizing that he was at fault and smoldering with resentment, had to let out his anger on somebody; suddenly he broke off, went over to the piano, where Rubinstein had been accompanying admirably, took the slight man by the shoulders and shook him violently. Wagner blanched, bowed his head over the score, kept silent, and then, after what seemed like an eternity, said in a trembling voice, "Please, let us continue."

When the rehearsal was over, the artists were invited to the Wahnfried garden, which Cosima had decorated with paper lanterns and little flags. Wagner had recovered his equanimity, but Niemann had not. The gaiety of the company—which included Cosima and Liszt—grated on his nerves. He refused to eat. Teasingly Frau Jaïde (the Erda) speared a piece of ham on her own fork and reached it out to him. Niemann took it, ate it, and in turn helped himself to a bite from her plate. He then left the table. Cosima observed this. She, too, was overwrought and overtired, having had to open her house to a multitude of guests, some of whom she did not deem worthy of being invited to the holy halls of Wahnfried. Besides, she disliked Niemann, called him "a spoilsport, a peacock, demanding, uncooperative; he joins Richter in frequenting the taverns." Presently she went inside and sent Wagner's general factotum, a barber with the improbable name of Schnappauf, to summon Frau Jaïde to her. A few minutes later, the irate Erda emerged from the house, red in the face, and announced to all the guests: "I am leaving. What I have just been through I will relate to you at Angermann's" (the popular Bayreuth restaurant). Cosima had criticized her behavior, and she wasn't going to stand for it; she resigned. The next day the artists held a meeting, with Niemann as their leader, to protest against Bayreuth strictness. Niemann, too, threw up his role. "We were too happy," was Wagner's melancholy comment, as he tried to mollify "his children" without saying anything to Cosima. He turned on all the glitter of his charm —so irresistible when he wanted it to be—and after a while succeeded in quelling the palace revolt. Niemann and Jaïde resumed rehearsing. On August 13, Wagner finished the year's rehearsals and gave a party for all the musicians, at which Cosima managed to suppress her Red Queen instincts.

Yet further trouble was in store and it came, unexpectedly, from Richter. In Vienna the young man had given signs of a slackening of interest and now—eleven days after the end of the 1875 rehearsals—he wrote Wagner a letter which Cosima characterized as "so stupid and crass that one marvels how it is possible." It seems to have contained the proposal that he withdraw from working with Wagner because Cosima had offended him. (This is conjecture: the letter is lost.) No doubt, what Richter really wanted was to graduate from the role of amanuensis and pursue an independent career as conductor. But Wagner needed him badly. Who else could suddenly take over the festival? Richter's letter arrived on August 24. At first Wagner did not show it to Cosima; instead, he got up during the night and answered it. Cosima asked what was in the letter. Wagner told her. Early in the morning, without saying a word to her husband, she wrote Richter a long and remarkable letter.

Bayreuth, August 25, 1875

My dear friend:
In spite of all that I hear darkly whispered, I insist on using the above appellation, one which once in a serious and significant hour you earned. Remembering that hour, I will try to throw a ray of the light of reason into the present confusion. I have read neither the newspaper items, nor my husband's first letter to you, nor your reply, nor the last words of the Meister. I never even speculated about your peculiar attitude toward our house, because we always used to joke that you would rather be someplace else than with us and that you enjoyed yourself more with the children than with us. But now I have learned from my husband, who is greatly exercised over calumnies against myself, that he makes you responsible for them, at least partly. . . . Upon this you are supposed to have declared your misfortunes were due to a long hatred I had conceived against you. . . .

During the night, which my husband passed in anger and grief, I cogitated long and hard whether it was possible for me to halt the calamity. I will try to do so, I confess hesitatingly, and if you, my dear friend, were not involved, you could be sure that I would keep silent.

Now listen, and listen in a calm mood, to what I tell you . . . and remember the times in Triebschen when you lived with us as our child. Don't brush away those times, which you have often called the happiest of your life.

You surely must remember that when—after you assumed your position in Budapest—constant reports came to us that you behaved badly to my father, I said to our acquaintances: "I have no idea what happened, but of one thing I *am* sure—his probity and his fidelity." Do you remember? . . . Well, last year when you came to visit us, my husband was seriously perturbed over your failure to study *Götterdämmerung,* and he made no secret of his anger. This year came the concerts of Vienna, which were decided on the condition that you would work with him. This condition you could not fulfill, and what seemed to him gross neglect infuriated him to the extent that he did not want to go to Budapest. He went only because I begged him to, so as not to offend my father. . . . During the performance of the *Dutchman,* when he heard cymbal crashes in the Overture and again in the second act, he exclaimed audibly, "Oho! Richter is helping out my instrumentation," and at the end of the performance he expressed astonishment that you, even if you had to give his work in such a way, would invite him rather than . . . urge him to stay away. I was shocked by the constantly increasing disillusion with you on the part of my husband and in Vienna I wrote to your wife . . . my object being to keep you on the path of rightness. I could do this just then—when you were negotiating for the Vienna post—with complete confidence, knowing that I was your partisan. I wish you would ask anybody who took part in the negotiations whether a single syllable about our recent impressions was uttered there, even though my husband did express himself strongly within the confines of his circle of intimates. . . . I counseled my husband to tell you what he had let slip to others. He replied he would do so at an appropriate time. Then he asked me whether I had noticed that you were avoiding him. . . . So all of a sudden the gossip (as usual, false) arose that you would not conduct the festival. You know what my husband replied in answer to your inquiry. And in July you appeared, welcome as always and received with friendship. Your absence at several rehearsals, however, was observed by my husband with bitterness. . . . I regretted that you did not stay at our house. I continued to invite you and, mindful of our former Triebschen relation, I gave you hints when I observed that my husband was put out by your absence, since he had many an artistic suggestion to make to you. Did you not understand me? . . . Had you already swallowed the tittle-tattle? Why did you not come and demand an explanation? That much a relationship of eight years deserved, such a relationship that when we parted we had tears in our eyes as well as when we saw each other again. In all this time you might have observed that I feel no individual affections nor disaffections, but love only those whom my husband loves, and part from those from whom he separates himself.

This is the reward he earned for all the wonderful things he gave us and created for us! My name is being maligned in the newspapers and in his resentment over such abominable thanks he writes to you and demands your assurance that your attitude toward our house will no longer furnish a cause (or a pretense) for such viciousness. Dear friend, whatever you believed me capable of, whatever you thought of me, to him you should have conceded everything, to him you should have shown your fidelity. . . . Now I beg you, imploringly and in recollection of those Triebschen hours when you knew for certain what we meant to you and you to us, wipe away your neglect. As soon as you receive this letter, written in the night, telegraph my husband: tell him you are sorry to have listened to all that stupid chatter and promise to come and be the old Hans Richter. . . .

With all my heart I forgive you everything you may hold in your heart against me. I do not find it easy to judge somebody evil whom I once knew as good. I will merely ascribe the guilt of your confusion about me to your temperament, so very impressionable and excitable. And if it gives you satisfaction to think me wicked, you may think so, even say so—would you be capable of that?—but don't let my husband hear you, otherwise even I can do nothing for you. However, I am convinced that you will understand me, that my words have not become strange to you, that the time of the *Idyll* has not vanished, and that you will not deny a proof of high love to the Meister, who now feels hurt in his grief. . . . If I have ever offended you I regret it sincerely. But when could that have been? . . .

Well, be worthy of our past, come back to us free, glad, open as before, remembering the good, forgetting the evil. Let me greet you in the expectation of a profound and secure understanding.

Cosima's letter had its effect: immediately on receiving it, Richter telegraphed, asking to be forgiven and promising his "lifelong devotion." In November of that year he conducted the Viennese performances of *Lohengrin* and *Tannhäuser,* which Wagner staged—and the following year, the first festival.

Cosima's thoughts were concentrated on that event, planned for so long and fought for so strenuously, which finally promised to become reality. When her mother died, on March 5, 1876—the year of the festival—she did not pretend to a grief she could not feel. Her heart was in the theater; Marie d'Agoult was but a memory.

6

"I did not think you could bring it off," said Kaiser Wilhelm to Wagner as he alighted from his train on August 12, 1876, the day before the festival was to begin.

He had been preceded by King Ludwig. The citizens of Bayreuth had known their king was arriving. The town was beflagged and il-luminated, the houses and the theater bedecked with flowers. But Ludwig had stipulated: "I am coming to . . . refresh myself in heart and spirit, not to be gaped at by the curious or to offer myself up as an ovation-sacrifice." At one o'clock in the night of August 6, Ludwig's train halted at a little wayside station a few kilometers from Bayreuth. There Wagner met him, the king shook hands with him, Wagner bowed to Count Holnstein, the king looked at Wagner and Wagner looked at the king. They had not seen each other for eight years. Both looked older—but it was with the king that time had dealt unkindly. He had grown flabby and heavy in figure, his new beard only partly concealed his jowls, his eyes looked weary; at thirty-one, he had reached middle age.

For the dress "rehearsal" of *Rheingold* (it was a rehearsal in name only), the theater was virtually empty. Wagner escorted Ludwig to the royal box. "Where is Cosima?" the king asked. She was in the theater and at once she came to him. "You are the one," he said to her, "who never doubted that I would remain faithful." For the following eve-ning the king wanted the theater filled, to test whether the presence of the audience would improve the acoustics. Immediately a black market for tickets developed and every seat was taken for *Die Wal-küre* (August 7), *Siegfried* (August 8), and *Götterdämmerung* (August 9). Ludwig remained hidden, and after the fall of the curtain on the ninth, he returned to Hohenschwangau. Cosima noted: "The King prohibits all demonstrations, yet seemed puzzled when none was forthcoming."

The festival began on August 13, and from then until the end of the third series of the *Ring* performances on August 30, Cosima found herself in the eye of the social hurricane. No wonder the entries in her diary are but the briefest jottings; she was far too occupied with the grand receptions of the grand visitors and—what was more difficult— the placing of the big and little sovereigns in the theater so that none should take offense. Who was more important, the Grand Duke of Schwerin or the Grand Duchess of Baden? Where should Countess Andrássy's place be in relation to Robert von Keudell's, the German ambassador in Rome? How did one separate the Bavarian from the Prussian dignitaries, the French from the Austrian? Three times a week Wahnfried opened its portals to selected guests, one of the most select being His Majesty Dom Pedro of Brazil, who when registering at his hotel gave his "Occupation" as "Emperor." At the Margrave Palace, fifty-nine royal personages were quartered, not counting Kai-

ser Wilhelm's suite of thirty-eight courtiers. The Grand Duke of Weimar asked Cosima whether Professor Helmholtz (the famous physicist
who was working on electrodynamics) was conducting the orchestra.
More knowledgeable visitors came to witness the miracle, some, like
Camille Saint-Saëns and Anton Bruckner, to be wholly admiring;
some, like Tchaikovsky and Hanslick, to voice reservations; some, like
Grieg and Gounod, to be both impressed and puzzled.

Wagner had become so newsworthy that numerous representatives
of the world's press—including those of the New York newspapers and
American magazines such as *Macmillan's* and *Scribner's*—descended
on a town the name of which they had not previously known. From
their reports it appears they were more concerned with the problem
of getting food and the problem of where to sleep than with the
problem of understanding the Music of the Future. The price of a
hotel room ordinarily costing one mark rose to five. Private families
with mean rooms to let tried to charge the same, but when the irate
seeker after shelter refused and left, somebody from the family ran
after him and offered the room at half price. Barbers charged double
for a shave, concierges cheated on changing dollars into marks, there
were no cabs to be had—Bayreuth had only seven cabs—and on rainy
nights the price quadrupled, if a vehicle could be found. Cosima appealed to Feustel: the festival was being desecrated—could nothing be
done? Nothing could be done.

Any Bayreuther who provided free lodging for a member of the
orchestra was entitled to one free seat for one performance—in the
back rows. Most of these seats found their way to ticket speculators.
Cosima protested publicly and vehemently, of course in vain.

A young girl from Boston, Grace M. Tilton, who later married the
music publisher Gustave Schirmer, wrote her impressions of the hostess of Bayreuth in action:

> Mme. Wagner is exceedingly gracious and affable. She is a magnificent-
> looking woman, a perfect queen (some call her a despot), and dresses
> elegantly, always with a great deal of expensive white lace, and is never
> seen in the same dress twice. She is at home mornings from eleven to
> twelve and gives a reception to the Patrons once a week. They are very
> grand affairs, and all the great people attend them; she begins to show
> signs of her tremendous care and anxiety, and appears much fatigued. If
> it had not been for her support, encouragement and aid, Wagner says he
> never should have accomplished the enterprise.

A reason other than overwork was responsible for Cosima's look of
anxiety, apparent even to a stranger. Judith Gautier was in Bayreuth.

She had been divorced, and in her new freedom she appeared to Wagner more beautiful and desirable than ever. Ideas for *Parsifal's* music were even then, in the midst of a hundred problems beating down on him, gyrating in his imagination, and as was consistent with his nature, he needed someone, some woman, to quicken the creative process and to give exhilaration to his inner life. It had happened before with Mathilde and *Tristan,* it was happening now with Judith and *Parsifal.* Again as before he considered, or fabricated the illusion for himself, that the infatuation was of Olympian significance. Writing to Judith in 1877, he called his love "the most exquisite intoxication, the highest pride of my life, the last gift of the gods, whose will it was that I should not break down under the misery of the delusive glory of the *Nibelungen* performances." He almost sounds an echo to his frequently voiced regret that he was united with Cosima fifteen years too late, when he tells Judith: "Why in heaven's name did I not find you in Paris, after the failure of *Tannhäuser?*" After Judith returned to Paris, he asked her to order for him satins, velvets, and strong perfumes to help him on his "three years' work on *Parsifal.*" These were to be sent to Schnappauf.

Cosima knew. She was wise enough not to let him know she knew. The hurt she felt she hid from him. Not a word did she say or write in the diary—until it was almost over, and even then she wrote in oblique terms:

> The sorrow which I feared did not fail to arrive. It broke in from the outside! God help me! Pain, you my old comrade, come back to me and live with me; we know each other! How long will you tarry with me, my most faithful, steadfast friend? [February 12, 1878]

The blow Judith dealt Cosima was an especially stunning one, since the two were—or had been—good friends. Judith had been present at the *Rheingold* dress rehearsal in Munich in 1869 (about which she reported: "I thought I would die with rage," which was just what Cosima and Wagner wanted to hear). On that occasion she had talked to Liszt. Being a girl who knew how to use her beauty, she was not afraid of any man, and she had boldly broached the subject of his daughter's marital dilemma. You must not place any obstacle, Judith had pleaded with Liszt, to Cosima's obtaining a divorce. Liszt consented, and Judith immediately wrote to Cosima. "If I sleep tonight," Cosima replied, "I shall have you to thank for it. I embrace you with my whole heart."

The Judith affair lasted only a little more than a year. It was a temporary solace, a transitory aid, a last sexual excitement for the man who was creating the Kundry of the second act—and Cosima condoned it. Judith passed, Cosima remained.

For the third and final cycle of performances, Ludwig was once more present and he again hid himself from the people. However, on the thirtieth of August, after the performance of *Götterdämmerung,* Wagner persuaded him to step to the front of the loge. Cheered by the audience, the king applauded Wagner as he appeared before the curtain. Wagner spoke quietly, thanking Ludwig and his artists. Whether the festival would be repeated he did not know. But perhaps it had demonstrated that a new "German art" could be possible, if they, the German people, wanted it. He then accompanied Ludwig to the train. King and composer conversed with quiet emotion. At a signal from Ludwig, the train began to move. They waved good-bye. Neither knew how long it would be before they saw each other again.

The visitor whose absence Cosima regretted was Nietzsche. In February 1876, he had sent Wagner and Cosima the second of his series of essays *Thoughts Out of Season* ("Schopenhauer as Educator"). Wagner was disappointed in it, possibly because the essay dealt with Schopenhauer rather than with Wagner, and acknowledged the work with lukewarm enthusiasm, while Cosima assumed a schoolmarmish tone, criticizing Nietzsche's style. He later remarked that if Cosima, a foreigner, was desirous of correcting the style of German writers, she might do well by beginning with her husband's. However, his fourth essay, "Richard Wagner in Bayreuth," had hailed Wagner as the first artist to fuse all the arts into a great synthesis and urged all Germany to realize the significance of the festival. The essay arrived in Wahnfried in July 1876 and Cosima, with all she had to do, spent half the night reading it. The next day she sent Nietzsche a telegram, thanking him for the refreshment of spirit he had given her. Nietzsche came to the Bayreuth rehearsals and to the first performances, but long before they were over, disillusion eclipsed his pleasure. He now saw the festival only as another sport spread before wealthy "culture Philistines," resembling the promenade at Marienbad or the horse races at Baden-Baden: a beer-and-sausage "contemptible German affair." He felt Wagner had betrayed his own creed. Those great theatrical effects —what were they but "opera," held together by the mucilage of a pseudo philosophy? He was tired of "undisciplined rhapsody" and "idealistic lying." He could not discern—or chose not to—the few (and necessarily they had to be few) who listened, understood, and were exalted. And so he fled—from Wagner, from Cosima, and in a sense from music. Of course Cosima never forgave his apostasy. But she missed him. One more friend lost.

On the last day of August it was over—except for paying the costs. Cosima:

Many farewells, nevertheless our evening Reception very overcrowded. Many Englishmen, among them a Reverend who, though very Jesuitical, declares himself to be enraptured. [Diary, August 31, 1876]

7

To Cosima, as to hundreds—whether they had actually been in Bayreuth or not—the first festival represented the greatest triumph an artist could achieve. To Wagner it did not. He could condone the imperfections of the performances; what he could not forgive was the imperfections of the public. The deficiencies of the staged realization —the meager illusion of the swimming Rhine Maidens, the incomplete dragon in *Siegfried,* the mistakes in changing scenery which disclosed to the audience the stagehands scurrying around in shirtsleeves, Richter's insecurity of tempi, the vainglorious behavior of the baritone who sang Wotan—these he would correct at the next festival, or if not then, "one day when I will stage *Walküre* in heaven at God's right, and the old man and I will watch." He knew better than anybody that he had failed to set his people on a higher path, that he had been unable to "redeem" their mediocrity through the "nobility of art." (Of course, *his* art.) Germany had let him down; it was decadent and moribund. Looking back, he cried to Cosima:

"I have no illusions left. . . . I inquired if 1,000 people in Germany could be found, each willing to spend 300 marks for such an enterprise. How miserably was I answered! I arrived at the most disgraceful time through which Germany has ever passed, with that pig-demagogue [Bismarck] as its head. Nevertheless I accomplished it, I built the great Theater, no man has done anything like it in the entire history of art. Through the force of my personality I was able to summon the best artists we had and to bring about a performance commensurate with their talents. What was the result? Bah, bah! I thought at least they would pay the deficit! They came—the ladies swishing their tails, the gentlemen with their mustaches. Everybody had a good time and, since Emperor and King were present, they asked: My God, what more does Wagner want? Does he want still more? . . ." [Diary, March 18, 1880]

The festival ended in a deficit. A weary Wagner would ordinarily not have cared two straws about that—but the creditors cared, and began to march up Theater Hill, making threatening noises. Cosima, and Cosima alone, had the courage to face the situation. Feustel knew it and it was to her that he wrote:

Bayreuth, January 15, 1878

Most honored lady:
Conditions unfortunately compel me to bring the matter of the outstanding deficit to your attention, since I wish to spare your husband, occupied as he is in artistic creation, the unpleasant facts.

You know the deficit amounted to M147,851.82. Of that M49,823.25 was paid,* leaving a debt of M98,028.57, which sum has been somewhat enlarged by defaulting on the interest.

All measures undertaken since to raise this sum have failed. I spare you their recital. Nothing was left untried. Now I am being pressed for the money. Even if I can spar for time for a little while before the matter will be taken to court, the end is not far off.

I see but one possibility to avoid the catastrophe. That is, that the Royal Theater in Munich would grant your husband an advance of about ten years' duration, at 10,000 marks a year, to be applied against his royalties. With such an arrangement one could build a capital by which—in addition to the money from the sale of the larger restaurant—the debt could be disposed of. I am ready to submit the pertinent documents which will show that I have calculated very exactly.

I have come to this proposal and this conclusion only after cogitating fully on the situation.

I hope to discuss this further personally with you and remain for today your very devoted

Friedrich Feustel

The very next day Cosima sent this letter of Feustel's to Ludwig—without Wagner's knowing anything about it—accompanying it with a letter of her own, of the sort she knew well how to write:

Bayreuth, January 16, 1878

All-noblest, all powerful King!
All-gracious King and Lord!
Your Majesty will graciously forgive me if in the deep need of my

*Cosima contributed 32,000 marks, out of her inheritance.

heart I know not where to turn except to him, so generous of his benefits, who has for years acted as protector of our beloved.

I lack the courage to tell my husband, occupied with the plaint of Amfortas, about this other plaint, which is sure to upset and depress him and would choke the first plaint. Would my most gracious lord take it ill were I, who have so little courage, yet to muster enough of it to place these lines [Feustel's] at your feet, you the beneficent one? I would not have dared to do it had I not harbored the hope that my action would be kindly judged, and looked at with the penetrating ray of Royal pity, that ray which shines on the life of the poet of *Parsifal.*

I hope that my step will not be disapproved by my most gracious lord, whom I have ventured to approach with the most respectful and grateful feelings, and for whom I remain unto death

> His Majesty's
> most obedient servant
> Cosima Wagner-Liszt

Ludwig granted her request. Generous to the last, he responded promptly. Considering the size and complexity of the project, the deficit was not all that large—less than half of Sarah Bernhardt's annual income. It was paid off as Feustel had proposed, but that took longer than anticipated. The last of the debt, every Mark of it, was paid into the treasury of the Munich Opera House in June 1906.

8

It was in those final years, the years of *Parsifal,* that Cosima exercised her greatest influence and fulfilled her finest function. Her presence and her love fortified Wagner in what he felt was his most difficult artistic task. When he complained that he was too old to accomplish what he had in mind, she told him that she would supply him with the youth he needed: "That is the only thing I brought you, a little youth, now not quite so young." When he was in a positive phase and was certain that he would not only finish *Parsifal* but compose symphonies thereafter, he would hum: *"Ça ira, ça ira, j'aimerai toujours ma Cosima."* One should never take the autobiographical pronouncements of a genius too literally, but one may accept his assertion that he would not have written another note had she not been there and that it was she who gave him the strength to construct the Temple of Monsalvat. This man, who as a man still stands as a conspicuous example of the disconnection between talent and character, had the good fortune—and the determination—to find the woman exactly right for him, a woman who herself shared some of his less attractive traits, however much she surpassed him in suppleness, grace, and elegance. The coming together of two negatively charged beings helped to produce positive results: the completion of *Götterdämmerung,* the composition of the *Siegfried Idyll,* the creation of Bayreuth, the creation of *Parsifal.* "You knew how to help," he told her, and she wrote it proudly in the diary. "All my friends thought I could no longer be helped, I would no longer work. You knew that I could be helped. And you did it."

> I asked him yesterday if he was content. "Immeasurably," he answered. That answer and the accent in which he pronounced it covered me with enchantment. Blissfully I passed from waking to sleep. He lay peacefully beside me and "Immeasurably" resounded in my heart.

To many a visitor at Wahnfried, Cosima presented a changed aspect. Her prejudices grew stiffer. Her Francophobia made her now find Molière "abstract and lifeless." More frequently than before, she said something nasty about the Jews. Suddenly Rubinstein "showed the saddest characteristics of his race," the synagogue in Nuremberg bothered her as being "insolent and show-offish." Ludwig Schemann, a passionate adherent of Wagner, who knew her well in these years, wrote that moderate people complained of the etiquette, the salon atmosphere, the "regimen of women" which reigned in her home.* But to Wagner she remained, alike behind her tears and her self-importance, all love, all dedication. There, in spite of defects and deficits, stood the Festspielhaus. "Every stone in that building," he said to her, "is red with my blood and yours."

*Ludwig Schemann, *Lebensfahrten eines Deutschen* (Leipzig, 1925).

CHAPTER IX

Toward *Parsifal*

A GOOD GERMAN seeking refreshment, sunshine, and gaiety goes to Italy, Venice preferred. Cosima and Wagner could hardly wait for the doors of the Festspielhaus to be locked and the servants at the theater restaurant to disperse to other employment before they started packing. Cosima was especially anxious to avoid another wet autumn in Bayreuth, with its obbligato of children's sneezes. Two weeks after the last *Götterdämmerung,* the whole family, plus servants, were on the way to Verona, then to Venice—where they received the first shock of the news of the deficit—and then by way of Bologna and Naples to Sorrento. There they remained for a month, followed by another month's sojourn in Rome.

In Rome they met Count Arthur Gobineau, with whom they were to form a close friendship. As a diplomat, he had served France well in Athens and Rio; he had studied the religions and philosophies of Central Asia and had published a good book on the Renaissance. Yet the mind of this learned man turned presumptuous, climbing the high horse of ethnological arrogance. He believed in the inborn superiority of "the Nordics," the Germans above all, and developed this belief in a long work—four volumes, no less—on *The Inequality of Human Races.* Predictably, the book was a failure in France, a success in Germany. Even there it had been virtually forgotten until Wagner called attention to it. Cosima found the author "decidedly important and interesting" and enjoyed conversing with him in French.

Slowly the *Parsifal* drama was taking shape. Wagner discussed it with Nietzsche, who concluded that Wagner had "sunk at the foot of the cross," and he discussed it with Cosima in greater detail. He told her that he was creating this work solely and completely for her. The present world could not and would not understand *Parsifal:* it would consider it nonsense. She would understand.

In Kundry—surely the most provocative character Wagner created —we can discern something of Cosima's nature. She is a representative of human contradiction, forever present. Obviously she is not a "portrait," any more than Proust's Albertine or Chekhov's Irina Arkadina or other figures into whom their creators have woven biographical threads. Yet there is much of Cosima in Kundry, and not only in the Kundry of the first and third acts, where her role is *dienen,* to serve, but in the Kundry of the second act. As Cosima was, so is Kundry a creature of ecstasy, the ecstasy of servitude, the ecstasy of guilt, and the ecstasy of atonement. That Wagner was not unaware of the affinity is indicated by one of those lovingly joking remarks he was fond of making to her: "Don't exert yourself, don't do anything, just remain being Madame Klingsor."

In those years, as Wagner lost hope in the German spirit, as he realized that the repetition of the *Nibelungen* planned for the following season would be impossible (it hurt him so keenly that he said, "If somebody pronounces just the syllable 'Ni—' I go mad"), as he carried the burden of the deficit with him wherever he went, as Nietzsche departed from his life, he drew closer than ever to Cosima. Their mutual adoration deepened. Not for half a day can he do without her —or she without him.

> R. to me: "You form my life into a complete benediction. When will we wander into our graves?" I answer: "Whenever you wish." [January 7, 1878]

> R. visits me when he returns from his walk and tells me: "You are a gift from heaven. Because of you I believe in God." [January 30, 1878]

Wagner and Nietzsche talked for the last time in Sorrento in October 1876. It was clear by that time that the two, who had much in common, stood far apart in their "artistic endeavors" (as Nietzsche later put it). But Cosima knew that however Wagner stormed, saying, "It is no great honor that this man has praised me," he grieved over the melting away of the old intimacy, and she continued to try to patch up the relationship. She wrote to Nietzsche: "You know my naïve receptivity to art. I read the second part of *Faust* and even the *Divina Commedia* without a commentary, abandoning myself freely to the power of the poet. Similarly, in my youth I learned to love the *Ring of the Nibelungen* [the epic] without having the faintest notion of German mythology." Could he abandon himself to the *Parsifal* poem? Nietzsche answered her, somewhat noncommittally: *"Parsifal* promises to offer us consolation wherever we have need of consolation." (October 10, 1877) His real opinion was less kindly; he thought *Parsifal* "a lapse of taste, an offering to Cosima's Catholicism."

At the end of April 1878, Nietzsche sent them his *Human, All Too Human,* with its sideswipes at them both. After glancing at it, she noted: "Firm decision not to read the book by friend Nietzsche, the perverse strangeness of which was apparent at first glance." But she did read it, and then she wrote to Elisabeth Nietzsche that evidently her brother had "gone over to a well-fortified enemy camp." She gave up sadly.

Wagner read the completed *Parsifal* poem to Cosima on April 20, 1877, a gloomy day. She had just taken Isolde away to a special school: the child had developed curvature of the spine and it was hoped that gymnastic exercises might help. Isolde resisted and wept. Nothing had been settled about Bayreuth. But she listened to the poem with feverish excitement. It was "my greatest solace."

Wagner's health was worsening, as much because of his psychological depression in the hours when he was not immersed in *Parsifal* as for physical reasons. Cosima was haunted by forebodings:

> I shudder when I think there could be a life, a world, in which he would no longer be, in which he would no longer show me the way to my salvation. Our mere "Good night," the separation of only a moment, calls forth this specter of fear! [January 28, 1878]

But invariably, hiding her fears, she assured him of what he himself really believed—that he had lost nothing of his creative power. When she heard him again at work, "it seemed to me that the heavens opened as I listened to the sounds, unique in the world." At one moment he declared he was dissatisfied with all the *Parsifal* music he had composed so far and he was going to tear it all up. She quoted the French proverb: *"Château demoli est a moitie reconstruit."* And at once he began the "reconstruction." All he then wanted was to be "forgotten by the world," dreaming of Kundry and Amfortas.

Yet when he received what looked like a most promising offer from London, he bestirred himself. He was to give twenty concerts in the Albert Hall, the profit being estimated at a certain five hundred pounds a concert, Wagner's drawing power being now so great that he could easily fill a hall holding some ten thousand people. Before the negotiations were concluded, the extravagant proposal had shrunk to eight concerts, for which Wagner was guaranteed a total of fifteen hundred pounds, subject to that amount being earned. Though Cosima was not much in favor of Wagner's subjecting himself to so great an exertion, and though she distrusted the London agents—as did many of their friends—Wagner accepted. He would use the money to pay off a little of the Bayreuth debt. On April 30, 1877, Cosima and Wagner left Bayreuth for London. He engaged Richter as his coconductor, Seidl and Fischer as his assistants, and eight soloists. For them Wagner stipulated high fees: he was always generous with his artists. And of course everything had to be done in grand style.

In London, he and Cosima were the guests of Edward Dannreuther, a prosperous musician who had helped at Bayreuth and was now living in a pleasant house in Bayswater. Dannreuther acted as an interpreter between Wagner and the orchestra.

Cosima's first impression of London was the fog, which evoked in her "the dreamlike quality of life." She loved the city's vitality, its feeling of freedom. "If I had to choose a large city, it would be London." At once they learned the damaging news: the project had been mismanaged, the agents were "on the verge of bankruptcy, the second concert (May 9) brings in a scant six hundred pounds—there is no question of even covering the costs." "The whole of Israel is once more working against us," Cosima noted; how, she did not explain. The tenor, Unger, got hoarse, programs had to be changed, "the public, already intimidated by the press and by Herr Joachim [the great violinist, Brahms's friend—and a Jew] and consorts, will doubtless become even more timid."

The truth was that Wagner, in his depressed state of health, could not do his best. Albert Hall was not filled, but the audiences that did attend were enthusiastic. Every time Wagner appeared, he was given an ovation.

Socially, Cosima had a thoroughly good time. She met George Eliot, "who makes a noble and pleasant impression." Cosima had read both *Silas Marner* and *The Mill on the Floss* with much admiration. Eliot said to her: "I hear your husband does not like Jews. My husband is a

Jew."* What Cosima replied history does not record, but she accompanied Eliot to the concerts, where Eliot shed tears during the scene in which Brünnhilde announces to Siegmund that he is destined to die. (Sir Hubert Parry, the composer, noted this in his diary.) Cosima also met Robert Browning and Heinrich Schliemann, the latter "not very impressive," and the scientist Sir William Siemens. In addition to the usual tourist rounds—the Tower, the Crystal Palace, the Aquarium, the Zoological Gardens, Kensington Palace, Westminster Abbey, Greenwich (where she and Wagner greatly enjoyed a fish dinner)—Cosima was tireless in visiting the museums by herself. "At the National Gallery I make the acquaintance of Reynolds with pleasure, gain a juster impression of Hogarth, and receive light and warmth again from the Italians." (May 5) On free evenings they went to the theater, to *Richard III* and to a new play, *Rip van Winkle: "superb* performance by an American, Mr. Jefferson." She was taken to the studio of Sir Edward Burne-Jones, who liked her looks and decided to draw her. She sat for him several times.† On May 17, the Wagners were received by Queen Victoria. The queen recorded in her journal:

> After luncheon the great composer Wagner, about whom the people in Germany are really a little mad, was brought into the corridor by Mr. Cusins. I had seen him with dearest Albert in '55, when he directed at the Philharmonic Concert. He has grown old and stout, and has a clever, but not pleasing countenance. He was profuse in expressions of gratitude, and I expressed my regret at having been unable to be present at one of his concerts.

For all his work and worry, Wagner cleared a scant seven hundred pounds; these he contributed to the Bayreuth Fund. He had to admit to Feustel that he had been a deaf dupe to go to London and had done so because he wanted to show his well-wishers in Germany that "neither laziness nor love of ease" would prevent him from doing his best to save Bayreuth. If it could not be saved, he told Cosima, he would renounce the land he had loved and emigrate to America. Could he build a New Bayreuth in Minnesota? Cosima was ready. The king, on hearing the news, was "beside himself."

*He was George Henry Lewes, an eminent philosopher, whose *Life of Goethe* had a worldwide success, being highly valued even in Germany. But she was not actually married to him: they lived in a free and happy union until Lewes's death in 1878, the year after Cosima met Eliot.

†On inquiry to the Tate Gallery, the following information was given: "Burne-Jones, according to his wife's biography, did make a drawing of Cosima Wagner, but the whereabouts of this drawing are unknown. Lady Burne-Jones recorded that Wagner was too busy to sit, and that he and Burne-Jones did not meet." Does anybody know what happened to the drawing?

2

"R. is *working!* For me this word is the fountainhead of all gladness,"
Cosima wrote on August 29, 1877. Back in Wahnfried, after submit-
ting himself patiently to a cure at the spa of Ems, and having his teeth
fixed by an American dentist named Jenkins, who refused to accept
any money, Wagner and Cosima purposefully forgot London's yawn-
ing Albert Hall. He now began to set to music the high mystery which
he knew could be expressed only in a new style, a style whose ances-
tors were Palestrina and Bach and for which he would—as he told her
—"lay aside his old paint pot." That day in August could be defined
as the typical beginning of a creator's happiest period, the period of
sketching the work on paper, as yet erasable and changeable, yet
definite enough to convey its essence. For many months, and in spite
of many night thoughts, the sun was shining in their lives. They were,
Cosima felt, as happy as they had been in Triebschen.

On September 26 and again the following day, he plays her the
Prelude. They talk for hours, both invigorated. He tells her, "I also
have some bits for Mademoiselle Condrie [Kundry]; for instance, I
have her laughter." *Parsifal* was going to be his greatest achievement
and for it he was going to abjure all rough magic, all "polyphonic
games," and in the Good Friday scene—the idea for which came to
him *not* on Good Friday nor on any holy day but merely on a pleasant
day—he would return to the simplicity of the *Idyll.* With Cosima he
reviews his works: *Tristan*'s third act—"almost no tenor can manage
it"—may "exceed what is allowable in the theater," and the second act
is too heavily orchestrated. *Holländer* is too repetitious, too noisy, and
when he can get around to it he will recast it in one act. But she must
be there, every moment at his side. He recalls "how much we have
already achieved together." He assures her, "You and I will go on
living in men's minds." She answers, "You, for certain!" He laughs at
being called a reformer. He didn't reform anything—that word would
be applicable to Luther—but he has developed music to "a new ex-
pressiveness." He has no use for the new composers who don't know
how to invent a singable melody.* "They produce wood shavings from
which they fashion a lion's mane." Schumann ought to write a pendant
to the "Trout" Quintet and call it "The Herring." Berlioz is a chaser
after effects: Cosima hears the Berlioz *Requiem* and calls it ear-split-
ting.

*Cosima noted a remark of Wagner's about melody: "One cannot make music without
melody any more than one can speak without thoughts. Melody is thought in music."

Every evening Wagner played for Cosima what he had composed that day. By late January 1878, he told her that "soon I'll be able to satisfy my Monsieurs with a Radetzky March," meaning that he was composing the procession of the Knights of the Grail. By February he finished the first act, "with her help," and she surprised him with a gift of a bedspread decorated with roses. So the work went on, a task with which he was to be occupied for more than three years. Quiet descended. "Nothing can bother us if we are just by ourselves," Cosima wrote in March, "not even the eternally covered sky." Still, she continued to worry about his health. He was drinking more cognac than he used to and she begged him not to. He would sleep badly after having a glass of beer late at night. He in turn asked her please not to fret; he is strong and he still has a few ideas left, though she is his best idea. After *Parsifal* he was going to compose nine symphonies, the ninth with chorus, the theme to be an ode not to joy but to pain.*

While the ingenious Angelo Neumann carried Wagner's works to German cities—Cosima noted that *Lohengrin* brought in the most royalties—while the entire *Ring* was performed in Munich in November 1878 (without any protest from Wagner) and Leipzig in January 1879 and Vienna in May, and even a small town like Trieste gave *Tannhäuser* . . . while, in short, Wagnerism grew, his own theater was rotting. There and nowhere else would he stage *Parsifal,* and he began to discuss the problems with Cosima. How, she wondered, could the scene be realized in which Klingsor attacks Parsifal? It is one thing to *imagine* Klingsor throwing the spear and the spear hovering over Parsifal's head, but quite another matter to bring this off in the full light of the magic garden. How, Wagner asked her, should the Flower Maidens be costumed? Above all, where in all the operatic world could he find the tenor with the voice, the youth, the acting delicacy, to come near to doing justice to his central character? The exchange of thoughts and plans continued daily. When spring arrived, the whole family went walking:

The green meadow glitters, the children exult, in the shadowy thicket the young tender birches begin to green, the sun laughs through the dark and the light patches, the dogs are frantic with joy, the birds want to tempt us again to return to the woods, just as we have decided to walk home by the edge of the forest. One twitters to me, "Stay here, stay here." Above the meadow, lost in the blue, the lark ascends. . . . [April 28, 1878]

*He wrote down—as a joke—the opening lines: *Schmerz, schöner Höllenfunken—Püffe gabst du uns and Stösse, einen Feind beschmiert mit Kot.* (Pain, hell's bright spark—You gave us storms and blows, an enemy covered with dirt.)

Between the pages of this entry she pressed some violets which Wagner had plucked for her.

Fidi was their special delight. The boy was musical, drew well, was curious about everything, and adored his father, who interrupted himself in sketching the Kundry-Klingsor scene to play Indian Chief with him. Cosima bought him a telephone, because Fidi was interested in all new inventions. They discussed his education and his future: perhaps he ought to become a physician and help the poor people of Bayreuth—of course without pay. There would be enough money so that he would not need to earn his livelihood. In the meantime, she didn't want him to go to a public school, "where they will besmirch the image of his father," but to receive private instruction. She searched long and hard and it wasn't until October 1879—Fidi was ten —that she found the man she judged to be the right one, who would bring him up "devoutly Christian, completely un-Jewish." Heinrich von Stein, only twenty-two years old, was young enough to understand a boy. He was "slim and blond like one of Schiller's young men," as Wagner wrote the king; he was cultured, good-natured, sensitive, and, as it turned out, free of the Wagnerian prejudicial venom, so that he managed in the two years or so that he remained at Bayreuth to instill in Siegfried tolerance and understanding.*

Wagner, jingoist during the Franco-Prussian War, author of the poem "To the German Army," now, with Fidi growing up, railed against militarism. Was it necessary to support 1,200,000 soldiers, just so that the French wouldn't steal the country? As far as he was concerned, let the country be sold to the French: he was going to Taormina! He determined to use whatever influence he had to get Fidi excused from military service.

> The thought of offering a son for a war, whether with France or Russia, is abhorrent to him. "The feelings of the people have been outraged. While the poor dying soldier tells his sergeant, I die for Germany, they [the German leaders] drink champagne in Versailles. . . ." [February 10, 1880]

Cosima too, who once waved the flag, now exclaimed against the "stupidity of the uniform."

To her girls she was as devoted as ever; Daniela had become more tractable, Boni was charming, though her marks at school left something to be desired, Eva was perfect, but Isolde remained a *Sorgenkind*, a problem child, often ill, melancholy, and uncom-

---

*Later Stein taught at the universities of Halle and Berlin, but he died young, at thirty.

municative. Bülow kept up the fiction that Isolde was his child, writing, *"Nos trois filles en commun,"* and in apportioning certain sums of money he had set aside for "his girls," he treated each of the three equally. When he sent a gift to Isolde, he addressed it to "Fräulein Isolde von Bülow." From time to time, Cosima wrote to him, telling him what measures she was taking in educating Daniela and Blandine, and he answered in letters that were distant and somewhat formal in tone, invariably expressing his "respectful admiration for all you are doing for our children, an admiration which includes full and complete approval." For many years, however, he did not want to see them.

3

At the beginning of 1879, Wagner was thinking of the Good Friday scene. He felt, as he told Cosima, that it "could not be merely an episode," but needed to express the quintessence of the work. "It is going to be most beautiful—I already have many sketches," he said, though much time was to elapse before he gave the scene its definitive form. Cosima, more than usually excited, wondered what she could do to please him, and decided she would have her portrait painted by Lenbach as a birthday gift. For this she had to go to Munich. Wagner was at once ready to accompany her, but she begged him not to: he was overtaxed and didn't need such a journey. (It was not easy to get from Bayreuth to Munich, especially in the winter.) As long as she was going to Munich, she wished also to consult an ear specialist—her ears had been giving her trouble of late—and to visit her dentist. During the three days of her absence they both behaved as if the separation were three months long: no fewer than fifteen telegrams were exchanged between her and Wahnfried. The first she dispatched from Bamberg ("Have got here safely," etc.), the second from a tiny wayside station about two hours later ("One more word of greeting today in unending inexpressible unity"). And she came back earlier than expected, having traveled all night, sitting up in the train. He told her that during her absence "all music had departed from him, but now his head was again filled with themes." (Diary, February 26, 1879) On May 22, she arranged to present her portrait to him. Fidi, dressed as a painter, stood before the easel, making believe that he was putting the finishing touches on Lenbach's painting.

All through 1879, Wagner worked on *Parsifal,* in addition to writing several prose works, so that by the end of the year he, Cosima, and the doctor felt a prolonged absence from Bayreuth not only advisable but urgent. His eyes bothered him, from time to time and for no apparent reason he was gripped by a cramp in his chest, and his old complaint, erysipelas, staged a return bout. Accordingly, the family set out on December 31, from Munich, using a "salon coach" (a private railroad car) Wagner had hired. He took quarters at the sumptuous Villa Angri in Posillipo, near Naples, leasing it for six months. Cosima had her hands full: the household had grown to eleven people, including two governesses, one Italian, one English. Wagner wrote to the king—with whom he and Cosima were in frequent correspondence and whose love for Wagner had taken on new strength—that the expense of the salon coach had rather strained his purse, and Ludwig, taking the hint, granted him an additional allowance of 5,200 lire, "to help prolong his stay in Italy." The new court secretary, Ludwig von Bürkel, who was friendly to Wagner (or thought it prudent to be so), was instructed to tell Cosima that "no pressure on the Meister and his family about returning to chilly Germany was to be implied."

They remained in Italy for some eleven months, going to Ravello, where, walking in the beautiful garden of the Palazzo Rufolo, Wagner exclaimed, "I have found Klingsor's garden"; then to Siena, the cathedral of which he thought would make the right setting for his *Parsifal* temple, and again to Venice; but his health showed no marked improvement. On October 30, 1880, they returned to Munich. The king had arranged performances of *The Flying Dutchman, Tristan,* and *Lohengrin* to please Wagner: he wanted Cosima and the children to hear these works. At the *Lohengrin* performance of November 10, a private one, Wagner sat with Ludwig. It was the last time they were fated to be together, though it was arranged that two days later, in the morning, Wagner would conduct the *Parsifal* Prelude for Ludwig.

Wagner conferred with Hermann Levi, now the conductor of the Munich Royal Orchestra, and Cosima discussed the *Parsifal* costumes with a painter named Seitz (Böcklin, whom she wanted, refused to do the costumes). Wagner, overtired, showed himself at his worst. During the rehearsal, he was happy with the orchestra—and they with him. But then the king was late, Wagner fretted, and when the king did come he asked that the Prelude be played *twice.* Wagner had no choice but to do so. Would he now play the Prelude to *Lohengrin?* asked Ludwig. Wagner, in his *Parsifal* mood, could not jump to the earlier work and asked Levi to take over, while he fled to the greenroom, where he called for Cosima. Together they returned to the hotel. A few friends came to call, including Lenbach. "Unfortunately," wrote Cosima, "Lenbach begins to speak of Bismarck and R. bursts into a fury against that bulldog face which has been so often portrayed." Cosima sensed that his fury was really directed against Ludwig. Lenbach, deeply hurt, left at once. Late that night, Wagner went for a walk, somewhat calmed down by Cosima, but he slept badly. Four days later, they went to Lenbach's studio; they had been told that he had nearly fallen ill grieving over the incident, and Wagner apologized, no doubt at Cosima's suggestion. The next day they were back in Bayreuth, with Wagner still in a horrible mood. "I am the plenipotentiary of perdition," he said. Cosima understood. She knew that what troubled him was due to an even deeper cause than his irritation with the king or Lenbach or Bismarck; it was due to an emotion every artist feels. "He is troubled about *Parsifal*," Cosima observed; "he wants to compose it afresh from the very beginning." They both slept fitfully and in the morning he said to her, "Yesterday I felt anew the sadness of life. Those who deride the idealists and the heroes are in the right. Mephisto. Sancho Panza." But in music he remained an idealist and after a few days he sat down at his desk and continued to work.

4

There was one task which Cosima had put off time and again: to come to an understanding with Bülow about the future of Daniela and Blandine. She and Wagner both wanted to adopt the two girls legally. In practice, if not in law, they *were* Wagner's, having lived virtually all their lives in his household, regarding him as their father, while their real father was but a name to them. In 1881, Daniela had grown into a young woman of twenty-one; sooner or later she would be married. Blandine, too, was as interested in her male contemporaries as any eighteen-year-old, though Cosima chaffed her for being too standoffish. Their status had to be regularized.

Cosima put the question to Bülow by letter. Several letters. Bülow refused to discuss it, whether as revenge for the old hurt, or because of the impish stubbornness which so often induced him to say no when he was urged to say yes, or because he could not come to a decision. Whatever his reasons, he proved as obdurate as a Berlin policeman.

In April 1881, Daniela was in Berlin, visiting Marie von Schleinitz. Liszt was there too. Bülow came to Berlin, and at Cosima's suggestion, Daniela went to see him. Liszt went along. It was the first time in twelve years that Bülow had met his elder daughter. They looked at each other, they embraced, she stammered a few words—and she quite enraptured him. That one meeting made him write the most affectionate and warm letter he had written to Cosima in many a year. The "adorable child" (she was no longer a child) touched him as a father who had been a father only in absentia. The next day he sent off this letter:

Berlin, April 28, 1881

Once more, Madame, may I express to you my most devout thanks. What an adorable child! What a mind you have formed! It makes me weep to think of her, and I think of her without ceasing. This day, April 27, was a revelation to me. I thank Providence for having given me this inexpressible joy, a happiness which is such that it cannot be vitiated by any of the bitterness, regret, or remorse connected with it. Teach me, most generous and noble woman, what duties I have to fulfill as a father toward this much loved being, who has conquered my whole soul in one moment! I should like to build a shrine on the spot where your father brought her to me. I understand Père Goriot— pardon, I am wandering from the point, because what in him was madness would for Daniela be merely supremely right, a divine enthusiasm.

Thank you, thank you, thank you! I am indebted to you for a happiness without compare, painful as it may be.

P.S. A thousand blessings on you, wonderful woman! Daniela's bearing admirable in all circumstances. Worthy of her mother! May I express my admiration, gratitude, and deep respect?

Daniela as well was deeply moved. She telegraphed home: "Meeting today shook me terribly. I ask for your counsel. . . . Lulu."

In June, as Cosima and Richard were once more discussing the question of adoption, Wagner suggested that perhaps Daniela could make Bülow listen to reason. She was then in Weimar with Liszt, and planned to accompany her grandfather to Rome. Cosima asked her to go and speak to Bülow before departing for Italy, and knowing how perturbed the girl was between two "fathers," carefully prepared her for the meeting by writing her a long letter on July 2. The gist of it was: Yes, of course you have a real father, whom you must try to compensate for the cruel blows fate has dealt him and who has a right to ask for your devotion; but . . .

But here [in Bayreuth] you have a fatherly protector before whom you may incline in full gratitude. It was he who made it possible for me to fulfill my duty as a mother. . . . Up to now you have not found the noble and open words which are commensurate with this relationship [to Wagner]. But now you will find them, I know it, I sense it. . . . As certain as I am that all of us belong together, in spite of the separations life has produced, so certain am I that I ought to meet your real father halfway. Look, my child, I believe—I hope—I have been a good mother, albeit a serious one, strict, perhaps hard. The joy and the patient mildness of my calling—those I owe to your second father. In the truest sense of the word it was he who brought you up, as he strengthened, consoled, encouraged me. . . .

The results of Daniela's interview with Bülow were these: he would not consent to Wagner's initiating any proceeding for adoption, but he would be willing to discuss the situation—with Cosima *alone.* Would she come and see him?

Cosima was willing to go anywhere Bülow wished, but finally she chose Nuremberg as the meeting place, because "I could get there and back in one day." On July 10, 1881, suffering from a toothache, she was taken to the station by Wagner and Fidi in time for the 8 A.M. train. At one o'clock she arrived in Nuremberg. Daniela met her at the station.

Hans with me from four to half past six. I tried to calm his waves of violent emotion and to overcome his injustice toward Daniela. A vain task! He asks me to remain until tomorrow morning, as he has not succeeded in telling me his proposal as he wished. I consent.

She telegraphed to Wagner:

Good mood but until now little accomplished. Tomorrow morning another discussion. Assume your permission. Then will take train. Perhaps dentist. My whole being greets you.

Wagner wired back the next morning:

What is there to permit when everything has been permitted in advance, the location having been ceded to the other? Received telegram yesterday half past nine. Let justice prevail!

Cosima in the diary:

Second interview. He doesn't know whether white is white, black black. Hans said he has no star to guide him now. He was seized with nervous twitching. We bid farewell. I fetch Daniela. I would have liked to have another talk with him. He doesn't want it. Tearful journey home with Daniela. Arrival in the "harbor." R. happy to have me again. He says he arranged a game of whist yesterday but was in a shamefully cranky mood.

Everything I have to report is sad. Yet I am at home and we can discuss matters without hysterics. . . . I enter this house as if a new life were to begin for me. No consolation but peace. [July 11, 1881]

Nothing was settled until after Bülow's death. By that time it hardly mattered.

5

By May 1881, only the first act of *Parsifal* had been orchestrated, but Wagner, now feeling confident that the work would be finished in time for a Bayreuth performance in the summer of the following year, was gathering around him the usual group of devotees as well as new converts, ready to give their best. In Italy he had made the acquaintance of a Russian painter, Paul Joukowsky, who had once given promise of a considerable talent (Henry James thought well of him), but wealthy and weak-willed, he had not developed his gift, and James, disappointed, called him a "delicate dilettante." Turgenev called him a "naïve epicurean." Joukowsky fell completely under Wagner's spell and Wagner thought him the right artist to design the scenery for *Parsifal.* Cosima was not so sure.

Engelbert Humperdinck had been living at Bayreuth since January, copying the score. Carl Brandt came in June to excogitate the technical problems—the Transformation scenes, the collapse of the magic garden, the illumination of the Grail, etc. Josef Rubinstein was still there, and for some reason he took a dislike to Joukowsky and was often rude to him. "Malvolio Rubinstein," Cosima once called him. In addition, Stein was occupying a room with Fidi and had to be kept content. Various visitors, such as Julius Kniese, a most able chorus master, came and went. In this solarcentric universe, it was Cosima who had to keep the little planets from colliding.

The most important of the new Wahnfried inhabitants was the conductor Hermann Levi. He had proved himself a superb conductor and the kind of intellectual and introspective man with whom Wagner could ordinarily be friends. Besides, as Wagner wrote Ludwig, he knew of Levi's "passionate devotion" to him. However, he had one black spot: he was a Jew. So at first Wagner considered other conductors for *Parsifal,* then he tried to persuade Levi, son of a rabbi, to allow himself to be converted, "though how that operation would have

Family snapshot, 1881. Front row, from the left: Isolde, Daniela, Eva, Siegfried; back row: Blandine, Heinrich Stein, Cosima, Wagner, Joukowsky.

improved Levi's conducting is not clear" (Ernest Newman). Levi did not take kindly to the proposal. Wagner was then told in no uncertain terms that he could not have the Munich Orchestra—which was a sine qua non—without its official music director. So he settled for Levi, announcing the fact in grandiloquent phrases to the king, who replied:

> I am glad, dear Friend, that in connection with the production of your great and holy work you make no distinction between Christian and Jew. There is nothing so nauseating, so unedifying, as disputes of this sort: at bottom all men are brothers, whatever their religious differences. [October 11, 1881]

Wagner and Cosima must have swallowed hard when they read this missive. He answered that the king could only think so because for him the Jews were "only an idea, for us they are an experience."* To this morsel the king made no answer. Cosima excused Ludwig, saying that sovereigns are forced to take such an attitude. But Levi it had to be, and once the decision had been taken, Wagner worked with him harmoniously.

Levi to his father, from Bayreuth:

> I have spent three wonderful days here. The Meister was in an excellent mood and we discussed many things for next year. . . . It is no longer a secret that I will conduct the work. [April 14, 1881]

At the end of June, Levi returned to live at Wahnfried. He had been there only two days when Wagner received an anonymous letter begging him "to preserve the purity of his work by not allowing it to be conducted by a Jew"; in addition, the letter accused Levi of sexual relations with Cosima. Wagner brought the letter to Cosima:

> HE: Look—a *pretty* letter!
> SHE: Something nasty?
> HE: You'll see—
> I read, I marvel, then join him in laughter. But when he shows the letter to the poor Kapellmeister, he can't believe his eyes. Such indignities are new to him! [June 29, 1881]

It might have been more tactful had Wagner *not* shown the letter to Levi. At any rate, Levi bristled with fury, packed his valise, left Wahnfried, and asked Wagner to release him from the agreement to

*That "experience" included some of Wagner's and Cosima's most devoted friends: Tausig, Levi, Angelo Neumann—who Wagner himself said "regards it as his mission to force the musical world to recognize me"—and the difficult but loyal Rubinstein; not to mention those music lovers who from the beginning were among his adherents. When this was pointed out to him, he replied (according to Cosima's diary), "Yes, they are like flies. The more one chases them the more do they come around."

conduct *Parsifal*. Immediately Wagner wrote him: "For God's sake, return at once and learn to know us. Lose nothing of your faith, and strengthen your confidence. Perhaps you will experience a great change in your life. In any case—you are my *Parsifal* conductor!" He followed this up with an urgent telegram. The next day at one o'clock, Levi was back. They sat down to lunch. Cosima noted: "Very unconstrained, indeed lighthearted, atmosphere at table. R. orders Jewish wine." (July 2)

The man they insulted wrote to his father the next year:

April 13, 1882

He [Wagner] is the best and noblest of men. Naturally, the world misunderstands and berates him: the world always blackens the brilliant. It was the same with Goethe. But posterity will realize that he was as great a human being as he was an artist. Those who are close to him know this already. His fight against what he calls "Judaism" in music and modern literature is prompted by the noblest motives. That he harbors no small-minded *risches,* like a Junker or a Protestant bigot, is proved by his attitude to me, to Josef Rubinstein, and by his former intimate friendship with Tausig, whom he loved tenderly.

Wagner and Cosima had demonstrated the "nobility" of their anti-Semitism some months previously on the occasion of the terrible fire of December 8, 1881, in Vienna's Ringtheater, when hundreds of people lost their lives. Cosima noted in her diary: "That 416 Israelites perished in the conflagration does not increase R.'s sympathy for the tragedy." (December 17, 1881) Not a word of disagreement from her, and in her letters she warned Blandine against the Jews: Stay away from them! And yet she greatly respected Levi as an artist and grew fond of him as a person, and Levi loved her almost as much as he loved Wagner.

In September they received a surprise visitor: Judith Gautier. Cosima was nervous. What was his feeling? "I don't yet know whether [her visit] strikes R. as welcome or embarrassing." The beautiful Judith joined him at a game of whist and wanted to be his partner. She also wanted him to play *Parsifal* for her. He did, and Cosima left the room. But the infatuation had passed. Wagner tried to discuss the situation with Cosima, but she changed the subject and talked about the children. He was disturbed and told her that if anything came between them he would be finished. She confided to the diary that she felt the whole tenderness of his being going out to her, understanding of her fear. "There is a stranger in the house," she wrote. But that stranger soon departed and Wagner was glad of it. *"Ma chère enthousiaste, prenez pitié de moi,"* he said to Judith. A mild light once again shone in Wahnfried.

6

Once again they were longing to leave for Italy, not only for reasons of health but to get away from Germany, which Wagner now described as "a beggar armed to the teeth." He wrote the king:

> Not a day passes without my being gravely disturbed by a trouble that has been with me for the last five years . . . and now, after another year, in this refractory climate plaguing me almost without interval. It is a nervous complaint, a cramp in the chest . . . which shows itself at its worst in this continuously raw and inclement weather. . . .
> [October 1881]

The Wagner family—including this time the ever useful Schnappauf—took quarters at the Hotel des Palmes in Palermo, a luxury hotel with luxury prices. Cosima, happy to be relieved of the housekeeping chores, had hardly begun to draw a free breath when Fidi somewhere and somehow caught a serious infection and developed a high fever. The boy was nursed day and night by his frantic mother, but it took the better part of three weeks before he recovered.

Even when Fidi was once again smiling, making friends with the Sicilian boys, and sketching Palermo's houses with a new-found passion for architecture, Cosima's worries did not cease. Wagner's cramps were becoming more frequent and he suffered intestinal pains. A specialist they consulted told them that Wagner's organs were perfectly healthy: all he needed was a strict diet, lots of fresh air and sun. Sun they got, and "everywhere we looked, gardens and groves of orange trees laden with fruit." In those intervals when he was free from pain, Wagner worked with a will. He began scoring the third act on November 8, just three days after their arrival in Palermo. Cosima and he were now talking of selling Wahnfried and of settling here in this blessed spot—in spite of the mosquitoes.

Yet on her part this was make-believe. Watching her husband from day to day, recording every morning whether he had or had not slept well, seeing him now and again press his hand against his chest, she knew how ill a man he was, though not to anybody, not even to herself, not even in her diary, would she pronounce a portent. Not a word about the true situation did she write to Daniela, to whom she sent a letter every three days in November 1881: merely that "Papa is not feeling well. A little mistake in his diet. . . ."

Wagner had hoped to finish the score of *Parsifal* by Cosima's birthday. Another intestinal attack kept him from working for a few days. But he could not bear to disappoint Cosima, so he resorted to a loving little fraud. He finished the last page, leaving a few preceding pages blank, and presented the work, with a dedication to her, on December 25, 1881. He wrote on the last page, *"Für Dich"*—"For you." It was a combined Christmas-birthday gift, and not a meager one.

CHAPTER X

"I Was Aaron to Moses"

PALERMO, JANUARY 13, 1882. It is Joukowsky's birthday; he has become a member of the household, popular with both grownups and children. In the evening, music is played in his honor. Suddenly Wagner excuses himself and leaves the company. Cosima, worried, tiptoes after him and peeps into his room. He is all right, sitting at his desk and writing, and Cosima, reassured, rejoins the others. After a while Wagner comes back, carrying a weighty manuscript, which he hands to Cosima. It is the score of *Parsifal:* the work is now completed! "It didn't leave me in peace," he says. All of them, children, friends, Joukowsky, break into shouts of jubilation. A toast is drunk, they sing the *Tannhäuser* March, and Cosima gives Wagner a vase, decorated with Monreale motifs, which she has secretly obtained for just this occasion. Late that night, after the friends leave, they reminisce. Reminiscing is now their favorite pastime. Wagner tells her how often he was haunted by the conviction that he would not live long enough to finish *Parsifal.* He looks at her, now forty-four years old, and she is to him the same young girl he saw in Zurich. She looks at him, now sixty-nine, his hair gray, his face deeply lined as with an actor's makeup, and sees only "a head as young as Fidi's."

The work is achieved which Thomas Mann has called "the most extreme of his works . . . that surpasses at the close even Wagner's usual standards," and he knows that he will write no more music dramas. Cosima knows that it has been created while his body could no longer easily obey his will; she knows both the hardship and the joy of the genesis; and she knows that but for her it would never have been completed. As she has written to Marie von Schleinitz, her role has been that of Aaron holding up the arms of Moses during the battle.

It remained to bring the work to realization on the stage. That could happen only in one theater. But they were loath to leave the lemon and orange trees, to confine themselves once more within the wooden O of Bayreuth, to pump his conceptions, more mystic and "extreme" than ever, into opera singers, to tame imagination to the limitation of wood and canvas. They remained in the south as long as they could, moving from the hotel in Palermo to a villa, later to Arcireale and once again to Venice, where Cosima and he looked over the stately Palazzo Vendramin. They liked it so much that they promised to rent its entire mezzanine floor for the following winter, once *Parsifal* had been launched. They could afford it: Schott, Wagner's publisher, paid him 100,000 marks for *Parsifal,* a sum equivalent to more than $200,000 in today's purchasing power.

One great joy was vouchsafed Cosima in the spring: in Palermo, Blandine had met Count Biagio Gravina, the younger son of the Sicilian prince of Ramacca, and had fallen in love with him. He was a handsome and laughing young man and Cosima liked him, though he didn't care much about music and though—as Cosima's immediate inquiries disclosed—the financial situation of the family was far from rosy. It didn't matter: she saw that the two were very much in love, and Biagio was clever enough to act respectfully toward Wagner. She gave her consent, stipulating only that Biagio was "to take up an occupation."* They were married in Wahnfried, first in a civil ceremony on August 25, and the next day in a Catholic ceremony (the count being a Catholic).

> The bridal child very excited and darling. At 11 o'clock marriage in church. The priest, seemingly not in a good mood, hardly bothered to be suitably dressed. His speech, spiked with professional clichés and indecent indiscretions, embarrassing. . . . Only when Biagio slips the ring on Blandine's finger and looks at her do we feel that we are witnessing a holy ceremony!
>
> R. . . . gets irritated by everybody and everything and can't conquer his black depression, even after the guests are gone. [Diary, August 26, 1882]

*He probably did not. He died in 1897, only thirty-four years old.

Wagner's outbreaks had become worse as he grew older, his "black depression" covering him at the very time of *Parsifal*'s completion. When in a lighter mood, he himself recognized his fault; he told Cosima that Talleyrand exclaimed after an altercation with Napoleon, *"Quel dommage qu'un si grand homme soit si mal élevé!"* and that this applied precisely to him. Cosima felt that of late his anger reflected a premonition of death—death which he said he desired and which in fact he feared. On the day of the wedding she noted:

> In the afternoon, as he sat at his desk, I approached him to question him. He tells me he longs for death. Late at night when he has a bite to eat in the dining room, I sit alone in my room. I ponder and I ponder until my tumbling thoughts lull themselves to sleep. And I know quite well what things are going to be like—one day! [August 26, 1882]

Yet there was youthful news as well. Daniela, like her sister, fell in love; she became engaged to Fritz Brandt, the capable son of capable Carl. Cosima was delighted, at least at first. Soon she knew better. It appeared that Fritz was a troublemaker; when he came to Bayreuth he did all he could, both by carrying tales and by innuendo, to exacerbate the enmity between Kniese and Levi. Clearly, he wanted to step into the rift and make himself indispensable to Wagner. Fritz was handsome and he beguiled Daniela, but by and by the young Lothario wearied of her and the romance ended abruptly. Daniela, puzzled and unsure of herself, was miserable. Was she ever going to attract a man? Cosima wrote her wise, tender, and, for once, unpreachy letters and succeeded in restoring Daniela's morale: "all experiences, good and bad, enlarge us. Let this one serve you as an episode, as the beginning of a new chapter." That was going to happen soon, she predicted.

A new chapter had opened for Bülow: he had met a woman with whom he felt comfortable and who understood and loved the lonely man. That year, he married Marie Schanzer, an actress at the Ducal Theater in Meiningen. "How very friendly on the part of Fate," Cosima wrote Daniela, "to allow us to perceive a ray of happiness in your father's life."

Cosima and Wagner had left Venice on April 29 at one o'clock. The sun was shining and the two gondoliers, singing all the way to the railroad station, mingled their voices with the swish of the big gondola; the sight and sound brought curious spectators to the bridges, wondering who these peculiar people could be who were leaving paradise at lunchtime. The next day they arrived in Munich and Cosima took the children to the theater to see *Around the World in Eighty Days.* "Bad piece, badly acted." On May 1, they arrived in Bayreuth and were greeted at the station by a huge delegation. Four days later, Levi arrived, and rehearsals began. Carl Brandt had died in December of 1881; it was a great loss. But the flirtatious Fritz proved himself almost equally energetic and resourceful. Daniela and he hardly addressed a word to each other.

Presently Cosima began to assist at the rehearsals, proposing various positions for the backstage voice of Titurel, arranging the grouping of the knights, etc. "I feel as if I were dreaming. I can't grasp how it happened that I was awarded the happiness to assist him and be part of it!"

To be on the safe side, Wagner hired three tenors for Parsifal, "one better than the other, or at least two better than one." The Transformation scenery was moving too slowly to bring it in concordance with the music. Brandt asked him to compose some additional bars and he grumbled, "They always complained that my music is too long; now it is too short!" Humperdinck wrote a few bars and timidly submitted them to Wagner, who looked at them and accepted them—to everybody's astonishment, including Cosima's.* All the artists promised to be punctual for the first rehearsals, except Amalie Materna, who wanted to visit her mother. Wagner sent her a telegram: "Whoever is not here for the first rehearsal cannot be expected to sing the first performance." That was all that was needed. At the first rehearsal with the singers, "R. begs the assembled worthies to observe his rhythms exactly. 'I am a poor composer, but my rhythm is excellent.' He is in a wonderful mood." Everyone connected with the production worked with total enthusiasm, and with every rehearsal, things went more smoothly.

Cosima, who of course knew every word and note by heart, was present at every rehearsal and the artists, inspired by Wagner's direction, accepted her as well. After a day of two rehearsals, one of which lasted from half past nine in the morning to half past two, the other —for the orchestra—beginning at 5 P.M., Wagner was still fresh and lively. Late in the evening, Cosima discussed *Parsifal* with him. How superbly Levi was conducting! How lofty and moving was this creation! How wondrous "every sound, every gesture!" He answered: "We have done much together, you and I."

On the day after the dress rehearsal (July 25), a banquet was held

*Later the scenery was made to move faster and Humperdinck's contribution could be dispensed with.

at the theater restaurant. The guests sat at a long table, Wagner in the middle, Cosima and her father facing him. Next to Wagner sat Judith Gautier—whom earlier in the day he had refused to see, pleading fatigue—and with whom he now kept up a laughing conversation, she in French, he in French-German. While all the other women were dressed in evening toilette, Judith wore a simple sailor's blouse with a flame-red scarf. After the usual speeches, Wagner ended, saying, "Children, tomorrow is the day! Tomorrow the devil walks. All of you who are taking part, make sure the devil gets into you!"

The first and second performances, on July 26 and 28, were reserved for the Patrons. Fourteen further performances were given, most of them sold out. At the first performance, a storm of applause broke out at the end of Act I and again, with even greater strength, after Act II. Wagner stepped forward in his box and asked the audience not to insist that the singers take a bow. Some misunderstood, believed that he wanted no applause at all, and some spectators shushed the clapping at the end. This was the origin of the tradition of silence after the first act, and the customary approval after the second act and at the end. Wagner discussed the business of applause with Cosima the next day, on the evening of which Wahnfried was illuminated for a huge reception: "Schnappauf thinks 300, I think 200 people." Yet that day, with all the turmoil, Wagner had the leisure (and the power of concentration) to read some of Hume's *History of England,* so well did Cosima organize everything. At the second performance, there was again confusion over when to applaud, and at the end Wagner made a little speech thanking his artists. Cosima: "This time the mood is more peaceful than the first time. Our being together with my father is quiet and friendly." That did not last long: Wagner was livid when Liszt left, believing that he ought to have remained for *all* the performances. (Liszt returned for the last performance.)

The next day, Cosima received the owner of the restaurant, who complained of poor business and threatened to close his place. He was no sooner gone than she had to welcome delegates of the Wagner Verein, who had various grievances. For lunch she entertained the singers.

Aside from Liszt, many celebrities attended, most of them making demands on Cosima's hospitality. Bruckner was there, Leo Delibes and Camille Saint-Saëns, Lou Andreas-Salomé, the young Gustav Mahler, Hanslick—the ancient enemy, now remarkably laudatory— Angelo Neumann, etc. But Ludwig remained absent; much as he longed to hear *Parsifal,* he could not bear to face the staring crowds. Only illness, he assured Cosima, had kept him away.

During the festival, Wagner suffered one of his worst heart spasms. He was alone in a room with Emil Scaria, the Gurnemanz, when suddenly he sank down on a couch, his face purple, the veins of his forehead visible, gasping for breath and making helpless movements with his hands as if he were fighting Death itself. After a minute or two the attack passed and he begged Scaria not to say a word to Cosima.

The diary confirms one of two famous anecdotes: that at the eighth performance, the Flower Maidens sang so beautifully that a man in a box shouted a loud "Bravo!" It was Wagner himself and he was promptly shushed by the shocked audience. But an incident at the final performance (August 29) is reported differently by Cosima than by Wagner's official biographers and by Newman, who say that Levi was not feeling well and that Wagner, to relieve him, slipped into the orchestra pit and, unknown to the audience, conducted the work from the end of the third-act Transformation music to the final chord. Cosima records nothing of Levi's indisposition. It seems that Wagner, perhaps prompted by a premonition that this was the last time he was to be present in the theater whose walls he had erected through his own imagination, wanted once more to be united with his orchestra and his singers. Levi was standing beside him, evidently feeling quite well, as he reported the incident two days later to his father:

> At the end the public broke out into a jubilation which beggars all description. The Meister did not show himself, remained seated among the orchestral musicians, cracked terrible jokes, and when after ten minutes the noise showed no sign of abating, I shouted with all my might, "Quiet, quiet!" The shouts were heard above and some sort of quiet ensued. Now the Meister, standing on the conductor's podium, began to speak, first to me and the orchestra; then the curtain was raised. All the singers and the technical personnel were assembled on the stage. He spoke with such warmth that everybody began to weep. It was an unforgettable moment!

Cosima:

> Our return home is silent and solemn. I believe we may be grateful, though assuredly the achievement has been bought at a heavy cost, and we have sacrificed to it almost all of life's ease. Yet his activity is a necessity to R. and with all its sorrow the only one suited to him. In the evening we relate the incident [his conducting] to the children. It was obvious how

differently the orchestra played under his leadership, how incomparably different was Reichmann's [the Amfortas] delivery of the words "To die, the only benison." [August 29, 1882]

The next day:

And so they are ended, those sixteen performances, and not once did the spirit of toil and dedication on the part of the artists abate. The public, too, felt the sense of the exceptional to the highest degree. I believe one may be satisfied.

2

Cosima could not acknowledge to herself the whole truth about her husband's condition. She suppressed what she sensed, which made her watch all the more carefully his every frown, his every breath. Remarkably enough, as soon as they were installed in the Palazzo Vendramin in Venice, where they arrived on September 16, his health and spirits seemed to improve. He was as intellectually curious as ever, taking a new interest in Buddhism, studying Persian history, and reading an analysis of Balzac's work, despite his long-ago vow never to read another French book. He was still fabricating labored puns, and still uttering capsules of unleavened judgments, such as that "nothing could be expected" from the phonograph Edison had demonstrated in New York, that the Impressionists painted "nocturnes in ten minutes," that what the Russians needed was an unprincipled strong man like Bismarck, etc. Cosima recorded them all. She herself became attracted to Russian literature when she read Turgenev's *Fathers and Sons,* and she waxed enthusiastic about *War and Peace.* Promptly Wagner tackled it and was captivated by the scenes with Kutusov. . . .

They loved Venice more than ever, the city in which the light so often dances. What she loved most was to go walking with him, losing themselves in dark byways rounded by silent dark canals, and emerging finally in the splendor of St. Mark's Square. They drank their coffee at Florian's and as soon as the maestro saw him, the municipal band played selections from *Lohengrin* or *Tannhäuser.* The band played execrably, but he didn't mind. On warm days they took Fidi to the Lido and watched him swim on his back while he whistled snatches of his father's music. Or they visited San Rocco, where Tintoretto's *Crucifixion* was one of Cosima's favorite "great works." Wagner walked more slowly now, and once, on the way from the Piazzetta to the Rialto, he suffered a spasm, a brief one, which she pretended not to notice. She liked to return from the walks to a little boudoir she had furnished for herself in the huge palazzo. There she felt "like a lapdog in a lion's cage."

In 1858, when Wagner had fled from the Asyl to Venice—it was the year of *Tristan*—a comet had streaked across the sky. Now, in 1882, the year of *Parsifal,* another comet lit up the nocturnal lagoon with its fiery tail. Cosima and Wagner watched it, wondering whether it was a bad omen. Soon after, they received the news of Gobineau's death. They mourned their friend, and on Wagner's suggestion Cosima wrote a memoir for the *Bayreuther Blätter,* the periodical Wagner had founded. Too many friends, Wagner wrote the king, have disappeared around him; yet "something in me remains young and vital." He told Cosima that he hoped he would have sufficient strength to give the *Ring* again, and she assured him that he was the youngest of them all.

Cosima saw to it that there was always at least one guest whom Wagner liked and to whom he could expound. The Schleinitzes, Heinrich von Stein, Humperdinck, Rubinstein, Joukowsky, Levi, came and went. When they went he called them "selfish." A young art historian began to call with increasing frequency; Heinrich Thode had fallen in love with Daniela and was making himself agreeable to Wagner, with whom he discussed Aeschylus. Daniela, delighted to be home, now helped Cosima as hostess. Blandine, married, was living in Palermo; Wagner and Cosima missed her. Liszt was with them during much of the autumn and winter. As always, the two men liked and disliked each other; Liszt's way of rushing from one palace to the other grated on Wagner's nerves more than ever. The alternation led to quarrels with Cosima, who herself alternated between defending her father and regretting that she had opposed her husband. Joukowsky wrote in his memoirs: "When they [Liszt and Wagner] talked together, neither paid attention to what the other was saying: they would both speak at the same time, and this often led to the strangest quid pro quos."

In December, Cosima learned that Bülow, who had been ill for some time, had fallen in his bathtub and injured his head. She believed he had suffered a stroke, and all her latent guilt broke through in lacerating self-accusation; she tormented herself with the "horrible vision" of the sick man, unable to lift his arms:

> I see Hans before me, alone in the hospital, and I want to scream, scream to some God for help. . . . I do not believe that one happy moment will be granted to me from now on, nor that I deserve one. [December 18, 1882]

Wagner, deeply troubled himself, comforted her. She wrote in her diary—and for once that determined handwriting trembled—"With all my soul I embrace R. I think God will have pity." The situation proved not so bad as it had seemed at first; it had been a very slight stroke and Bülow recovered, nursed by his new wife.

Toward the latter part of December, Wagner went off alone several times, giving Cosima various excuses, none of which she believed. She guessed what was going on: he was preparing a birthday surprise for her. A symphony he had written when he was nineteen had long been lost, but the parts had turned up in Dresden and he now intended to have it performed for Cosima, with Seidl as conductor. He had leased the Fenice Theater for the evening of December 24; the students of the Venice conservatoire, the Liceo Benedetto Marcello, were to play. Seidl could not come and so Wagner had to take over the rehearsals himself. Cosima: "At supper he tells us that he had cramps at the Liceo, nevertheless he has to go there again tomorrow. When he says he has no conductor and I appear surprised, he blurts out" the secret. Cosima couldn't wait for the performance and sneaked into a rehearsal, unseen by him. He told the young musicians: "It is an old piece, composed fifty years ago. If you want something new we have to play a symphony by Beethoven or Haydn."

The weather was beautiful on Christmas Eve and Cosima, the children, Liszt, Joukowsky, and Humperdinck went to the theater in three gondolas. At the Fenice, brightly lit, they found a few other guests, the director of the conservatoire, and some friends Liszt had invited at the last moment. Wagner stepped briskly to the podium and raised his baton. The performance was of course a great success, Cosima thanked the young musicians, they toasted her, and then Wagner whispered to Liszt, "Do you love your daughter? Then go to the piano and play!" At once Liszt did so and played for a long time, to everybody's delight. "Around eleven we journeyed home through a Venice of blue haze. The children jubilant over the evening, R. very satisfied."

3

In the first months of the new year Wagner had his good and bad days. Liszt left, Humperdinck left, and Wagner bade them unwilling farewell. Levi came in January for a week; they discussed plans for the Bayreuth Festival the following summer, Wagner suggesting a production of *Tannhäuser,* and when Levi departed Wagner kissed him, much moved. Soon he complained to Cosima of being idle: "I am like Othello; my occupation's gone." The bitter clump in the caldron of his being had not dissolved. He did not have the strength to begin a new work and he hated himself because he had once again talked about the Jews in Levi's presence and Levi had fallen ill with melancholy. Nothing was right now; he thought he was "plaguing" Cosima. It was raining and cold in Venice. He longed for warmth; it had been a great mistake "to build his beautiful house in a shitty climate"; the best thing that could happen to him would be to be exiled to Ceylon. He felt as if he lived in a permanent winter, "even the Festival now seemed absurd." Yet the next day, February 11, he began to write an essay, a "highly spiced" effort, the first page of which he read to Cosima. His mood had improved because he was working.

On the evening of February 12—the day Levi left—Wagner read Fouqué's *Undine* to Cosima and the family. Joukowsky was present. Cosima passed him her notebook, and he made a quick sketch: "R. reading." Then Wagner went to the piano, improvising a little, and played the theme of a scherzo he intended to compose. Cosima retired. She was already in bed when she heard him in his room, speaking loud and volubly. She got up, went to him, and he said, "I was speaking with you." They embraced long and tenderly. He said, "It happens successfully only once every five thousand years." Once more he went to the piano, remembering the Undine-like creatures who long for a human soul, and played the song of the Rhine Maidens at the end of *Rheingold.* He said, "I am fond of them, these small beings of the deep, with their longings."

These were the last words Cosima wrote in her diary.

The next day, February 13, 1883, when Wagner got up he said, "I'll have to be careful today." He stayed in his room, working on his essay on the feminine component of the human psyche. Joukowsky came for lunch as usual and Wagner sent word that he was not feeling very well, they should begin lunch without him, but there was nothing to worry about. Nevertheless, Cosima asked the maid Betty to remain in the

room next to Richard's. Betty heard him sigh and moan from time to
time. Suddenly he rang the bell violently. Betty rushed in and then ran
to the others, shouting that Wagner wanted "the doctor and my wife."
Cosima jumped up, flew upstairs unseeing, collided with a half-open
door with such force that it nearly split, and took her husband in her
arms. He collapsed and a watch she had given him fell from his vest
pocket to the floor. He mumbled, "My watch." Those were the last
words he spoke. When the doctor came, he laid Wagner on the couch
and tried massage, saying, "We must not give up hope," while Cosima
clung to Wagner's knees. It was no use. Wagner was dead. He died at
3:30 P.M.

Mute and almost motionless, she sat by the dead man's side, waving
away anybody who approached. She refused food. She refused to
speak to her children. She sat. Now and then she took the corpse into
her arms and whispered useless words; now and then she dozed in
spite of herself. For twenty-five hours she would not budge from the
room. Wagner's death mask could not be taken until afterward, and
then only by hiding the fact from Cosima. At last, late the next day,
she emerged, still silent, on Daniela's arm. Liszt, who was in Budapest,
telegraphed asking if she wanted him to come. Through Daniela she
declined; he was glad of it. The coffin was brought. Cosima cut off her
hair, the adornment Wagner had loved, and placed it in the coffin.

The news was kept from Bülow, scarcely recovered from his illness.
Finally, on the evening of the fourteenth, his wife felt she had to tell
him and did so—in the presence of his doctor. She wrote to her
mother:

> The news . . . had so shattering an effect on my husband that the
> atmosphere here since then has been one of the profoundest
> melancholy. Even I had no idea of how passionate was the love he felt
> for Wagner, in spite of everything. [February 15, 1883]

Some days later, when Bülow heard that Cosima was trying to destroy herself and refusing food, he telegraphed her: *"Soeur il faut
vivre."*

Nietzsche wrote: "You have not in the past refused to listen to my
voice in grave moments. Now . . . that you have suffered the gravest
experience of all, I know of no other way to pour out my feelings than
by directing them wholly and solely to you. I look upon you today, as
I have always looked upon you, even from far away, as the woman my
heart best honors."

Ludwig, when the news was brought to him, exclaimed, "Horrible!" and asked to be left alone. He wrote to Cosima, hoping that God would give her the strength to "bear this terrible test." With justified pride he issued a statement: "I was the first to recognize the artist whom the whole world now mourns; I rescued him for the world." The *artist* . . . he said nothing of Wagner the man. Only three years were to pass before he himself was to perish, dethroned and judged mad, in a death the mystery of which has never been solved.

Venice, too, mourned Wagner, though few Venetians had known him. "We will remember the star which sank under the musical horizon," the *Gazzetta di Venezia* said on the fourteenth. On the seventeenth, the Liceo closed and the municipal band did not perform in St. Mark's Square. The *Gazzetta* reported that Cosima "took some nourishment yesterday."

Daniela had telegraphed to Feustel and he asked his son-in-law Adolf Gross and Gross's wife to hurry to Venice. It was Gross who shouldered the task of keeping journalists, officials, and acquaintances away from the Palazzo Vendramin, as well as making the arrangements to have the body transferred to Bayreuth. On the morning of the sixteenth, a group of gondolas draped in black, in one of which Cosima sat alone, hidden from view, proceeded slowly to the railroad station. Gross had persuaded the authorities to close the station to the public until the train left. Cosima rode in the compartment that carried the coffin. The window shades were lowered. There she was, and there she remained on the long journey, still silent, still deaf to what was going on around her. Richter, who had at once left Vienna for Venice, took care of the children. Wherever the train stopped, people gathered to express their sympathy, but she neither saw nor heard them. At three o'clock in the afternoon of the seventeenth—about twenty-four hours after it left Venice—the train arrived in Munich. The huge station was filled with people bearing torches and bringing flowers. Not until close to midnight did the train reach Bayreuth; there a throng had waited for the return of the town's most illustrious citizen. Cosima wanted the coffin to be taken at once to Wahnfried. That proved impossible, and it remained at the station during the night, under a guard of honor. When she herself arrived at Wahnfried, she suddenly noticed that her wedding rings were missing. Joukowsky drove back to the station to search for them. He couldn't find them. Later they were found in Cosima's room: they had slipped from her finger without her noticing.

The next afternoon, a Sunday, a last public ceremony took place at the station. Muncker and Feustel spoke of the man who had brought obscure Bayreuth to the world's astonished attention. A regimental band played Siegfried's Funeral March. The king's deputy laid a wreath on the coffin, but Ludwig did not attend his friend's obsequies. The long procession, with the coffin in a hearse drawn by four black horses, slowly made its way to Wahnfried through streets along which every house flew a black flag. It was cold when they arrived, and as the coffin was carried to the place in the garden that Wagner had designated long ago, a light snow was falling. Twelve men carried the coffin, among them Muncker, Feustel, Gross, Seidl, Joukowsky, Richter, Levi.

Cosima had absented herself from these ceremonies, but now, as the friends dispersed and darkness fell, she came from the house, leaning on Gross's arm. In her presence, the coffin was lowered into the grave.

CHAPTER XI

Silence and Sound

"I TELL YOU," Liszt wrote in December 1883, "that my daughter, hugging to herself the thought of death, is doing everything possible not to outlive Wagner." More than nine months had passed.

For the first two months following February 13, Cosima sat swathed in silence, most of the day locked in her room, where she reread her husband's prose writings, where she looked at his portrait through swollen eyes, where she reviewed, willingly and unwillingly, memories which flickered at her from an uncertain distance. She had closed her diary and she never opened its pages again, not once in her whole life. What was the use now of keeping a record? "Why live we idly here?" She read neither Shakespeare nor the newspaper. She received no visitors, refused to glance at condolence letters. When, at her physician's insistence, she went out for a little walk, her head shadowed by a broad hat, and people greeted her, she bowed her head but did not return the greeting. After a few minutes in the daylight of spring, she returned to the darkness of her room. Why was her wish to die with him not granted?

It was even painful to speak to the children. She could not bear their consolation. She communicated with them through written messages, and when spring arrived she summoned the strength to write a long letter to Daniela (who was in the next room), a letter that was an exhortation, an injunction to be obeyed after her death, a death she still hoped for and expected:

> My darling children—live from now on for Siegfried! All your thoughts should be concentrated on this task, at once heavy and glorious. You will accomplish the task—and then you will feel me present among you.
>
> I hope that in the time that I lived among you I was able to show you how greatly I loved you, how I rejoiced with you, how I blessed you, what elation I derived from your development and well-being. If now I must part from you do not regard this parting as a loveless leavetaking. Do not think my soul has not been happy being with you. There was not an hour in which I did not acknowledge the blessing of possessing you. It is only that the blow dealt to me has exceeded my strength. I might well have been able to live on for years and to help us all to bear our lives, exhausted though I sometimes felt, but now— God must decide. I submit my soul to His will. However He decides, wherever He leads, I will deem it good. You, my children, must think and feel that with me. Take care of Siegfried: that is my first word and my last. Your first thought on waking, your first action, your gladdest care—may they be for him!
>
> Darling children, if I have to leave you, look upon our resting place with friendly eyes and say to yourselves: "They are reunited." Yes we are, united for eternity— [April 10, 1883]

More than four months after Wagner's death, Daniela managed to pull her mother—at least intermittently—from her state of jumbled tears by appealing to Cosima's sense of responsibility to her family: the children needed her, in a Wahnfried in which everybody was walking on tiptoe. There were no meetings now, no discussions, no music—and very few visitors. Daniela described it to Joukowsky, who had let her know that he could not—or would not—come to Bayreuth. Nobody now seemed to want to come:

> . . . Yet I understand the feeling which makes you hesitate to come to Bayreuth, because were I to follow my instinct I would rather be in India and converse with elephants than with our best friends. . . . Our days pass in a silent flight. We call ourselves "the mothers" of Mama. We take care of her and make her nourish herself. The daily worry about her helps us over the heaviest hours of our darkened lives. God be praised, she is not really ill. Occasionally she even speaks to us of Papa's illness and the 13th of February. A few weeks ago that would not have been possible. Together we read from his writings, and I study Schopenhauer with her. She gives some lessons to my sisters and Fidi, and does some work for Boni and Manfred. Not one second is she idle. But, of course, she has resigned from life. She no longer

wants to see grandpapa [Liszt]. He isn't coming this summer. The
poor man! He has outlived himself. He is horribly lonely—not a single
thread connects him with the world in which he has to live. Even the
Glasenapps can't make themselves come here this summer. Too bad,
though I understand very well. Why do you subject us to this
deprivation? . . .

In August Cosima was still in a precarious state. Siegfried had been
sent to the seashore for a little holiday, just to get him away from
Wahnfried. Cosima wrote him a letter which must have been highly
embarrassing to a fourteen-year-old boy:

My blessed child!
My thanks and again my thanks. I would like to speak to you with
voices of angels, my dearest one. Blessed be your every step, your
every word, your every breath! You, my joy, my blessing, my
Siegfried, peace of my heart, triumph of love—how can I address you
in order to satisfy my heart, in order to express to myself what you
are to me? . . . Sleep sweetly. . . . [August 5, 1883]

That summer, *Parsifal* was given in twelve performances under
Levi's direction and with virtually the same cast as in 1882. Cosima did
not attend any of them. However, when the season was finished, a
knowledgeable observer—his identity is unknown—prepared a forty-
page memorandum for her in which he compared the 1883 performances with those under Wagner's direction. The substance of the
analysis was that "the incidental characters (Knights, Acolytes, Flower
Maidens) transgressed the measure," the result being that "the principal interpreters overacted as well. The same gestures were repeated
two or three times . . . and thus the whole performance lost conviction." In instance after instance, the observer detailed exaggerations
and vulgarities.

Studying this memorandum, while she revolved her mourning
thoughts so often that in the end they became immobile, she began
to realize that her life *did* have a purpose. Eva, Isolde, and even Fidi
would soon be old enough to take care of themselves. She had other,
farther-reaching, work to do: as in the past, so in the future she would
have her mission. That mission was the preservation of Wagner's creations in his theater. She would return to his interpretations, keep the
heritage intact, stop those head shakings and arm stretchings "which
have been smuggled into the performance," and see to it that "the
Flower Maidens would not play to the public, instead of paying attention to Parsifal." (From the memorandum)

In the meantime, an astonishing proposal had been put forth in

Bayreuth: Cosima being too shaken to act effectively—such, at least, was the pretext offered—the direction of the festival was to be taken from her. The theater was to be run by a consortium, headed by Liszt and Bülow. They were to be supported by a business manager—everybody knew by that time that Bayreuth would become "a business"— while Cosima would be fobbed off with an honorary title. Levi, whose loyalty to Cosima was untouchable, was to be got rid of. Curiously, Daniela was in favor of the plan, which of course caused a temporary rift between mother and daughter. The principal author of this scheme was Julius Kniese, who was as rotten a character as he was excellent as a chorus director, who hated Levi, and who felt that by undercutting Cosima he would increase his own power. Kniese would use Liszt's and Bülow's names for glamor, his own name being unknown.

This was the kind of battle Cosima relished. It acted as the stimulant to awake her from despondency, a tonic that aroused her from her shapeless languishing. A "stranger" touching her husband's legacy— it was presumption not to be borne. A year after the death in Venice, she bestirred herself and, first consulting Adolf Gross—whom she regarded as her most faithful adviser and ally—she pointed out: (1) That though Wagner had left no testament, he had beyond possibility of doubt intended that Bayreuth was to be her "inheritance"—and she could prove it. (2) That Liszt and Bülow had their own careers to pursue and could not devote all their attention to this task which, God knew, required somebody's full attention. She—and *only* she—would have both the time and the dedication necessary. Therefore (3) she had every intention of assuming the direction of the enterprise. She was, and meant to remain, the keeper of the keys. Did she not know, had she not absorbed, every gesture, inflection, and expression from the creator of the works? With the ice-hard politeness Cosima could summon, she asked Kniese to leave.

Parsifal was again performed in 1884. Cosima had a closed cabin built and placed in the wings of the stage. From that observation point she watched, unseen by the audience, every one of the ten performances. At every performance she issued notes which came to be known as "Performance Notes" *(Regiezettel)*. A typical one:

> The Prelude a trifle more delicate so we don't lose the inner voices. The crescendo even and continuous. The colloquy between Gurnemanz and the two knights a little too slow. The orchestral figure at Kundry's entrance sharper, the crescendo more marked. At the words "without permission!" the orchestra too loud.

She did not confine her contribution to Beckmesser-like jottings. Presently she conceived her task as fundamental: not only should the performances be washed clean, but Wagner's entire artistic philosophy must be kept alive for posterity. His influence on music would be enormous: that was evident to her, and by this time to many others. His influence on literature she could only prophesy, but she was sure of it, and she was right. It was Wagner's ghost which lured D'Annunzio's Giorgio to commit murder and suicide, prompted Thomas Mann to illustrate German decadence by the incest of the twins and to symbolize disease by his *Tristan,* aroused sexual longing in George Moore's Evelyn Innes, caused Virginia Woolf's Mrs. Dalloway to faint at *Parsifal,* overcome by beauty and humidity, furnished Shaw with the material for a primer on revolution, moved T. S. Eliot to drift Wagnerian characters through *The Waste Land,* and most deeply inspired Proust, as Saint-Loup remembers during the war the warble of Siegfried's bird and the Guermantes mock *Tristan.*

So Cosima proposed not only that Bayreuth was to preserve "model" performances, but that it was to become a center, a Jerusalem, where Wagner's creed would be preached to the world. For such an undertaking, money—a lot of it—was needed and Cosima felt, as her husband had felt, that Germany, and indeed the whole world, had a duty to support Bayreuth financially. As she wrote to Glasenapp: "Forty millions, that's what I need to give the Germans the Festivals. Perhaps one of these days a good soul will give them to me, a Jew who wants to atone for the evil of his race."

As Cosima reentered life, as she became aware that a task was awaiting her, both the practical and the mystic strains of her personality strengthened. While some were saying that Bayreuth was finished and the festival should be transferred to Vienna, she evolved a careful plan for the performances of the next five years. Her choices for the musical direction were Levi and—as chief conductor—Bülow! *Tristan* she planned for 1885—it was actually postponed a year—and as Isolde she wanted either the proven Materna or the untried Theresa Malten. "Ask Fräulein Malten to study the part with Frau Schnorr," she noted: Frau Schnorr, her enemy. She herself assumed the direction on stage, moderating every gesture, insisting that the singers play to one another, that there be no unnecessary to-ing and fro-ing—"Please! No promenades!" she used to say—and that the words be clearly pronounced, a style that later, when overdone, came to be known as "consonant-spitting." She insisted on *"Ruhe,"* quiet acting, in which miming was to be carefully considered *before* a phrase was sung, since "unarticulated feeling gains in spontaneity." The chorus was never to indulge in meaningless participation—making signs to each other, faking astonishment, etc. She often jumped onto the stage and acted out various parts, and she was so good an actress, Siegfried wrote, that he could compare her only to the one actor who had impressed him most, Salvini in *Othello*. (Obviously, his was hardly an unprejudiced judgment.)

When away from the theater, she immersed herself in dim religious thoughts. She wrote to Daniela:

> Not among graves, among spirits do we wander. The way is lofty. Our task is to seek redemption, here on earth. For our guilt stands the Redeemer, bleeding. We are freed of guilt through faith. Our suffering because he [Wagner] is dead is compensated by immortality —Compensation must grow within ourselves. In our hearts is Eden. We must guard it against weeds and the serpent. . . . [February 24, 1885]

She added a postscript: "When I loathe myself from the bottom of my soul I look toward you, toward your love, and am transfigured."

Ludwig inquired about her with sympathy and sent a further contribution to the Bayreuth Fund. She knew that the best way to thank him was to give him all possible reminders of Wagner. She prepared a new book, containing memorabilia she had acquired. Among these were Wagner's letters to Theodor Uhlig, a composer and a violinist in the Dresden orchestra, to whom Wagner poured out his heart during the first years of his banishment. The letters reflect Wagner's hotheadedness in those revolutionary days of 1848. Wagner had asked Uhlig's daughter Elsa to make him copies of these letters. This she did, but withheld some. Cosima now asked her for the remaining letters. Elsa duly sent them and Cosima included them in her compilation for Ludwig, first, however, striking out offending passages.*

Mrs. Burrell bought the letters and John N. Burk (in *Letters of Richard Wagner*) compared the bowdlerized version with the originals:

> We can look over the shoulders of Cosima . . . as she deletes the passages on page after page, crossing out anything from a name or an expletive to an entire letter. Only 23 out of 93 letters were allowed to appear intact.

*Both Cosima and her daughter Eva tried to persuade Elsa Uhlig to destroy *her* copies of the letters. "Destruction would avoid indiscretions," she wrote, and again, "I repeat my advice to destroy the copies." Legal action was threatened by Wahnfried if she published them. However, there being no legal ground for such a prohibition, the letters were published (in 1888), though in the censored version.

Yet her editorial misdemeanor—or if one prefers a harsher term, her editorial falsification—does not appear all that heinous, as one reads the originals and understands the reasons why she wielded her blue pencil. Wagner in his perturbed condition expressed himself freely, now with momentary irritation, now with deep-seated resentment, against some of the people who had helped him. Most of these were still living; for example, the Ritters. Alluding to Karl Ritter's homosexual tendency ("the main feature of his character is weakness") or to Liszt ("This Liszt is almost crazy!") or to others made it well-nigh impossible for Cosima to allow full publication. More blameworthy was her suppression of Wagner's revolutionary comments: she tried to pretend that his participation in the Dresden uprising of 1849 was minimal.

These letters, then, along with other notes, poems, etc., Cosima assembled for the king. With them she sent a letter which gave Ludwig a sketch of her current life and activities:

Most noble and most potent King!
Most beneficent King and Lord!
I feel unable to lay at His Majesty's feet adequate words of my thanks! Would Your Majesty graciously permit me to express my feeling solely through this book which I submissively offer you today? My gracious Lord will find there again many a page which twenty years ago I had the happiness to copy for our King, thrice blessing him as I did so. As I return these notes to the most faithful of friends, I realize that I am restoring them to their true owner. For how could our lives have continued in an unending stream, had it not been for the protection you granted—granted in spite of all obstacles—a deed which I can never cease to regard as a miracle? My soul, even in dying, will continue to praise and pray.

To my silent thanks I wish to add a few words, hoping that I have not misinterpreted the encouragement which I read in your immeasurably kind words.

She tells him that she has chosen *Tristan* as the work to be performed the next season. She perceives an "arcane connection" between that work and *Parsifal.* She goes into mystic detail to explain this connection, quoting Wagner's first sketches. Then:

There is a practical reason as well for my choice: the scenic investment would be relatively small. The scenery will be virtually the same as that used by Your Majesty's Court Theater. Only in the third act do I want to bring the castle entrance further downstage, to render the fight clearer.

May she now give him some personal news, asking his pardon should such news prove uninteresting to him?

After a serious and indeed dangerous illness Siegfried is sufficiently restored to go back to the gymnasium. I did not send him there with a light heart, because there the sense of what is great is dulled rather than stimulated. At least I think so. However, I felt it important that, young as he is, he mingle with boys of the same age. I sought for him a counterweight to the seriousness of Wahnfried. He likes school and learns willingly, though for the present he has to give up his predilection for architecture. He has shown talent with his carefully done drawings and original ideas for churches and chapels. I ask myself over and over again whether I should let him finish the gymnasium or transfer him to a polytechnical school where his gift could be developed.

As to the girls:

There is no change in Isolde's or Eva's life. They are with me and help me by their love and openness. On the other hand, my eldest child [Daniela] had to undergo many a trial. When last year she became engaged I thought that a sign from heaven and I thought she would devote herself to the cause of Bayreuth. I believed her happy and I believed that I had found in her fiancé somebody to whom I could confidently entrust the management of the Festival, at least until the time when Siegfried would be old enough. Nothing came of it, the experience was sad, and I believed that my child—still so young and full of life—would be condemned to frustration and resignation.

That, too, has changed: now she is engaged to a man who seems to me to possess all the characteristics which would enable a woman to enter, freely and in friendship, a noble marriage. Dr. Heinrich Thode, an art historian, is about to publish his book on St. Francis of Assisi. The theme of this book agrees with our view of the world. [I quote:] "The art of the Renaissance was not fructified by the excavations, nor by Antiquity, but by the impression made by a great and holy man in whom the life, suffering and death of our Savior was echoed by his own life, suffering and death."* I gladly opened my house . . . and entrusted my child to a man who could feel and think in such terms. He is also publishing a periodical, the purpose of which is to reproduce little-known paintings by the old masters, and to gather material for a new history of art. . . .

Cosima wrote not a word about Blandine, who had become a stranger to her. She is sending a "modest" photograph of her children to

---

*This is misty nonsense. Thode was a better art historian than would be concluded from this quotation. He became a well-known teacher, lecturing on the history of art at the University of Heidelberg. He died in 1920.

the king's secretary, "while asking His Majesty's pardon for everything, for silence and for words." She concluded her letter:

> With all the fervor with which I pray to God that He excise all
> egotism in me so that the spirit whom I must serve will reign
> supreme in my soul and enable me to accomplish that for which I am
> still held on earth, with all the fervor with which I try to achieve the
> temporal well-being of my poor children as well as their eternal
> salvation, with that same fervor I ask God's blessing on the anointed
> head of my King and in this spirit of worship this letter is sent by—
> > Your Majesty's
> > in gratitude expiring
> > most humble servant
> > Cosima Wagner
> > Wahnfried, September 27, 1883

How strange it is that the proud woman would write so fawning a
letter! Perhaps not so strange: it was addressed to a man who now
needed to be fed on honey. Ludwig had lost all interest in the government of his country, had ceased conferring with his ministers, whom
he now called "rabble" and "vermin," and listened only to servants
and stable boys who told him how magnificent he was. He said that
"eight white elephants" would not now drag him to Munich. On June
8, 1886, two government-appointed medical commissions—not one
member of which had actually examined Ludwig—declared him insane. Two days later, he was deposed and held in "protective" captiv-
ity, first in Neuschwanstein, then in Berg. On June 13, escaping his
captors, he drowned. Cosima had not seen him for more than five
years and had only read the account of the declension to which the tall
figure had shrunk, his body clogged with drugs, his hands so unsteady
that when he ate he "splashed gravy and vegetables all over his
clothes" (from the medical report). Like the Empress Elisabeth,
Cosima did not believe him to have been insane. "He should have
been treated with kindlier feeling."

Yet Cosima had neither the emotional strength nor the time to
mourn him for long. Daniela had for months been pressing her to lay
aside her widow's weeds, and make arrangements for her wedding
with Thode. In October of 1885, Cosima promised that Daniela could
marry the following Easter. Yet she still delayed, and it was not at
Easter but on July 3, 1886, less than a month after Ludwig's death, that
the wedding finally took place and guests were welcomed in a reopened Wahnfried.

2

When Cosima decided that *Tristan* was to be her initial venture, she was at first not altogether sure of her own capabilities. Obviously, the man who could best help her was Bülow, the godfather of the work, the man who had conducted its premiere, the man instructed by Wagner. She wrote to Daniela:

> If he [Bülow] happens to talk with you of Bayreuth, and you could manage it *without in the least exciting him*, I wish you'd tell him that I have often thought of applying to him to help me clear up some dubious points. . . . If he agrees, I wouldn't bother him with letters but would ask specific questions. Not many. If he does not agree, let's forget it. I am not all that insecure and I have unlimited confidence in the force which protects our cause. [March 3, 1885]

Bülow said no.

She chose new interpreters for two of the three important participants, for Isolde a young and passionate singer, Rosa Sucher, and for the conductor the young Felix Mottl, who had been one of Wagner's assistants and had then become conductor in Karlsruhe, from where Cosima received enthusiastic reports of his talent. She now called him, telling him that if he wanted to work with her, the word "holiday" needed to be stricken from his vocabulary. She conceived "the enormous" difficulty of a *Tristan* performance to be in the fact that the music expresses so complex an interior life as to render any attempt at outward gesture absurd. "No 'action' could be commensurate with the power of orchestral sound, least of all the 'realistic style,' however well meant. . . ." We must banish everything banal—conventional— and create a new, a loftier convention of our own. Rehearsing with her, Mottl noted in his score many of her instructions. From it we learn with astonishment that Cosima, while preaching fidelity, made changes. Most frequently in the love duet of the second act, she depressed the dynamics, fortissimo becoming forte, forte mezzoforte, etc. This is especially true of woodwind and brass, though often new decrescendo signs were inserted for the strings and at one point, instead of all the lower strings, only *two* violincellos and double basses were to play. She went further: in the last bars of the second act, a slight alteration is made for the first and second trumpet. At the end of the first act she eliminated the cymbal crash.*

---

*The cymbal crash was eliminated in subsequent editions of the *Tristan* score and everybody forgot about it. When Toscanini began his first rehearsal (in 1930), he stopped

Her stage instructions demand "moderation here," "little move-
ment," "suggest only by moving head—no arms," "only one arm," etc.
When in the first act Isolde bids Tristan to wait on her, Cosima noted:
"Movement only with one hand. Proud, aristocratic, *not* exaggerated.
Isolde is used to command."

In general, her efforts, then and in the future, were pointed toward
making the words understandable. One may conclude that she responded more easily to the poetry than to the music.

Rosa Sucher was a fortunate choice; Cosima wrote her as fine a letter
as any artist could wish to receive:

> How often had I been astonished when I heard . . . certain artists
> praised for their dramatic fire and pathos, only to feel coldness and
> opposition within me, which swelled in proportion to their
> exaggerations and efforts! With you, dearest friend, it all seems to
> come so naturally, in art as in life. You give out beauty and warmth.
> . . . [October 22, 1886]

3

Tristan was an artistic success but not a box office draw. Quite a few
seats remained empty that year. But the silence was broken and
Cosima's ambition grew. She would stage *Tannhäuser* next, her conception differing from previous interpretations. She planned new
lighting effects and had the theater converted from gas to electricity,
at a cost of seventy thousand marks.

In a period of activity which extended from 1886 to 1906 and for
251 performances, Cosima worked with nine conductors. To say that
eight of the nine were difficult—the ninth being her son—is to say the
obvious. She felt closest to Felix Mottl, whom she described to Daniela
as "soulful, talented, and firm in character. In addition he has been
endowed with the gift of charm." She judged him to be "a real stage
conductor, who knows how to make the connection between scene
and orchestra." She called him "my minstrel" *("mein Spielmann").*
No doubt she liked his devotion to her, as he expressed it in response
to her invitation:

---

and asked, "Where is the cymbal crash?" Everybody assured him that no such crash was
called for in the score. They showed him various editions. No crash. He insisted on
having Wagner's manuscript brought. There was the crash.

Most Honored Lady:
It goes without saying that I would dedicate my strength and
capabilities in the service of the great cause of Bayreuth! Dispose of
me—I am as ready to conduct *Tristan* as to superintend the opening
and closing of the curtain. . . . [Vienna, June 14, 1886]

Perhaps he was too devoted to her. Felix Weingartner, who that
year assisted at the performances, thought so, thought that he too
readily adopted the broad tempi Cosima preferred. Those broad
tempi became ever broader until she herself objected. Once, she is
said to have exclaimed in her sleep, "Faster, Mottl, faster!" She gladly
paid him five thousand marks a season, not a small sum, especially in
those seasons when Bayreuth was not all that rich. (Other conductors
served without remuneration: Levi, Richter, Karl Muck, later Knap-
pertsbusch and Toscanini.) Over the years, she entrusted many of the
most important first performances to Mottl, yet when he went to New
York one year, in 1903, and later accepted the direction of the Munich
orchestra, the aged Cosima spoke of "betrayal," and though he conducted *Tristan* in Bayreuth in 1906, she refused all his overtures of
reconciliation.

Hermann Levi was the greater artist, and she knew it. It is as easy
to understand why she liked him less as it is difficult to understand his
character. She worked with him, joked with him, ate with him, discussed her sorrows and hopes with him—and plagued him, pressing
on that one "defect" until he became ashamed of it and got to be, if
only unconsciously, an anti-Semitic Jew.

He tried to escape her, but couldn't; like an intellectual Circe, she
held him in her sway. One night four years after Wagner's death, it
came to a serious disagreement. The next morning she wrote him a
long, long letter, replete with pleas—and with real affection:

Yesterday I could not find the right words and not even a tear could I
shed to console myself. In former years I would have run after you
and would have talked so long, tried so hard to persuade you,
complained, scolded—until you would have gone crazy. Now I am old
. . . and the only ability I still possess is that of introspection. . . . Weak
as I am and miserable, I will try to free you of the delusion which
obsesses you. I would not do it, I would merely lament and grieve, if
you were not an artist, and as such, part of an art which is a religion.
You need no other. Just because you serve this art in terrible pain,
you are chosen as its most apt servant. Just because you do not feel
yourself worthy to perform this sacred service—as you ingenuously
confessed to me—you prove that you are destined for it.

Consider the road you have come: you ought to praise heaven! You
belong to a race which is completely worldly and seeks its goal in

reputation, fame, etc. Yet you have arrived at a complete
understanding of our art, while totally belittling your own merits.
How do *we* look, we who in our early youth were given the benefit of
teachings and examples which we then forget? . . . There is nothing
sadder than the "Now-and-then Christian." [August 6, 1887]

She went on for pages and it all came down to "Remain with me,
for the sake of Wagner."

When Levi was attacked, as he often was during his long stewardship, Cosima ignored the attacks contemptuously. She defined his
usefulness to Bayreuth in four points: "1. His great intellectual culture,
which enabled him to understand the *Collected Works* [of Wagner].
2. His conscientiousness in practical matters, so that he lightened
Adolf Gross's complicated task (i.e., the engagement of orchestra players). 3. His generosity, not only refusing a stipend but contributing
largely to our Fund. 4. His comprehension of the purpose of our
School." (Cosima established a school for performing artists. It never
amounted to much.)

She valued him and yet could not conquer the feeling that he was
a "stranger." He loved her and yet could not conquer the insecurity
and resentment she had fostered in him. He wrote her: "I do not know
what will become of me when one day I will approach *Parsifal* not
from the artistic, but from an even higher standpoint. For the present
I won't let it overwhelm me, just as I firmly march past church doors,
though—or rather *because*—I am irresistibly drawn to enter." (September 3, 1887) She wrote to him: "How can you be so fainthearted?
You, who have devoted your whole being to our cause and have
accomplished your task brilliantly? I am afraid that my way of expressing myself . . . has added to your perplexity, but never should my
virulence be interpreted as condemnation or a wish for separation.
. . . Nobody could serve our cause better than you. I do not believe that
the Prelude to the third act of *Parsifal*—no, the whole third act—will
ever sound as magnificent as under your direction." (August 6, 1887)
He answered: "To whom should you let yourself go if not to me?"

And so he remained not only her *Parsifal* conductor but her chief
artistic adviser. At the end of the 1891 festival, he told her: "I have had
enough—let me go. My shoulders are now too weak. You said to me
often, seriously and jokingly, that I am the cross you have to bear to
the end. But when is the end? Why not today?" (August 30, 1891) She
answered: "I meant it in full earnestness when I said that we two must
bear each other—however we differ in our points of view, however
different are the roads we pursue. . . . You are ill and wounded? My
God, who is not? Have we not learned to look on life as a wound?

. . . No more than I could voluntarily end my life could I separate myself from the task allotted to me." (September 3, 1891) Again she cast her spell. He remained for another three years. In 1894, he wrote to her:

> It has become a dogma in Wahnfried that a Jew has certain physical characteristics, that he thinks in a certain way, acts in a certain way, and above all that he is incapable of unselfish dedication. Everything I do and say is judged by this precept, everything is considered offensive or at least strange. I will not censure anybody for this judgment. I know quite well the content of *Judaism in Music* and share the view of that glorious book [!]. But to demand that I ascribe all the characteristics of the Jews to myself—that I protest against. I know that my own nature is very different.

Her relation to Hans Richter was quite unproblematical. Since he had been taught by Wagner and since he conducted the first *Ring,* she decided he had to be retained as one of the Bayreuth regulars. But she was skeptical. She felt he was too easygoing, too *"gemütlich"* in temperament, too Viennese. He was a stout, foursquare man with a foursquare beard. What's more, he was very sure of himself, and when she called him for *Die Meistersinger* in 1888, he was supposed to have told her that he would come only if "nobody was going to meddle in musical questions." She seems to have been afraid of him, though she acknowledged that he knew "the tradition," and though she lauded him to his face. When he was inspired, he was able to produce passionate and beautiful performances. Mottl, Bülow, and Mahler voiced some reservations about him, but the judgments of fellow conductors can hardly be taken at a baton's value. Richter was active in Bayreuth until 1912.

In 1892, Cosima invited Karl Muck, that thundering disciplinarian of the concert hall, to Bayreuth. He conducted a rehearsal of *Die Meistersinger,* smoking one cigarette after another, and Cosima didn't like what she heard. Without hesitation, she got rid of him, ignoring his plea that he had not shown himself at his best in unfamiliar and confusing surroundings and that he be given a second chance. Not until 1901 was he recalled, and then to conduct *Parsifal.* But Cosima never liked him personally. A Teutonic panjandrum, he was not easy to like.

It was different with Richard Strauss. She engaged him in 1891 as rehearsal conductor and three years later he took over *Tannhäuser.* She quickly recognized that "his personality is most impressive, his intelligence high, his ability undoubted." She became fond of the high-strung young man, as thin as a rope but strutting with energy, who when he was not conducting played cards all night. She was supposed to have said to him, "Well, well, so modern, yet he conducts *Tannhäuser* beautifully." He worked in Bayreuth only one season and did not return until 1933, taking over *Parsifal* after Toscanini had refused to have anything to do with Hitler's Germany.

To her decisions as to who was worthy of lifting the baton, unseen in the sunken pit, she admitted little tolerance or allowance for temporary nervousness. When Siegfried, her beloved Siegfried, first faced the orchestra in 1896, there she was, criticizing him with such severity that his sisters deemed it "an act of immeasurable hardness, even cruelty." In 1900, Isolde married Franz Beidler, a conductor. Four years previously, Beidler, like Strauss before him, had functioned as musical assistant. Mottl and Richter taught him. Richter thought well of him. Cosima asked Mahler in Vienna—the Mahler who was "unusable" for Bayreuth—to take him on as a "voluntary helper" so he could gain further experience. She studied *Tristan* with Beidler. He went to Moscow to conduct Wagner, with apparent success. Then, in 1904, came the trial by fire: he was to conduct the *Ring*. Cosima fretted, and after the performance in 1906 she dismissed him, dismissed him with wounding words: "You have an aptitude for being a decent conductor. Technically you lack a lot. . . . Try for a position where by working hard you can acquire what is missing. You have precision, certainty, force. What you don't have is tenderness, feeling, ecstasy." (August 11, 1906)

4

The wish to discuss consecutively Cosima's relations with her principal conductors has disturbed the chronology. To return to her second effort: she had a special love for *Tannhäuser;* it was not unlikely that she felt in herself something of Elisabeth and something of Venus. She was oblivious of the work's faults: the whipped-up Meyerbeerian close of the first act, the pompousness of Landgrave Hermann, the cloying sentimentality of Elisabeth's prayer. Wagner had written many years before that he had created the work as a musician who was striving toward the drama, and he realized that he had not been entirely successful in forging the union. Cosima now wanted to prove that she could give the work homogeneity. She not only studied text and score afresh, but she reread the poetry of the German troubadours, the Minnesingers, and she collected forty-four photographs of the "Clothed Aphrodite" in the Pergamon Museum to help her dress the Venus. She was in touch with experts on the Middle Ages in Dresden, Paris, and Vienna, to advise her on the materials, ornaments, emblems, and weapons that the guests in the Wartburg were to wear. She conceived *Tannhäuser* as a drama of two opposing ideologies: the sensuousness and decadence of the antique world versus the idealism and purity of the Christian Middle Ages. To stage the Venusberg scene, she consulted, among others, Wilhelm Bode, the famous art authority, under whose direction the Berlin Museum grew into one of the great museums of the world. In the bacchanale she presented, in explicit pantomime, Leda and the swan, Europa and the bull, the three Graces, Hercules and the snake, Hebe and Ganymede, plus an assortment of sixty-four cavorting fauns, satyrs, bacchantes, sirens, nymphs, naiads, tritons, all being athletically seductive. Judging by the extant photographs, the scene, overgrown by exotic foliage, was a mess. A similar overpopulation beset the "Christian" acts: 116 guests, each followed by three servants, were invited to Landgrave Hermann's party, to mingle with thirty knights. With patient effort, Cosima tried to give individual characteristics to each guest and to vary each greeting. She wanted no bedraggled supernumeraries. She had called back Julius Kniese to train the chorus musically, ignoring her feud with him. The shock of the guests at Tannhäuser's revelation, their attack on him, the fervor of the pilgrims (seventy-two of them), the great climax of Act II, were superbly realized. Yet, to quote Nietzsche, too much industry enchained the imagination. The act reminded one critic of a military drill.

Mottl conducted. The Elisabeth was a good-looking young girl, a newcomer, Pauline de Ahna. When Richard Strauss conducted *Tannhäuser* three years later, he fell in love with her and married her. Ernest Newman tells us that one interpreter of Elisabeth wished to enter the Hall of the Minstrels, the *teure Halle*, with her arms raised ecstatically. Cosima said, "No!" During the rehearsals she obediently kept her arms down; her singing teacher, however, advised her that on the night of the performance she should indulge in the "effective" gesture. The night came, the singer tried to reach for the ceiling—in vain! Cosima had sewn up the sleeves of her robe.

Cosima was extremely sensitive to criticism of her work. Three weeks after the last performance of the 1891 season, when she was recuperating from her efforts in Lucerne, she wrote a ten-page letter to Georg Davidsohn, editor of the *Börsen Courier* of Berlin (the letter is now in the Morgan Library):

> It is inevitable that the musical opulence of the first scene render that of the subsequent scene pallid, not to mention the second and even the third act. Therefore if we succeeded in presenting the [Christian] figures in their tragic fate, as well as the life of the Middle Ages, our effort would serve as an antidote to the magic Venus music. The sincerity of the welcome given to Tannhäuser [in the second scene], the simplicity and clarity of the language, the avoidance of everything . . . which could remind one of a [conventional] Septet, such was our goal. Only those who have lived through the usual performances could suspect how much work is hidden in this seemingly simple scene. . . .

Whatever Wagner might have thought of this, and whatever Herr Davidsohn thought of it, there is no question that *Tannhäuser* was a great success with the international public which was flocking in increasing numbers to Bayreuth. Cosima wrote to her friend Bodo von Knesebeck, head of the German Red Cross:

> A curious satisfaction lies in observing crowds of people approach, silent but determined. The demand for reservations for the Festival indicates just that. In April we had more than three and a half times the number of requests than for the preceding Festival. . . . And I'd like to mention that in 1882 (shame on the world!) we spent 13,000 marks for advertising, in 1886, 7,000 marks, and this year virtually nothing. . . .

> What crazy notions come along with the requests! A few wish to inspect Wahnfried, including inhabitants, but care nothing about the performances. Others want to undergo a cure in the mountain air of the Bavarian Alps, near Bayreuth. A Mrs. Burnett, who is supposed to be the richest woman in England, wants to rent my house—price no object. Some American girls are disappointed: they braved the perils of the crossing *only* to see Alvary as Tannhäuser [two other tenors sang it in addition]. . . . [May 8, 1891]

Yet in spite of sold-out houses, the staging of *Tannhäuser* proved so costly—some sixty thousand marks—that the season showed a deficit.

CHAPTER XII

———————◆———————

The Chatelaine

"For there is in this world in which everything wears out, everything perishes, one thing that crumbles into dust, that destroys itself still more completely, leaving behind still fewer traces of itself than Beauty: namely Grief."—Marcel Proust

THE WIDOW'S GRIEF had become an illusion, expressed in her still wearing black more often than colors and in her avoiding current fashion, presenting herself in clothes cut in the style of a past decade, which signalized to those who saw her that she had come from afar. Her hair had grown back the purest white; she covered it with a black lace shawl. She was very pale and had grown thinner, and though her eyes seemed smaller and her nose larger, her face was still unwrinkled and retained much of its beauty, had, in fact, gained in impressiveness. She bore herself as erect as ever, and her walk was still decisive.

Having passed her fiftieth birthday, she wrote to her old friend Ludwig Schemann, who was ill. She adjured him "not to let anything distract him from taking care of himself." As to herself:

My health is quite good, but my eyes have become so wretched that I cannot read anymore. At first this seemed a great privation, now it seems an advantage, since I hear everything through the melodious voices of my children. Apropos "distracting"—my grandchild [Blandine's Manfred] takes care of that. He couldn't care less if my day is filled with worry or anxiety—what he wants is to be constantly entertained. That helps. . . . [August 1, 1888]

Her dedication to Wagner had turned into a memory consciously evoked. It was no longer—it could not be—a clutching hurt which came unbidden, but rather a gentle tremor she summoned when she wanted to. She was now, so to speak, "on her own," no longer his missionary but an independent oracle. After the years of adapting herself first to Liszt, then to Bülow, then to Wagner, she now expected the world to adapt itself to her, and she used past grief to force obeisance and obedience from her workers and her children. The festival became a "property," belonging more to her than to its founder. "We have decided." "We know the tradition."

No doubt, Cosima honestly thought she was continuing Wagner's wishes with pristine correctness—the Wagner who said after the first *Ring*, "Next time we'll do everything differently." She worked tirelessly, with long rehearsals and long discussions, to preserve what she believed to be the "purity" of the performances. But at best these performances were carbon copies, often very legible carbon copies, but carbon copies all the same. "That was how we did *Tristan* in Munich," she proclaimed. "Isolde stood at the left and made this gesture." To Carl Perron, who was the Gurnemanz in 1889 and who wanted to discuss with her "his concept" of the role, she said: "My dear friend, we have no 'concepts' in Bayreuth. Phrase according to sense, pronounce each word distinctly, observe the indicated rhythm exactly! Then you've done your part; everything else is contained in the work itself." To a degree, that sounds reasonable. But not really. It ignores the recreative contribution of the actor, the personal commitment, without which a performance becomes devoid of life. No good stage director would ignore the individuality of the man or woman up on the stage. The interpreter *must* have a "concept."

Besides, Cosima did not have all that many examples on which to draw. What had she witnessed? The superb *Tristan* under Bülow, a good *Meistersinger*, one experimental *Ring*, an incompletely realized *Parsifal*. Hardly enough to establish *"the* tradition" on which she insisted. That tradition, such as it was—or rather such as she *thought* it was—developed hardening of the arteries. In the years of her stewardship, acting styles changed, the change led by Otto Brahm in Berlin and by Konstantin Stanislavski in Moscow, while Gordon Craig was waiting in the wings. They served the new plays: Ibsen's *The Wild Duck, Hedda Gabler,* and *Ghosts,* Tolstoi's *The Power of Darkness,* Strindberg's *The Father* and *Julie,* Chekhov's *The Sea Gull* and *Uncle Vanya,* Wilde's *Lady Windermere's Fan* and *The Importance of Being Earnest,* Shaw's *Mrs. Warren's Profession* and *Candida,* Wedekind's *Spring's Awakening,* Hauptmann's *The Weavers*—all produced before the turn of the century.

Lording it over conductors and singers, Cosima was impervious to the new influences. If Wagner's works were to be regarded not merely as "concerts" but as music *and* drama (as he had wanted them to be regarded), they needed to be brought into accord with new stage conceptions—and new audiences. This was recognized by some who were not overawed by Bayreuth's temple aura, among them Bernard Shaw, who wrote that Cosima "has no other function except the illegitimate one of chief remembrancer." Shaw, the perfect Wagnerite, wrote as early as 1889:

> The law of traditional performances is, "Do what was done last time"; the law of all living and fruitful performance is, "Obey the innermost impulse which the music gives, and obey it to the most exhaustive satisfaction." And as that impulse is never, in a fertile artistic nature, the impulse to do what was done last time, the two laws are incompatible, being virtually laws respectively of death and life in art. Bayreuth has chosen the law of death. Its boast is that it alone has the pure and complete tradition—or, as I prefer to put it, that it alone is in a position to strangle Wagner's lyric dramas note by note, bar by bar, *nuance* by *nuance.* . . .
>
> Wagner is now dead, absent, and indifferent. The powerful, magnetic personality, with all the tension it maintained, is gone; and no manipulation of the dead hand on the keys can ever reproduce the living touch. Even if such reproduction were possible, who, outside Bayreuth, would be imposed on by the shallow assumption that the Bayreuth performances fulfilled Wagner's whole desire? We can well believe that in justice to those who so loyally helped him, he professed himself satisfied when the most that could be had been done—nay, that after the desperate makeshifts with which he had had to put up in his long theatrical experience, he was genuinely delighted to find that so much was possible. But the unwieldy toy dragon, emitting its puff of steam when its mouth opened, about as impressively as a mechanical doll says "Mamma": did that realize the poet's vision of Fafner? And the trees which walk off the stage in *Parsifal:* can the poorest imagination see nothing better by the light of Wagner's stage direction in the score than that? Is the gaudy ballet and unspeakable flower garden in the second act to be the final interpretation of the visionary bowers of Klingsor? . . . [*The English Illustrated Magazine,* October 1889]

*German caricature, 1890. Cosima as a Valkyrie bringing home the tenor
Van Dyck; the inscription on the flag reads "Gold seduces."*

Returning to Bayreuth five years later, Shaw observed:

It is true that German singers at Bayreuth do not know how to sing: they shout; and you can see them make a vigorous stoop and lift with their shoulders, like coalheavers, when they have a difficult note to tackle, a *pianissimo* on any note above the staff being impossible to them. . . .

Singing there, in fact, is exactly like public speaking in England—not a fine art, but a means of placing certain ideas intelligibly and emphatically before the public without any preoccupation as to beauty of voice or grace of manner.

The music-dramas are, so to speak, effectively debated; and the exposition of the poetic theme has all the qualities of a good Budget speech; but there is just about as much charm of voice and style as there is at a conference of the National Liberal Federation. [*Music in London,* August 1, 1894]

He was not alone. Lilli Lehmann returned to Bayreuth in 1896 to sing Brünnhilde in a new *Ring* staging by Cosima. Lilli had plenty to say about these performances in her book of reminiscences, *Mein Weg.* She thought most of the actors behaved like "soulless wooden dolls." While the swimming machinery worked better than in 1876 (when Lehmann sang one of the Rhine Maidens), the costumes for the daughters of the deep were ridiculous—Shaw, too, observed that they were clothed as proper Victorian girls out for a stroll, and if they had carried parasols it would not have been amiss—while Freia looked "Japanese like Yum-Yum."

Lehmann praised Cosima's intelligence and industry, but "heart is missing." In 1876, "Individuality played an important role. The Master allowed everybody to express his own." Now: "All roads lead to Rome—only one to the Bayreuth of today: slavish submission!" One would be tempted to take her remarks with a grain of salt, since it is obvious that she disliked Cosima, were it not that others echoed her. In 1888, the distinguished critic of the *Allgemeine Musik-Zeitung,* Otto Lessmann, wrote:

Tradition—it is a tricky thing. Without fresh spirit it leads to stagnation. And stagnant was, e.g., the first scene of the *Meistersinger.* The exaggerated play of facial grimaces between Eva and Walther during the church service struck one as highly inartistic. . . . Magdalene would have had to be an idiot—or a determined procuress—if she failed twice to notice the knight addressing Eva. . . .

If one remembers what grace informed the scene of the Flower Maidens in 1882, one is shocked by the present lack of charm in a scene which so easily can become a caricature.

In 1899, when the young Thomas Beecham paid his first visit to Bayreuth with as much awe as inspired a journey "to some shrine such as that of Thomas à Becket at Canterbury in the Middle Ages," he found that "the singing, playing and stage production all fell below the level I had previsioned." Besides, he observed that "the inevitable crowd of cranks and faddists swelled the ranks of worshippers and the bookshops overflowed with literary curiosities, some of them linking up the music dramas with every 'ism' in philosophy, politics, science, and even hygiene, one bright effort going so far as to allege that *Parsifal* was less of an art work than a piece of propaganda for the higher vegetarianism and not to be comprehended fully unless accepted as such."

New personalities, such as the conductor Felix Weingartner, took leave to differ with the views held by the chatelaine of the Festspielhaus, who acted as if she alone were privy to arcane secrets. He wrote:

Four laws reign in Wahnfried: 1. You must accept as Gospel whatever House Wahnfried decrees. 2. Even if occasionally you hold a dissenting opinion, you must under no circumstances voice such an opinion. 3. Siegfried Wagner is a great conductor, regisseur, poet, and composer. You are to proclaim him as such and you are to do your best to persuade others to think so. 4. He who does not obey the above-mentioned laws is to be persecuted mercilessly, calumnized, wiped out by silence, and under no condition are you to have any communication with him.

All that made no difference to the ever-growing success of Bayreuth. To undertake a pilgrimage to the inaccessible spot became the thing to do, and there was to be found, in Thomas Beecham's words, the "familiar crowd of knickerbockered sportsmen, gaitered bishops, and equine-visaged ladies." One needed to hear, study, discuss Wagner's work to be counted among the avant-garde of culture: in Bayreuth, where his music dramas were offered in their full version and often convincingly, whatever the shortcomings, one could best receive the revelation. Even Shaw, iconoclast *par excellence,* admitted that some of the performances seemed "miracles of preparedness" compared to those at Covent Garden, "at which half the attention of the singers is given to the prompter, half to the conductor, and the rest to the character impersonated." The least one may say in Cosima's defense is that she tried to preserve Wagner's ideal of taking the theater "seriously," of regarding it as a festival rite, as the Athenians did, in the hope that it would help audiences to live life more intensely and would lift men and women from the anxious humdrum to the secure realm of myth.

Cosima wrote: "The number of habitués is remarkable. They come from everywhere and the first rows is their habitat. All of them are demanding, especially the nobility, which shows its overweening insolence. Often enough I loathe taking up my pen when I have to write something agreeable to a presumptuous Highness or a hysterical Princess. . . ." She didn't do it often.

Her inflexibility as guardian was companioned by a set of hard-cooked judgments on diverse subjects, her opinions stemming not so much from advancing age, not so much from early-formed prejudices, as from a desire to keep alive the memory of, and feel close to, the great man she had loved. His opinions, right or wrong. Renoir was a worthless dauber, *Carmen* the acme of vulgarity (which had *not* been Wagner's opinion), the French had no national epic, no national hero, and while their poetry contained charm and pleasant ideas, it cannot be compared to the creation of the German Minnesingers. Perhaps out of the same loyalty, she was suspicious of *anybody* who brought new ideas to the theater. Albert Schweitzer, who admired her because she showed an astonishing grasp of Bach's music, brought Gordon Craig to see her. Craig, the great reformer of the modern theater, told her his vision of staging Wagner, conceiving certain scenes as wild phenomena of nature. She smiled tolerantly and commented, with a wave of her hand, "He is still very young." That ended the conversation.

She dismissed as peremptorily Appia's ideas in his essay "The Staging of the *Ring of the Nibelungen.*" "Nothing in it for 'us,' " she wrote, "since all the stage directions are clearly marked in the score. *Perhaps* something for France, but they, too, would do better to hew closely to the indications of the poem."

She did invite Isadora Duncan to mime the first Grace in a performance of *Tannhäuser,* and to restage the Bacchanale. She was not altogether happy with the famous Isadora: "While she thinks about the music, she is not musical and does not dance rhythmically. . . . She belittles the importance of the right costume and surely her figure needs a flattering costume. Nevertheless, contradictions, stubbornness, limitations notwithstanding, we have a personality before us of true artistic importance. . . ." Yet Isadora Duncan was not invited back.

Cosima was ever careful to polish away the smudges on her idol. The smudges being many, it was a task like that of the Sorcerer's Apprentice. In 1902, a new and large collection of Wagner memorabilia came to light, offered for sale by an autograph dealer for eleven hundred marks. Cosima wrote to Adolf Gross:

My faithful Adolf:
Once again I bespeak your counsel, indeed your decision. You are careful and will know, better than I, what we can do without exceeding the money at our disposal. . . . I'm willing to let everything go, however much I want to have everything, except those letters which would feed the appetite of the scandalmongers. If you think we ought not to spend the 1,100 marks this year, I would *renounce*—
   1. The letters to the King.
   2. Letters of the Schnorrs from the Tristan period.
   3. The 40 letters to Ludwig Schnorr.
I would buy—
   1. The letters to Frau Schnorr.
   2. The letters of Frau Schnorr to Bülow.
   3. The fantasies of that Fräulein Reuthern [*sic*] (chief font of the gossip).
   4. Correspondence between Herr and Frau Schnorr.
[September 17, 1902]

Obviously, Cosima was still trying to bury the Malvina Schnorr episode full fathom five. But it is curious that she was unwilling to spend the money it took to get all the documents. The personal fortune of the Wagner family that year amounted to two and a quarter million marks. Couldn't she afford eleven hundred marks?

Around that time, too, she was much occupied with thoughts of Nietzsche. Her hurt transpires in her remarks to Houston Stewart Chamberlain, on the occasion of the publication of Nietzsche's letters:

I marvel that nobody has recognized that a man such as he, he who decried all the people who were kind to him and indeed insulted them, he who derogates his fatherland, he who belittles his mother tongue without inventing one of his own, he who poses as a prophet, must be either a monster or insane. . . . I marvel as well that nobody has pointed out where he got his ideas. First in [Wagner's] "Collected Works," then Schopenhauer, the Encyclopedists, the British, etc. Even the word "Superman" comes from Goethe! The poor fellow was already ill when I met him: he constantly complained of headaches. . . . [August 14, 1900]

To her friend Prince Hohenlohe, she had written:

I am very glad that you found pleasure in Nietzsche's "Thoughts Out of Season." When he read the work to me, I found it profound in its

ideas, while its language could be regarded as classical. Of his later
published works I read nothing. I found him already in '76, when we
met him in Sorrento, diseased and at war with himself. It is difficult
not to indulge in irony when one learns that his *only* popular writings
are those influenced by disease. Or is there a connection here? Is the
popular conception of the Devil based on some truth? [February 4,
1894]

Soon after, Nietzsche was dead. Cosima wrote to Malwida von Mey-
senbug, her friend and Nietzsche's:

I have read your essays on "The First Nietzsche" (I would be tempted
to say "The *Only* Nietzsche"), and I was deeply moved. . . . A truthful
portrait arose at the very moment when he finally, finally, was set free
of his suffering. . . . Most remarkable in "The First Nietzsche" is his
modesty. His later megalomania, as it showed itself in his letters to
Stein, proves that the poor and unfortunate man reached beyond
himself. He should have remained a teacher in Basel, as he confessed
to you so touchingly. [October 8, 1900]

Cosima misunderstood him, but now, letting time transport her
back to Triebschen, she wept for him. He was a tragic example of the
nearness of madness and genius, she wrote.

The poet Maria Ebner-Eschenbach said that as we grow old, our
hearts become a graveyard. Cosima was surrounded by cenotaphs.
Liszt had died in 1886, three years after Wagner. Now, twelve years
later, Liszt's letters were being published, and Ludwig Schermann
wrote a commemorative essay which he sent her. She thanked him,
but pointed out that he had criticized Liszt's operatic transcriptions
unnecessarily:

Concerning the transcriptions, I submit for your consideration (though
I quite understand your doubts) that my father made the mistake of
regarding the appearance of Meyerbeer as a significant sign of a
meaningful dramatic art. He saw in him a representative of serious
drama, against Italian opera and *opéra comique.* Only when he
became acquainted with our works [!] did Meyerbeer become a
stranger. Meyerbeer said bitterly: *"La seule scène d'Allemagne où Le
Prophète n'a pas été donné, c'est Weimar; il est vrai que j'y ai un
ami."* My father, faithful to his first impression, then transcribed those
motifs from *Le Prophète* which seemed to him the most adaptable.
These transcriptions belong to a genre of music which by their
masterful treatment and their ideas have so enriched pianistic
literature that no pianist these days plays a concert without including
at least one piece in his program. He wanted to demonstrate the
possibilities of sound which lie inherent in the piano and of what he
himself was capable in technique and execution. That I do not ascribe

any special importance to these pieces goes without saying. He didn't
either, even if he did work them out carefully and conscientiously (in
the last period chiefly for his students). [April 29, 1896]

The next year Brahms died, and she wrote to Richter:

My dear and honored friend:
The gentlemen of "The Society of the Friends of Music" did me the
honor to inform me of the death of Brahms. I know no one better or
apter to bring to them my expression of thanks than you, true friend
of our house. I ask you to do this. Because for many years I have
absented myself from concert life, I am totally ignorant of the works
of the dead man. With the exception of one chamber work, I have not
listened to the music which has brought him so great a reputation and
wide a fame. I knew him only casually, having met him in the
director's loge in Vienna, where he asked to be introduced to me. I
am, however, not unaware that his attitude toward our art was noble
and kind. His intelligence was too great not to recognize that which
essentially seemed strange to him. His character was too fine-grained
to indulge in animosities. . . . [April 7, 1897]

Was this one of her "diplomatic" letters? She had earlier called his
character gross, his music boring, and it is unlikely that she had
changed her mind.

With a melancholy half egotistical and half loving, she witnessed the
death of Friedrich Feustel in 1891. She remembered "with soft emotion his first visit in the autumn of '71, his energetic grasping of a cause
which then seemed hopeless, his counsel in all difficulties, and his faith
when all went awry. . . . One does not lose a being like him. One draws
the account of his worth and regards him with one's inner vision, when
the corporeal eye can no longer behold him." (Letter to Prince
Hohenlohe, October 13, 1891)

2

Her work kept her in life, her children brought her joy mixed with
worry. They had been so imbued with the pride of belonging to Wahnfried that they felt themselves royalty, and like royalty they were
jealous of one another but united in clustering around the throne. Fidi,
it was decided, would become not an architect but a musician. Cosima
sent him to Humperdinck in Frankfurt, adjuring the composer to
teach her son "a thorough analysis both technical and intellectual of
the classic works, including Mozart and the French School." She wrote
to Humperdinck:

I perceive from his joy—which is a great satisfaction to me—how well you have led him to the magnificent realm of Mozart. It would have pained me if my son had not properly appreciated the creations which preceded the works of the most perfect art. If you agree, study *Figaro* with him next, the opera which seems to me even more extraordinary in its use of the orchestra than *The Magic Flute,* though personally I prefer the latter because of its fullness of melody. Then, I think, you ought to take up *Fidelio,* which in my opinion is not the equal of Mozart's operas, though certain parts (Prelude to Act II, the final chorus) are truly Beethoven—which means that they are unsurpassable. After that *Iphigénie.* . . . [June 2, 1890]

In 1892—an especially strenuous year for Cosima, *Parsifal* being given with Levi, *Tristan, Tannhäuser,* and *Meistersinger* with Mottl, in all *twenty* performances—Daniela was married; Blandine of the sunny disposition was content with her husband in sunny Sicily; Eva, twenty-five years old and very pretty, danced attendance on her mother and became her favorite daughter; but Isolde, now twenty-seven, restless and resentful, suddenly wanted to secede and absent herself from Cosima's idea of felicity. She knew she was illegitimate and she felt her birth as shameful. There was no man in her life—none of significance, at least—and she never again wanted to hear a note of Wagner's music; she was sick of Wahnfried idolatry and Wahnfried solemnity; she wanted to get away, away into a world where she might wash off the thin layer of inherited fame and become Isolde Somebody, living on her own and earning her own livelihood. She packed up and went to Rome. Cosima would not, or perhaps could not, stop her. But she missed her, worried about her, and soon attempted to call her back:

My beloved child:
I remember the day when you greeted the world with a joyful scream. I remember your childhood as a beautiful gift awarded to me. How charmingly and willingly did you cling to me, from the first moment on! How content you were, demanding nothing, annoying nobody! You seemed to possess that rare and divine gift, harmlessness. And you possessed it so richly that I could not but believe that God sent you to me at a time when my own existence was full of harm, in order to assure me that everything would come out all right in the end.

However much I concerned myself with your elder sisters, pondering how best to guide them, about *you* I never worried. You seemed to have inherited from your grandfather [Liszt] that outgoing friendliness which accounted for his very special geniality. You were so malleable, so easily guided. Everywhere you felt at home, so that you reminded me of grandfather, to whom it was all the same whether he sat in a nest like Weimar or dwelt in Rome. I thought you were destined for what I define as true happiness.

Now you have fled from me. At every word I spoke to you I asked myself whether you were really listening to me. When you answered me in heated words, I had to realize that I had lost what once was so infinitely precious to me.

I thought about this. Every one of us is born with his individual character. The second phase is the coming together of one's character with the world. The third phase—the decisive one—is the interaction, the influence of the world on one's character. I believe that an exceptional character, like yours, is harmed by contact with the world. The world has bewildered you. Believe me, if I felt that you were content, I would not say this to you. You have placed yourself, so to speak, above the universal law. You make demands—and forget that all relations are based on mutuality.

It seems to me that you have come to the end of a cul-de-sac and I choose your birthday to try to recall to you the true purpose of our lives. Bayreuth is our plot of ground, from there springs our well-being. There is our blessing to be found, there Fidi completes his studies, there a daughter of Wahnfried can through marriage establish her own home. . . . Those are our circumstances, my child; away from Bayreuth we have no business, away from Wahnfried we can find absolutely nothing, and our pride must consist in knowing this.

Will you be able to accept the fact that I will, more ineluctably than ever, be bound to Bayreuth? Except for eight or ten days—which this winter I spent in Berlin, where we had little diversion, save seeing Kekulés [an archaeologist] and Helmholtz [the scientist]—I do not intend ever to leave my home. Do you want to share my lot, along with Eva? Do you want to aid my work? Do you want a home? Or do you want to lead your life in your separate way? Even if you do, I am convinced you can develop and ripen your gifts, provided you are not sullied by vain illusions.

When grandfather left us in Berlin—to be sure, under the most modest circumstances—he spoke to my sister and me with such harshness as to make us feel annihilated. We had been there hardly a month when we blessed his severity. Today I know that I have him to thank when I am able easily to get along with everybody. He said to us: "You are tolerably pretty and not untalented, but don't imagine that gives you the smallest right to expect anything from anybody. The only thing which would earn you such a right is the consideration you show everybody you meet, the respect for individuality, whether that of person, country, class or whatever." . . . Once somebody maliciously reported to him that we were comparing Berlin to Paris and were making fun of Berlin. He came from Weimar and asked us whether we didn't know how a guest in a foreign land ought to behave and who had given us the *"asinine right"* to judge conditions or people. He thought us exceedingly stupid and wrong-headed.

If I tell you this it is only to make you realize that everybody has to go to school, that all of us must ask ourselves who we are, of what we are capable, where we belong, so that we may find the right connection with others. . . .

It is most fortunate that Boni, through her husband, now belongs to the aristocracy—the most highly placed—and that in Italy she could introduce you into the world of which you are so enamored.

But this was but a worldly and superficial advantage, and would fail to offer Isolde complete satisfaction. No; her proper place was in Bayreuth.

. . . Let us suppose that today you close your second phase and turn, like the great geniuses, to the third, ascending with all your strength to your real self. All hail to the third period! In Beethoven it summed itself up in *Freude, schöner Götterfunken!*

Freude—that you brought me when you came into the world. Willingly would I bear any troubles if I could say to myself that today you were to return to joy and peace from the purblindness of estrangement. God bless you, my beloved child. May the rays of a mother's love and thought illumine your heart!

Mama
[April 10, 1892]

Isolde did return to Bayreuth after further and fruitless attempts at independence. After a while she fell in love with a man of whom Cosima disapproved violently; Isolde was not strong enough to stand up to her mother and the affair was broken off. On the rebound, she married the next man who showed any interest in her. Ironically, he was a conductor, Franz Beidler. On his part it was probably a union not compelled entirely by the transports of love. His career, such as it was, was helped by Cosima. He and Isolde had a son, Wilhelm, but the marriage was not successful, nor were mother and daughter ever truly reconciled. Siegfried, too, disliked Beidler. "About Bayreuth," he wrote him, "you comprehend virtually nothing." Isolde and Beidler moved out and established a home away from Wahnfried. Cosima, wounded but still seeking adjustment, wrote her daughter: "Let us be separated so that we may remain united." Isolde was to rebuff her crassly.

In official documents, such as her passport, Isolde had always been designated as Bülow's daughter; she signed herself "Isolde von

Bülow," and she had inherited part of Bülow's fortune. When she married, Cosima stipulated that she was to receive a yearly stipend of ten thousand marks, exactly the sum that Eva and Siegfried were receiving. Even more, whenever she wanted additional money, it was forthcoming without a murmur. (From 1910 to 1913, it amounted to nearly thirty thousand marks.) Her income was equivalent to the salary of a Bavarian state minister.

Time passed and in the year 1913 the copyright of Wagner's works expired. Isolde then demanded of Cosima that she be legally declared Wagner's child, so that on Cosima's death she could claim her share of the Wagner fortune, which at that time amounted to some five million marks. True, she wanted security for her son more than for herself—she was already stricken with tuberculosis and marked for death—true, she wanted the satisfaction of bearing the famous name; but it is safe to conjecture that she wanted still more to hurt her mother. Cosima begged her not to drag out for public scrutiny and the leer of the journalists the long-hidden secrets of "her most intimate life," and Siegfried, acting on his mother's behalf, offered to increase Isolde's income to 22,000 marks, pay for a cure in Davos, and guarantee sufficient money for her son's education. The bribe was proposed in vain. Isolde insisted on public and legal acknowledgment of her paternity. Should she be refused, she would "proceed with a lawsuit which would besmirch the name of Wagner ineradicably." Cosima answered: "My child, I received your letter and the enclosure. You have created a situation which must be handled by a lawyer. Therefore I have forwarded your letter to Counsellor Troll. Your mother."

When the case came before the court, Cosima had to testify that "from June 12, 1864, to October 12, 1864, she had lived in intimate relations with no one but Wagner"; but a housekeeper employed by Wagner in that year deposed that at Starnberg Cosima was still sharing a bedroom with Bülow when he came to visit. The court had no choice but to deny Isolde's request. For the newspapers the case was an appetizing morsel. They made the most of the family quarrel, accused Cosima of money-grubbing, accused Siegfried of having "let his mother be dragged into a law court," accused them both of "having insulted the German nation." The mail at Wahnfried was heavy with smear letters, mostly anonymous. Four hundred tickets to the festival were returned. Then the matter was forgotten in the shock of a graver incident: an Austrian archduke was assassinated in Sarajevo. Five years later, in 1919, Isolde died, never having found the "joy and peace" her mother had wished for her.

Cosima was too powerful a personality not to overshadow her children. Romain Rolland, visiting Wahnfried in 1896, observed that the daughters were splendidly dressed in silk, "Eva in red, Daniela in green, Blandine in white. Cosima spends nothing on herself and wears a black shawl which reaches to her feet and covers her hair and forehead." Yet she dominated everybody. He found Cosima

> grown older, but there is still something attractive about her, especially about her mouth and eyes. Unfortunately she does not behave naturally. When she plays the piano her face mirrors whatever she plays. She treats everybody charmingly and speaks excellent French. [Why not?]
>
> Her four daughters make a better impression on me than they did five years ago. Isolde is totally indifferent to everything that is going on. She is tall and strong, has quite a good figure, but a terribly Semitic profile, certainly not pretty. . . . Blandine is still pretty, though a little sickly and nervous, and has a better complexion than the other daughters. Eva, in spite of being very thin, is an elegant apparition.

Rolland discussed with Cosima the commercialization of Bayreuth. All those souvenirs that were hawked about—Wagnerian stickpins, neckties with Wagner's picture, Wagner beer mugs, wallets decorated with "A social evening at Wahnfried," *Tristan* teacups, dinner plates with scenes from the *Ring*, etc. Cosima could hardly be responsible for them. Yet, observed Rolland, "one may speak only of Bayreuth; everything else is competition."

Rolland liked Siegfried best. And indeed, Siegfried turned out to be the most likable of the children. His several operas, now forgotten, were faraway echoes of his father's style, but he was a fairly good conductor and as a man, liberal in thought, straight in behavior, kind in action. (Toscanini, who knew him well, was fond of him.) All the more strange, therefore, that he married Winifred Williams-Klindworth, an Englishwoman, who was later to become Hitler's friend. She was the most despicable of the whole clan.*

3

Cosima, her mind as mobile as ever, her curiosity as searching, her wish to exchange ideas and observations as pressing, needed a friend who could respond—respond on her level—playing a countermelody.

---

*"If Hitler were to walk in the door today, I would be just as pleased, just as delighted to see him as I was back then."—Winifred Wagner, from a filmed interview in 1975

Nietzsche was such a one in the early years; Wagner was such a one —complete and all-absorbing—until the day he died. Nearing her sixties, she found another to whom she became bound in an affection fed by her belief that "she could tell him everything and he would understand." This was Prince Ernst zu Hohenlohe Langenburg,* a scion of one of Germany's oldest families, yet by no means cast in the usual aristocratic mold, since he was learned, introspective, a student of philosophy, concerned with the common welfare, and skeptical about the principles of his caste. As a young man he had become enamored of Wagner's music and had gone to Bayreuth several times without approaching Cosima. Returned from the festival of 1891, he wrote to her, telling her of the magical impression he had carried away. She answered. Presently he came to see her. They liked each other at once. Later she visited his castle and he came to Wahnfried. But the visits were few. He entered the diplomatic service and was sent to various posts—London, St. Petersburg, Berlin as a member of parliament, and finally, during World War I, to the East Front. Wherever he was, he wrote to her and she to him. The correspondence extended over more than thirty years—during which he got married and became a father and she became a grandmother several times— and what they wrote about was not confined to music but ranged from family affairs to world politics. It is astonishing how many letters she penned—or dictated—and how long they are. Pages and pages. Where did she get the time? She wrote: "You tell me so charmingly, my dearest Prince, that my endless letters do not bore you, and so I continue to indulge. I am like the preacher in Laurence Sterne who preached so long that an old woman who was to be fetched by her carriage asked the coachman, 'Has he not yet done?' to which the coachman answered, 'Of course he has done, but he never finishes.' " (January 10, 1894)

Ernst Hohenlohe wanted to be a writer and tried his hand at a play, *Roland,* which she analyzed kindly but honestly:

What is amiss here is lack of conciseness. Three love scenes strike me as questionable. I am afraid of abstractions. In a play one needs the tangible, the conflict of passions; symbolism cannot be the mainspring. In *Rheingold* Alberich seizes the gold because the Rhine Maidens mock him. From the *action* the thoughtful spectator can deduce the conflict between power (gold) and love. . . . As an exercise in dramatic construction take a novella as a starting point—as Schiller did for *Don*

*Langenburg is located in the Swabian Forest, a beautiful region. The province is called Hohenlohe. The castle is still standing.

Carlos, based on the novel of Saint Réal—and eliminate all situations and characters which you think unsuitable. I would like to show you a sketch which I once, in an idle hour, wrote based on an idea of Prosper Mérimée. Perhaps you would find it usable. One needs to see both the protagonists of a play and the situations which arise through them so clearly that one could tell the story to a child. [September 11, 1892]

They discussed the Boer War, the Dreyfus case (surprisingly, Cosima believed he was innocent and *liberté, fraternité, egalité* had been trampled underfoot), the arming of Germany, the role of Bismarck, Queen Victoria, the home rule debates ("the Irish problem is like our Jewish problem"), whether or not the Czar could be trusted, the Hague Peace Conference.

The assassination of Empress Elisabeth of Austria shook Cosima terribly:

I felt as if while looking at the stars I suddenly found myself at the edge of an abyss! I felt as if I had suddenly seen the Medusa! I walked for many hours quite alone. At last I became calmer. On the 13th I could again face the daylight and greet you, my dearest Prince. . . . She died without pain in all her beauty, without foreknowledge of murder. Like Ludwig II she embodied the silent and mystic aura of kingliness. Thus she was chosen as a symbol and thus she was sacrificed. As in a saga she bled to death on the water. So did our King, wrestling with his last adversary. The crime sinks into its disgusting nullity. [September 16, 1898]

Contrary to what she had told Isolde,, she traveled quite extensively. To Italy for her health. To Paris to hear the De Reszkes, with the intention of engaging them for Bayreuth. (She did not succeed.) To London to hear Nordica, and to dine with Balfour. In Paris she saw Sarah Bernhardt as Tosca: "If you can picture an old female monkey you would have an exact idea of what I had to endure for four acts."

She did not conceal her troubles from him: "Worry and aggravation I have aplenty, but *'j'y suis faite comme un chien à aller nue tête.' "* When Biagio Gravina died, she at once

decided to rush to my poor daughter [in Palermo]. I found her miserable. The tragedy was worsened by the circumstances: there were mother-in-law and sister-in-law with their loud superstitious cries; there were five physicians, all being vituperated: if the sick man had recovered it would have been the work of the Madonna, that he died was the fault of the physicians. . . . [October 17, 1897]

The two correspondents vied with each other in recording the impressions they received from the books they were reading. Once again one notes with astonishment Cosima's gobbling up one book after another. Once again one wonders where she found the time, considering that usually her daughters read to her, at a slower pace necessarily than one can read by oneself. She went through the *Odyssey* and studied the *Edda,* she reread much of Goethe, including his correspondence with Zelter, she waxed enthusiastic over Otto Jahn's biography of Mozart, she read in Italian a new biography of Savonarola, in English Laurence Sterne, Scott, Richardson's *Clarissa Harlowe,* in French Pascal, Flaubert, and a new poet, Stéphane Mallarmé:

> He is today considered the most important of the French poets, most skillful in language. I was repelled by him. In the first place I found his language *contournée* and *alambiquée,* steering everywhere except toward clarity. Secondly, I found his melancholy an expression of sterility. . . .
>
> He affects me like a November dawn or as do certain obfuscating perfumes which have one guessing whether they are pleasant or unpleasant. I am troubled, both because I can feel the talent and because I know that he is a gracious partisan of our cause. [January 10, 1894]

She went back to Luther's writings, which inspired her, and then made her way through the Old Testament, which made her shudder. She wanted to learn more about the business of government and read a number of political works—some on the prince's recommendation —including Bismarck's memoirs and the letters of Maria Theresa. There were few personal experiences or artistic impressions that she did not impart to the prince. "My second hearing of *Death and Transfiguration* by our young talented Strauss displeased me again because its ideas are jejune and its technical mastery sovereign." . . . "I visited the exhibition of the Secessionists in Munich. I marveled over the confusion and cannot find the talent of which most connoisseurs speak." . . . "Isn't it curious that at the very time *Lohengrin* is acclaimed in Paris with indescribable enthusiasm, almost all the German theaters play *Cavalleria?*" . . . "Yes, I would like to read that book about Byron. I am interested in everything which concerns that fascinating personality." . . . "I am hard at work on *Holländer.* Van Rooy is so magnificent he constricts my heart."

Hard at work? She wanted to give the festival *yearly,* not every second year. She argued with Adolf Gross, who could balance income with outlay, saying to him, "We can't afford to be spendthrift with the years. . . . You told me recently that our financial situation would suffer. . . . God, dear unique Adolf, it is my fate not to be concerned with this;

perhaps it is my wish not to be concerned. I gladly contribute our well-being in order to gain and earn what is holy to me." But with some exceptions, Gross's counsel prevailed.

Each and every performance seemed to brace her, quickening her liveliness. George Moore visited her, was enthralled by her, and said to her jokingly, "Won't you run away with me?" James Huneker remembered:

> The last time I saw her was in 1901. With George Moore I stood on the esplanade facing the Franconian valley, and during an entr'acte of the *Ring* we discussed the mediocre conducting of Prince Siegfried Wagner and the fond, foolish affection of his mother. She passed. This time she rode, but that rigid spine, the proud pose of the head, the undimmed hawk-like eyes—I am the widow of Wagner and the daughter of Liszt! they seemed thus to challenge the gaze of the public—proved her still in possession of all her powers. And she was then past sixty. Truly an extraordinary woman this, with her name out of the Italian Renaissance, herself like some belated and imperious apparition from the Renaissance. [*Variations*]

CHAPTER XIII

The Escape of *Parsifal*

THOUGH IN THE BEGINNING Wagner had told Cosima that he was composing *Parsifal* for her alone and that it had best remain unperformed, at least until a far-off time when a public could be found worthy of so high a revelation, she did not really believe this self-denial of the creator. He called it a "Stage Consecrational Festival Play"; she noted the word "stage" and saw him address himself to the problems of staging it when the ink was hardly dry. He made his wish quite clear to her that *Parsifal* was to be given only in Bayreuth.

The first challenge to this exclusivity was signaled shortly after King Ludwig's death. Ludwig's brother Otto became king in name only, being hopelessly deranged, and their uncle, Prince Luitpold, was appointed regent. His foreign minister and minister of the household, Baron von Crailsheim, who had hated Ludwig—he headed the commission that apprehended the "mad king"—lost little time in summoning Adolf Gross to Munich as Cosima's representative. Gross decided to go alone, without even a lawyer, but with a briefcase full of documents. In Munich he faced a group of seven solemn officials, Baron Crailsheim presiding, who pointed out that Ludwig had contractually acquired the performance rights to the *Ring* and to *Parsifal* for the Munich Court Theater. These works could be performed only by permission of His Majesty's government, and there was no question that *Parsifal* could be reserved for Bayreuth, if Munich wanted to perform it. Gross fished out the documents, which showed (1) that Ludwig had relinquished his rights voluntarily and (2) that he had acknowledged that *Parsifal* would belong exclusively to Bayreuth. Crailsheim cleared his throat and announced: "Since King Ludwig was officially declared insane and deprived of freedom of action, his decisions—on whatever documents they might be based—must be regarded as null and void." Gross, boiling with anger, replied, "My documents were signed a year before you, Excellency, were appointed minister. If, then, my documents are null and void, so is your appointment." After the shocked shouts had died down, Gross declared that under the circumstances there was no point in continuing the discussion. He walked out.

On the staircase, one of the ministers overtook him and urged him to reconsider and to present his case to another commission. Gross consented. There followed long negotiations, which ended in a total victory for Gross and Cosima. It was agreed that "the performance rights of all hitherto published operas and musico-dramatic works, as well as of other musical works and writings by Richard Wagner, are not to belong to His Majesty King Otto, nor to the Royal Court Theater Intendant, but to Richard Wagner's lawful heirs." A special clause covered *Parsifal:* it was to be performed only in Bayreuth. However, should a performance outside Bayreuth be contemplated at any time, the Munich theater was to have first call on the work and a special interval was to elapse before it could be given elsewhere. All this sparring merely showed that by the end of the nineteenth century the Wagnerian works, including his last, were strong attractions; Munich wanted both the cash and the credit they would bring to an ailing Court Theater.

Before the beginning of the twentieth century, Cosima had to address herself to a second challenge. She was aware that the "period of protection" (as copyright was then called in Germany) would soon expire and she began a campaign to try to force through a new law which would prolong the protection. With elaborate pleas, in which the words "piety" and "honoring the wish of a genius" kept company with her avowal that it was not for gain that she wanted to retain the "holy work," she approached members of the Reichstag, even the Reich Chancellor himself, her influential friends such as Prince Hohenlohe, and Prince Luitpold. For the president of the Bavarian Ministry she prepared a long memorandum reviewing the history of Bayreuth and underlining its extraterritorial importance as a "world symbol of German art, indeed German culture." Finally she reached His All-Highest Imperial Majesty, Wilhelm II. The Kaiser told her not to worry: he would see to it that her request was granted. It was "his unshakable will that the work would never be given on any other stage. He would not permit it." Cosima, knowing something of the worth of Wilhelm's word, was astute enough to view this skeptically. "I know we are still far from a *lex specialis*. But at least it is something!"

She even wrote to a member of the Reichstag who represented the Social Democratic Party, which she disliked. This man, Fritz Kunert, was the only delegate who answered her plea, in return for which she overwhelmed him with a treatise of nine pages in which she philosophized that the benefit of art lay not in being made "superficially popular (cheap editions of the classics, etc.) but in being allowed to make its impress on profound minds." Moreover, "the ideals of a great artist must be kept intact, insofar as that is possible within the limits of earthly powers. Our present institutes serving art cannot do that."

Nothing helped. The law was not changed. At the beginning of 1902, Cosima, vanquished, wrote to Mathilde Wesendonck (it was the first communication in years between them):

> . . . your view (which you demonstrated by not signing the general appeal for the protection of *Parsifal*) has at least the advantage of swimming with the stream. The Reichstag, almost the whole press, the Goethe Association, the most eminent scholars, the most celebrated artists are against it. . . . [January 7, 1902]

As yet, however, no German theater planned to wrest the work from Bayreuth, partly out of respect, partly because of the difficulties the performance would entail. Munich considered it, but was not quite ready. In Amsterdam, a complete public concert performance was given, which was followed by a closed performance for members of a Dutch Wagner Verein. These were made possible because Schott had published a "study score," from which the orchestral parts could be copied. But there for the moment the matter rested.

2

In 1884, the Metropolitan Opera inaugurated the first of seven consecutive seasons of opera in German. The German population of New

York (then estimated at a quarter of a million and therefore larger than that of many German cities) wanted to hear the voice of their controversial compatriot. Perhaps some of the members of New York society in their boxes, a Jay Gould or an Adrian Iselin, could take the third act of *Tristan* or leave it alone; but there was no question that most of the general public, German or American, was fascinated by Wagner. His works, though not always well staged or adequately rehearsed, were superbly sung. The best German singers had been gathered by the Metropolitan: Materna, Brandt, Van Rooy, Schumann-Heinck, Nordica, Niemann, and above all Lilli Lehmann, at the height of her glory, who sang an Isolde "marvelous in its beauty of tone, its radiant color, its breadth, its tenderness. . . . Criticism is weak for want of superlatives."* The chief conductor of those years was Anton Seidl,† whose passion for the task reflected itself in reports to Cosima:

> Our *Tristan* performances were first rate. Jean de Reszke is the best Tristan I know, the most lucid, the most untiring. Nobody could be compared to him; he sings the second act magnificently, the third act truly astonishingly, because in addition to his enchanting voice he enunciates every syllable, indeed every letter, even in the most difficult passages, so that for the first time I understood the entire text. (Perhaps Schnorr managed it as well—I never heard him.) His Tristan is a human being, not a warrior forever boasting of heroic deeds—as most of the German tenors play him. . . . His brother Édouard has, since Scaria, the sole right to give Marke's speech. His is mighty singing coupled with understanding. Nordica was surprisingly good; she has grown and will grow further. Once she studies Brünnhilde she will become one of the greatest German dramatic artists. . . . The orchestra didn't drown the singers, but was powerful in the right places. In a word, it was music. . . . If you really want to hear *Tristan* sung, invite Jean, Édouard, Nordica to Bayreuth. . . . As to the cuts, there are fewer in New York than in any German city, Munich perhaps excepted. First act without cuts, second act one unfortunately rather large cut, third act two tiny cuts not worth mentioning. . . .
> [New York, May 25, 1896]

More than likely, such a report made Cosima jealous.

In 1903, Heinrich Conried became the director of the Metropolitan. He was a German, born in Breslau and trained as an actor in Vienna, but New York had long been his home. He directed the Irving Place Theater, where he gave the plays of Sudermann and Hauptmann. In his new capacity, one of the first things he thought of was the possibil-

*According to the critic W. J. Henderson.
†Leopold Damrosch, who knew Wagner and Cosima, was director of the first German season, but died in 1885.

ity of staging the first performance of *Parsifal* outside Bayreuth. That he was prompted by a desire to set before the public an immediate "sensation" (his other sensation of that season being the debut of Caruso) cannot be doubted. But Conried determined that if he was going to do it, he was going to do it right, and he not only imported a competent stage director from Munich, spent lavishly on scenery, and had the expert Alfred Hertz as conductor, but he assembled a superlative cast: Ternina as Kundry, Burgstaller as Parsifal,* and Van Rooy as Amfortas.

When Cosima heard of Conried's plan, her anger rose to a new level. Nothing in her life, not Bülow's erratic behavior, not Nietzsche's philippic, not Judith Gautier's luscious glances, had wrought her to such a pitch. One can hardly believe that fear of any financial loss caused her to cry anathema.† The loss of something that "belonged to her Bayreuth"—that is what hurt. Then, too, she shared the European attitude that competition is harmful and must be scotched. Otherwise, why would she have viewed with such hatred an effort to introduce that difficult work to a faraway public, the probable result of which would have been to tempt some auditors to hear *Parsifal* again—in the Festspielhaus?

But what could she do? No copyright agreements existed between Germany and the United States. Nevertheless, she instituted a suit in the New York courts, appealing for an injunction against the performance. The courts had no choice but to refuse. Further, she let it be known that any artist having anything to do with Conried's project would never again be permitted at Bayreuth. Next, she appealed to Walter Damrosch, son of Leopold, who was now one of the city's leading musicians.

> Dear Sir:
> I hear that Director Conried has announced a theater performance of *Parsifal*. The firm of Schott will not hand over the parts and I have protested against this performance. I hear as well that you have given concert performances of *Parsifal* and that you are in possession of the orchestral parts. I do not know where you got them. May I ask you, my dear sir, *not* to give these parts to Director Conried?
>
> I assume I need not give you my reasons for this request. Nor do I doubt that you, as an honorable artist, abominate this planned performance. [Bayreuth, March 29, 1903]

*He had sung the part in Bayreuth under Cosima's direction in 1899 and again in 1902.

†For that matter, Conried offered to pay Bayreuth a "performance fee." Cosima refused it indignantly.

She didn't let up. In July she wrote Damrosch in English:

Dear Mr. Damrosch:
I thank you very much for your kind lines and the expression of your feelings for Parsifal, who, of course, is never to be given out of Bayreuth; but also concerning the production at concert, that has been made a very limited choice of fragments, which is not to be extented. This choice, done by the master is as follows:
1. Prelude, close of the first act, nothing of the second.
2. Verwandlungsmusik. close of the third act.
3. Amfortas Klage.
4. Charfreitagszauber.

I am astonished, that for £50.—you got the allowance to enact the whole Parsifal in concert and will ask the publisher.

Concerning the performance on the stage, I still hope that the cultivated part of the public at Newyork won't agree to it.

Receive, dear Mr. Damrosch, with my best thanks, my kindest regards.

C. Wagner
Bayreuth, 6 Juli 1903

One other factor may account for her indignation. Improbable though it must have seemed even to her, she still hoped that *after* the decision of the Reichstag she could put through a "special dispensation," prohibiting other German theaters—including her pet aggravation, Munich—from performing the work. She wrote to Prince Hohenlohe:

I haven't the slightest doubt that the "Parsifal" New York affair was incited mostly by Munich. If the New York performance will really take place, I'll be deprived of all further measures I might want to take, relying on what has been reported to me of the sympathy of the Kaiser. I will lose several of my principal singers and they will be snatched up by the [Munich] Theater. The whole thing is quite cleverly schemed up. . . . [Bayreuth, August 18, 1903]

In New York, some sanctimonious disputations broke out. One devout Protestant protested, excoriating the performance of a work in which "not only is Christ's person represented, but the blood." When a music critic pointed out that nothing like it took place in *Parsifal,* others spoke of "profanation," while the Catholics stated through a spokesman that they were unwilling to take their ideas of sacred and profane from Protestant clergymen. Mayor Seth Low was petitioned to suspend the Metropolitan Opera's license.* All this only served to

*The facts are given in Irving Kolodin's *The Metropolitan Opera.*

Cosimama, Die Gralshüterin
Karikatur von G. Brandt aus dem Kladderadatsch-Album. 1905

Caricature, 1905. "Cosimama, guardian of the Grail."

whet the curiosity of a public able and willing to pay up to ten dollars
—double the usual price—for a ticket. Every possible space in the
house was filled. Richard Aldrich, critic of *The New York Times,* wrote
a full report of the occasion; its essence was:

> Dec. 25, 1903. . . . It may truly be said that the eyes of the whole musical
> world were turned upon this performance. . . . Never before, perhaps, has
> a stage production of any kind in this country so stirred the imaginations
> of so many people or been so widely discussed or so urgently debated. In
> many of its aspects it was one of the most important and significant
> musical events that Americans have been concerned with. . . .
>
> *Parsifal* was presented in a manner wholly befitting its distinctive charac-
> ter as a work of art—a manner that recognized and gave a full exposition
> of the solemnity and dignity of its theme, the lofty eloquence of its treat-
> ment, the overpowering impressiveness of the drama. . . .
>
> It was in many respects equal to anything done at Bayreuth, and in some
> much superior. It was without doubt the most perfect production ever
> made on the American lyric stage. . . .
>
> All the outward circumstances were calculated to enforce it. The per-
> formance began at 5 o'clock in the afternoon, the first act ending a little
> before 7. There was an intermission of an hour and three-quarters for rest
> and refreshment—meditation, if any were so disposed. . . . The house was
> shrouded in darkness while the pictures upon the stage were unfolding.
> There was a hush—if not a "Bayreuth hush," at least one to make it plain
> that this New York audience was quite as disposed as any at the Festival
> Playhouse to preserve the impressiveness of the occasion.
>
> The occasion was, in truth, profoundly impressive.

That season *Parsifal* was given eleven times, sold out each time,
which means that close to fifty thousand people heard it.

Cosima could not be appeased. She called it "rape," a "vivid proof
of the world's decadence." Two years later, Humperdinck was in New
York to attend the premiere of his *Hänsel und Gretel* (November
1905). He actually apologized to Cosima for daring to go to that pros-
cribed place! Cosima in reply commented on Humperdinck's comments on an emissary she had refused to receive, probably Edmond
C. Stanton, secretary of the Metropolitan, who had been sent to Bayreuth by Conried as a messenger of peace:

> I understand that America made a good impression on you. I too have
> retained my sympathy for the New World and have not let myself
> become confused either by what is called "Americanism" or by
> certain unsavory incidents. Recently I read a novel, "Leopard Spots"

by Dickson, which vividly pictures conditions in the Southern States
after the emancipation of the Negro. . . .

The man of whom you speak is not [a typical] American. He belongs
to the race of speculators such as are to be found here and
everywhere. In Munich he'd easily find *confrère et compagnon.* I am
sure that the crime against *Parsifal* was initiated there, with the
purpose of establishing a precedent which would despoil the work in
the future.

Well, we have lost the lawsuit, and those gentlemen who are hardly
burdened by ethical considerations can help themselves in all comfort,
whether they grab hold of an Offenbach piece or *Parsifal.*

I do not blame you in the least for going to New York. Life compels
us sometimes to a course which is not to our liking. . . . But I do wish
you had not spoken to Van Rooy: he knew what he was doing and he
didn't need to do it. . . . [Wahnfried, December 28, 1905]

She never forgave, never got over it, never derived any satisfaction
from *Parsifal*'s making its way to the stages of the world.

In 1913, when the centenary of Wagner's birth was being celebrated, she wrote to Hohenlohe:

That Germany could not manage to mark this memorial by granting a
protective law to *Parsifal,* that's the way things usually are done. But
that in Munich a Herr Possart wants to erect a monument in front of
the opera house, collects money for that purpose, and proposes to
invite *me* to its unveiling (partly, no doubt, to listen to his oration)—
that reminded me of Schopenhauer's words: "Life is a tragedy which
acts like a comedy." [Bayreuth, May 18, 1913]

The next year she wrote him that the Milanese, "those happy-go-
lucky people," found nothing profound in the work. They took its
mysteries as casually as they did the fall of a leaf. On the other hand,
"the Viennese were simply bored by it—and they are right, because
if it isn't a Consecration play it is a boring opera. The Berliners, at least,
are honest, admit that they perform it because it does business, and
pump out the poor work, evening after evening, with 'Bayreuth Singers' who have long since lost their voices."

The argument she advanced, that *any* performance of *Parsifal* outside Bayreuth was a desecration, could not be accepted as valid, since
it ignored the basic question: how worthy was the performance? Many
who at first sympathized with her began to see this.

She was so downcast that as she was writing her protests, she asked
herself "whether it wouldn't be better for me to let everything go and

to admit the uselessness of my endeavors. But I could not do it. And I cannot. However desperate one is, one continues to hope. 'Hope against all Hope,' says St. Paul."

To the end of her days, she hated the Metropolitan and the Munich Theater.

CHAPTER XIV

Cosima Moves Upstairs

THE BUILDING OF VALHALLA, the forging of the shattered sword, the hero who knew no fear, the God who knew no sanctity of contracts —these were the contents of the *Ring* that made a greater appeal to the audiences of new Germany than did Wagner's messages of the vanity of power and redemption through love. The Tetralogy had become the theme music of a people who believed themselves to be, or shortly to become, the leaders of Europe and perhaps the world. In this belief the burghers of Berlin strode in pride, their paunches before them, though they quickly stepped off the sidewalk to make way for any second lieutenant in uniform. Official building commissions designed local Valhallas, edifices as bloated as they were unoriginal. They bestrewed the city with monuments of muscular kings and muscular generals riding muscular horses. The Kaiser was Wotan, a maimed god, but a god nevertheless. Cosima thought of him as less than "All-Highest," since he showed scant interest in Bayreuth. (However, Wilhelm later had his automobile horn tuned to the "Thunder" motif from *Rheingold.*) She sensed the mood of her adopted country, and so in 1896 she staged the *Ring* freshly, emphasizing its grandiose aspects. The castle fashioned by the giants in *Rheingold* would have satisfied a Berlin architect; the shields of the Valkyries were massive platters, their spears three times as tall as they; Gunther's vassals were fit for military duty; the conflagration at the end as consuming as Sodom's. This staging was repeated the following year, in 1899, in 1901, and five times more in the first decade of the twentieth century, sixty-eight performances in all.

She looked up at the waving banners, more than ever firm in her patriotism, expecting great things to be created by the German spirit. Great things—except in music. She felt the summit of that art had been reached and she said so. What more, what better could follow? Of most of the music composed between the 1890s and the early 1900s she was ignorant, ignorant on purpose. She was contemptuous of Verdi, never heard *Otello* (1887) or *Falstaff* (1893) and did not acknowledge Verdi's death in 1901, though Verdi had written to Giulio Ricordi when Wagner died, predicting that this "great personality . . . will leave a potent impress on the history of art." (Then he crossed out the word *potente* and substituted *potentissima.*) She knew Debussy as a music critic, but she could make nothing of "The Afternoon of a Faun" (1894), which she heard, nor of his setting of the Baudelaire poems she had once read and admired, nor of *Pelléas et Mélisande* (1902), a work which seemed to her moist vapor. She did not much care for the songs of Hugo Wolf, worshipper of Wagner though he was, and she disliked the young Schönberg, then still in his Wagnerian phase, partly because Schönberg declared himself against the *"Parsifal* Monopoly," believing that "The whole world together ought to collaborate on solving the musical, instrumental, vocal, scenic and pictorial problems posed by such a work as *Parsifal.* . . . Any work needs to be freshly studied for new audiences and cannot be entrusted to one 'guardian' alone."

Of the important Wagnerian epigones whom she knew personally —Mahler, Bruckner, and Richard Strauss—she could not approve of Mahler, for the sole and simple reason that he was a Jew. She didn't want to see a Jew as director of the Vienna Opera and she opposed his appointment. Yet when he did become a director, and when he decided to accept for performance Siegfried's opera *Der Bärenhäuter,* she was delighted, although her delight was mitigated when she heard that Mahler was making some cuts in the opera. Mahler assured Siegfried that he had made these cuts only to improve the opera's effectiveness, telling him honestly that his last act was "mediocre and carelessly written." Siegfried took this verdict with a modicum of calm, but Cosima wrote Hohenlohe:

My son is now in Vienna to help stage *Der Bärenhäuter,* and he writes
me how much sympathy he is receiving from the entire staff of the
Opera. Director Mahler has shown great enthusiasm for the study and
presentation of the work, but has decided for some mysterious reason
—or perhaps one which is all too easily explained—to make some
quite incomprehensible cuts. For example, the whole of Luisel's
prayer, which is the very heart of the work, as well as all the passages
which create a mood of holy worship. My son asked him in front of
the whole personnel: "Does the religious content bother you?" . . .
The incident fits in curiously with a book I am reading, Chamberlain's
XIX Century, in which the author explains that what distinguishes the
Germans from the Semites is that the former have a strongly
developed penchant for religion while the Semites lack it altogether.
[March 12, 1899]

Mahler's origin, however, did not prevent her asking for his advice
and help. What did he think of Anna Mildenburg (later the wife of the
brilliant Viennese playwright Hermann Bahr)? Would she be a suitable Kundry? And would Mahler be interested in Siegfried's latest
opera, after he had rejected a previous one, *Kobold?* Did he want to
see the score of *Bruder Lustig?* "May I request a reply by telegram?"
One can imagine that Mahler became more of a Jew after he refused
Bruder Lustig as well. Of his music Cosima knew little—though by
1900 he had completed his fourth symphony—and cared less. Nor was
she much in tune with Bruckner's work, though Bruckner had adored
Wagner with his whole heart and though Wagner had sensed the great
talent in the few compositions Bruckner had shown him. Her opinion
was:

I would appoint that good man court composer. And every year I
would order from him one cantata, one festival mass, and one Te
Deum. I would be confident that he would deliver them punctiliously
composed. But when he tries to trumpet himself into a genius, he
becomes a Simple Simon.

Yet she treated the young Richard Strauss almost as a son, a son
whose behavior was not quite exemplary. She was genuinely fond of
him and he venerated her, consulting her about his life and career,
which rose rapidly from conductor to opera director in Weimar to
Bülow's successor in Munich. Richard's father, Franz, had been the
first horn player in the Munich Royal Orchestra. He had loathed Wagner, both as a composer and as a man, and he was offensively rude to
him. (Young Richard had to hide the score of *Tristan* from his father
when he was studying it.) Once during a rehearsal, Wagner had remarked jokingly, "Always dour, these horn players," to which Franz

replied, "We have every reason to be." But that had happened long ago, and now both Franz and Cosima took pride in Richard's talent and Franz escorted Cosima to a performance, arm in arm, the past forgotten. She was full of tenderness for Richard, the chemistry between them benevolent even when he caused her trouble. "No Christmas tree," she wrote him, "could shine brighter than does my heart with good wishes for you! Just get well! Then you can remain as pigheaded as you are and annoy me as much as you want. I know all the same how we feel about each other!"

Cosima dealt with Richard both as a conductor and as a composer. He was wildly ambitious, and wanted to take over the Bayreuth performances of *Meistersinger,* in addition to *Tannhäuser.* If he couldn't have both, he wouldn't come at all. But *Meistersinger* had been promised to Richter. Cosima reproved him:

> . . . My friend, what is important is that you become a member of our family. Only thus can we create a living relationship. And life is for the living. . . . I believe that you would be well advised to heed my call without making difficulties.
>
> I think you underestimate Richter. . . . Let us not forget that he is intimately connected with *Meistersinger,* that he was present during its composition, that he trained the singers, conducted the choruses, and once even sang Kothner. . . .
>
> If Richter disappoints your expectations, let me assure you that *my* expectations have been often enough set at naught. All the same, just as I will continue to work here, you can continue to conduct here. . . .
>
> But—just as you wish! I offered you what I am able to offer you. I never make a proposal without first thinking about it a long time. . . . Therefore I seldom retract it. . . . Every man carries his demon within him and if your demon urges you to quit me, I wish you to do so with an easy conscience, convinced that I will regret it deeply but that I will continue to hold you in affection. You must understand that with the best of will we cannot always ignore conditions as they are.
>
> Let me have your decision by telegram, since we have to make an immediate announcement.
>
> P.S. I fear I did not express myself with sufficient affection. It is late at night, and the day was fatiguing. Supplement what is lacking by your knowledge of how I really feel about you! [Bayreuth, May 18, 1892]

The next day Strauss telegraphed: "I come. Heartfelt greetings."

Much as she valued Strauss as an executant musician, she thought him too cerebral a composer. When his *Don Juan* appeared, she wrote him:

I believe that in music as in poetry the shape [*Gestalt*] is decisive. If the shape is clearly imagined, then one must try to scale it out with all possible terseness. Restlessness harms clarity and restlessness is a product, it seems to me, of a capricious intellect.

We have experienced the perfection of art: that very perfection teaches us simplicity. If, for example, you compare *Rheingold* to the other three parts of the *Ring,* you will observe with what economy of means it is fashioned, while later, with increasing action and the entanglements of passions, the music grows ever richer. . . .

In your "Don Juan" you seem to have been captured by the gestures of your characters; the characters themselves are not felt by you. This is the play of intellectuality versus emotion.

It is difficult to discuss these matters and everything I am saying seems to me somewhat faulty, because it is insufficient. Perhaps a simile may help: the shape is born in the artist as is the sculpture in Pygmalion. The passionate concern with that sculpture endows the work with beauty and movement.

Even the choice of your subject shows the predominance of intellectuality. You could not have been truly moved by Lenau's poem, with its satiety springing from boredom. . . . Now I say to you, don't pursue the beckoning of your intelligence further, but submit to whatever appeals to your heart, be it the gleam of the sinking sun, the surge of the wave, the hero doomed to perdition—or truth in its virginal innocence. It is precisely our art which leads us back to eternal motives and lets us recognize the truth behind deceptive appearances. [Bayreuth, March 6, 1890]

She heard *Zarathustra* "praised on all sides." Very well, she was happy for him. Yet: "I protest against using poor Nietzsche as the author for program music." He cannot defend himself, since "for more than twenty years he lies sadly ill."

When Strauss played her parts of *Salome* (on Good Friday, 1905), she exclaimed, "But this is madness." A few months later she wrote to him (it was to be her last letter to him; her interest waned):

The famous French poet Rostand wrote a play for the equally famous actor Coquelin in which the chief protagonist is a cock. Are you going to set it to music? You see, I'm joking to comfort myself: *on en rit pour n'en pas pleurer!* . . . No doubt it was the demonic element which attracted you to the subject. I can only keep quiet and continue to hold you in affection. . . . [Bayreuth, October 24, 1905]

It is astonishing that Strauss took all this in good part: he was too sure of himself to mind her strictures and he greatly enjoyed exchanging ideas with her. Often she had bits of wisdom to impart to him:

About singers and actors:

What is usually called "intelligence" has nothing to do with the stage
and often leads to all kinds of nonsense. [Acting] is a matter of instinct
and the most talented artists I have met were in a way stupid.
So-called intellectual criticism merely confused them. . . . [Berlin,
January 27, 1891]

She reread Liszt's biography of Chopin and while perceiving its
faults, she was stimulated to go back to the music:

I reviewed some of the works mentioned in the book, the Polonaise
Fantasy, the Prelude in F-sharp minor, the great Polonaise in the
same key with the Mazurka, and I derived immense pleasure from
them. The sureness and precision of form, the fullness of melody, the
originality of feeling—there is hardly a comparable achievement to be
found in the whole literature of the piano. . . . Still one asks oneself
what is this delicate edifice doing in our crass world? . . . [May 21,
1890]

2

Cosima's life had reached what was for her an even tenor. There
were no performances in 1905 and she was looking forward to staging *Tristan* the next season; the work had not been performed for
thirteen years and she was restudying it. In the winter she wrote to
Chamberlain:

A few days ago it was snowing gently and I walked alone up the
Festival Hill, where our Theater stands in its lofty silence and
loneliness. My glance wandered into its past, its present, its future. I
thanked heaven for the son given to me. Then I marched on, into the
forest which protects this edifice. I found myself amidst the green of
firs and pines. No light penetrated from above, but the blanket of
snow furnished illumination from below, as often in my life light came
to me from the depths when all around me darkness reigned. I met
nobody and nothing disturbed my thoughts, which swirled around me,
like friendly spirits. . . . [December 10, 1905]

The 1906 *Tristan* was a success, though at one of the performances a curious accident happened, which might well have caused
a panic. At the end of the third act, as Marke exclaims, "All is death!"
the electric lights went out, plunging stage, orchestra pit, and audi-

torium into darkness. Mottl continued to conduct, Marke to sing, the musicians, knowing the score by heart, kept on playing—and the audience sat quietly. "It was," Cosima wrote, "as if the world grew dark with Tristan's death." It was as well "an example of the Bayreuth spirit and discipline." After four minutes—which is an eternity in a theater—the lights came on again and Isolde died of love.

The preparation of *Tristan* was the last active work Cosima was to undertake. She had received a warning. In the winter of 1906, she was visiting Prince Hohenlohe in his castle, and on the last evening of her visit, he was reading aloud an essay by Goethe which dealt with the nature of artistic creation. They discussed the subject and Cosima retired late in a happy mood.

Early in the morning—it was still dark—the prince and his wife were awakened by a servant shaking with fright. Their guest had had some kind of an attack during the night; she was now moaning and only half conscious. Hohenlohe ran into her room, looked at her, and considered her condition serious enough to telegraph the children, asking them to come at once. They came with Cosima's physician, Dr. Ernst Schweninger, one of Germany's leading internists, who was also Bismarck's personal doctor. (Cosima called him "Magus.") Schweninger diagnosed a gall bladder attack, and found that her kidneys were involved as well. However, there was no immediate danger. She begged to be allowed to go home, and after a few days the children took her back to Wahnfried. Schweninger now issued stern commands, involving the kind of physical care a physician prescribes with little regard for the psychological. She was to be kept absolutely quiet, no visitors, no excitement, no travel, above all no work. No work of any kind. That decision meant, as she at once understood, stepping down from the direction of the festival. She wept. Worse, she was forbidden to be present at any of the rehearsals or performances. Again her tears flowed. But she dared not disobey orders, and she turned the management over to Siegfried, who, at thirty-six, came into the kingdom.

Presently she accepted her prescription. As she wrote to Hohenlohe, "He who must renounce can learn to renounce." The phrase served her but incompletely; for a long time she was not sure that Siegfried could manage.

To distance Cosima from the traffic that was constantly flowing through Wahnfried, they changed her room to a remote part of the house, a large room which had once served the children as a playroom. Now it became a personal museum. Cosima could survey the chronology of her life: there were the portraits of Liszt and Marie d'Agoult, her sister Blandine and Ludwig, all the children and her brother Daniel. The most prominent place in the room was occupied by Lenbach's portrait of Wagner—at first Cosima had not liked this painting, but she got used to it—and when she looked out the window she could see among the bare trees his grave, surmounted by a cold white bust. Dozens of little souvenirs dotted the tables. Wagner's *Collected Works* and a complete edition of Goethe were piled next to her couch. She had Wagner's watch beside her; it had long since been repaired and she used it to tell her when to take her medicine. Daniela got hoarse reading to her and Eva got writer's cramp taking her dictation for those endless letters.

After every performance she listened eagerly to the reports, but she never again entered the theater on the hill, giving up her "gorgeous palace for a hermitage"—except once years later, when she was secretly carried there and listened to one act of *Walküre*.

The wish to live—she said it was for the sake of Bayreuth—was still strong in her. In the spring she rallied and Dr. Schweninger recommended that she be taken south. Daniela wrote to Hohenlohe: "We would be eternally grateful to you if you would be so kind as to let everybody know that she is as yet much too weak to receive or talk to people. Only you, and the Princess . . ." In the next two winters Cosima went to Rapallo and to Santa Margherita. Wherever she was, she could not stop thinking about the festival. She wrote Hohenlohe:

> The coming Festival has been announced and this decision of my son seems to me right, since the demand remains lively. With the artists we again experience something we have known for thirty years: cynicism is their normal way to behave. Goethe knew what he was doing when he excluded actors from his school. . . . But we here must retain the ideal of a community *contre vent et marée*. My grandson Guido [Gravina] said to me: "In Florence I never look at the sky because it is always blue, and if for once it is overcast it clears up in a moment. In Germany I am always looking up." The idea that one ignores the beautiful because it is there made me laugh. With the artists I do the opposite: I don't look at the overcast and try to see the blue. . . . [Bayreuth, November 15, 1908]

But all she did with the artists was to receive their respectful calls. They stayed a few minutes and left.

3

One great joy was vouchsafed her. Eva, already forty-one years old, married in 1908. Her husband was the famous Houston Stewart Chamberlain, whom Cosima had first met in 1888. She wrote at the time that he was "a proud and original personality of great value. We talked continuously for five hours and neither of us got tired," and from then on a voluminous correspondence continued for twenty years,* though the style is more formal on both sides than is her correspondence with Hohenlohe. Chamberlain was a historian of much learning and almost no understanding. He was born in England, the son of a British admiral, educated in France and Germany, and then settled in Vienna, to turn into the familiar kind of German who is a scowling apostle of the doctrine, untouchable and undisputable, that virtue, valor, and all-round superiority are embodied in one race alone. It is strange that some of the most fanatic Teutons were born outside the *Vaterland.* His major work, *Die Grundlagen des neunzehnten Jahrhunderts,* was published in 1899 (in English in 1910 as *Foundations of the Nineteenth Century*). Misinterpreting Kant, completely misunderstanding Goethe, even mistranslating Wagner's philosophy (such as it was), Chamberlain postulated that the "world soul" was to be elevated to light and truth through the German spirit—provided the body housing that spirit remained unsullied. (No intermarriages!) He envisaged a blond young hero, a figure like Siegfried, ascending a steep path, threatened by two enemies, the Celtic race in the West and the Semitic race in the East, but finally emerging victorious. His symbolic figure bears a suspicious likeness to the Prussian uhlan, six feet two, cropped hair, pig eyes, and huge riding boots. Reading Chamberlain's book today, one marvels at its fallacies. Why was it taken seriously? Obviously because it blew the nationalistic trumpet, the sound his readers wanted to hear.

At any rate, the book made a great impression on Kaiser Wilhelm II, who invited the author to lecture at Potsdam and then decreed that it was required reading for all his generals. The Kaiserin, too, had to read it. Cosima studied it and admired it. Why not? Did it not regurgitate her own beliefs? She wrote him:

My Friend:
I begin this letter hesitatingly. I want to discuss your book with you—

*Their published correspondence fills a book of 695 pages.

and I am timid about it, since I did not have the time to sift the great number of impressions it gave me, so as to offer you a clear summary of my views. I will try to do so, asking your indulgence.

You have presented with admirable certainty your central theme, which is that we need only manage our heritage rightly in order to prove, not its oppressiveness, but its indispensability. We have inherited our art (and all this word includes) from the Greeks, our law from Rome, our religious truth from the revelation of a unique divine apparition.

What I wish to emphasize above all is your reasonable and convincing treatment of the racial question. . . .

I want to thank you especially for two points. First, your demonstration of the error that "everything has happened before." I am reminded of Goethe's word, "Nature is forever new." Second, for your warning against the Jews functioning in jurisprudence. But I was astonished that you ascribe "intellect" to the Jews. I would rather have thought "cleverness." They are anarchic (which Christianity is not).

I regret your chapters ["The Jews as Prophets" and "Christ a Jew?"]. I do not find your proofs convincing. I can see that you want to show yourself as an objective scholar in order to strengthen your wonderful thesis. But here is the marvel: Nature must be observed and discussed impersonally, while our Savior can only be approached and explained by devout worship. You began your chapter superbly. I wish you had ended it similarly. . . . [Bayreuth, May 7, 1899]

By this time Chamberlain worshipped Cosima too intensely to take an author's umbrage at her criticism. He had embarked on a biography of Wagner, which was about as objective as a sonnet to my lady's eyebrow. He defended himself against the accusation that he had used "private" information, made available to him by Cosima, by stating that he used only facts which were "generally known." That didn't say much for him as a researcher. He wrote Cosima:

After my book [*Wagner*] was published in 1896, you invited me to come to Bayreuth and to peruse the unpublished autobiography. That was the finest possible proof of your confidence in me and your benevolence toward me. . . . Yet with the stubbornness which you have known in me and which you, if you do not approve of it, at least excuse as a characteristic trait of my personality, I refused to glance at anything which was not common knowledge. . . . I believe that we suffer these days by an exaggerated search for documents. A great man ought to be judged by his works—and with few documents, the fewer the better. Up to now I have not read the autobiography. And though I know the iron safe in the small salon in Wahnfried where you keep the manuscripts and letters of the Meister, though I was present on one occasion when you opened the safe to search for something, nevertheless I have never, not once, looked at any letter preserved there. . . . [January 13, 1905]

In due course, Chamberlain met the girl sitting at Cosima's side. Eva was flattered by his attention, by the fact that a man so well known, so highly learned, and so elegant could be interested in her. For he *was* elegant with his made-to-measure glacé gloves and his Savile Row suits. Cosima brought them together often. But Chamberlain was married. He removed that obstacle by getting a divorce, and he married Eva in Zurich on December 27, 1908. He was then fifty-three years old. In marrying Eva he "married" Cosima and Wagner. From his honeymoon he wrote Cosima that "we confessed to each other that, over and above a love between man and woman sanctified by marriage, we felt that our relationship had something brotherly and sisterly about it, so that we found it difficult to imagine that we had not always lived together." One may read between the lines.

Eva and Chamberlain settled in Wahnfried. They did not want to get away from Cosima, they did not want independence. Both of them gave Cosima care and love, and he was thrilled by the pride of belonging to the "royal" family. But Fate dealt cruelly with Chamberlain. During World War I he was accused of being a British spy, he of all people. Indignantly he demanded public vindication and then applied for German citizenship, which was not granted until the Kaiser intervened. His fortune in England was confiscated and his relatives there called him a traitor. Worse followed: in 1917 he began to suffer from a creeping paralysis, which soon bound him to his bed. He could no longer speak, but he kept on writing. For ten years he lingered, nursed by Eva. When he died in 1927, the news was hidden from Cosima, who believed that he was too ill to see her. "People do not have to see each other to be together," Cosima said to Eva.

Similarly, Isolde's death was concealed from her. After the separation caused by the lawsuit, Cosima did not ask how or where she was except once, shortly before her own death. She had lost that daughter long before she lost her.

Slowly at first, and then with increasing speed, the circle contracted: Levi died in 1900, Mottl in 1911, Claire Charnacé and Marie von Schleinitz in 1912, Richter in 1916. To them she offered tributes in gracious and restrained words. Yet about the passing of the man linked to her early youth she seems to have remained strangely silent. Bülow's health had declined from uncertain to worse, he had consulted many doctors, who could advise nothing more than rest and quiet, advice he was unable to adopt, and finally he had gone to Egypt. Richard Strauss, who had journeyed there to cure a persistent catarrh, had told him that the sunshine would surely help him. Daniela saw him off: "His aspect seemed hopeless, he looked like a dying man, his eyes were lusterless, his bearing somnolent." On February 7, 1894, he arrived in Cairo. Two days later, he suffered a stroke. On the twelfth he died. Cosima said nothing, not to her children, not to her friends. Was it out of self-protection? Did she hide her grief? More probably it seemed to her an event geographically and emotionally removed from her, the relationship a far-off and long-ago piece of history which the years had turned into a pale fairy tale; one could not add more words to it. Much later she wrote a poetic recollection in his honor, the artificiality of which betrays the unreality of her feeling:

> . . . Rise, O weary one, to me
> As I sing you my festive song;
>
> All hail to thee, man of courage,
> My messengers, the sun's rays, greet thee,
> Behold my cloak which shields you.
>
> All hail to thee, noble one,
> The eye of heaven now absorbs you. . . .

4

Before the festival of 1914—*Parsifal,* the *Ring, Holländer*—ended, the war broke out. A total of 360,000 marks had to be returned to ticket holders. Yet, financially onerous though this restitution was, it did not seem all that tragic. The war would soon be over: the soldiers, the Kaiser assured his people, would be home by the time the leaves turned brown. Performances would soon be resumed.

For the four years of the war and for six years of its terrible aftermath, the theater on the hill was locked up. Ten years of silence descended on Bayreuth.

In the first war years Cosima was confident of Hindenburg. Who in Germany was not? Writing to Hohenlohe, who was working with Hindenburg, she cited Napoleon's words: *"Qui a gagné la bataille? Celui qui croit l'avoir gagnée."* But soon she understood that belief would not do it. She showed none of the bellicose spirit she had dis-

Cosima in her eighties, with Siegfried.

played as a young woman during the Franco-Prussian War. Now war seemed dreadful to her, "a crime against music." She managed by using her political influence to keep Siegfried from military service.

She had regained her health and vigor, remarkably so. And with it, her courage. One night a thief entered Wahnfried and made his way into her room. She awoke, thought at first it was somebody from the household, then realized what was happening, and had the presence of mind to keep absolutely still, pretending to be asleep. Even after the intruder had tiptoed away she did not sound an alarm, not wanting to frighten Eva and the servants. Blandine, who happened to be visiting Wahnfried, reported: "No trace of him. I doubt whether the Bayreuth police will demonstrate any remarkable detective skill. Precious memorabilia of the Meister are gone." Yet even after this incident, Cosima calmly insisted on sleeping alone.

The war seemed to go on forever:

As I stroll up to the Festspielhaus and I see that gigantic building standing there under a sunless sky, mute as a specter, I ask myself am I awake or am I dreaming? Will it again someday be filled with sound, to the delectation of a feeling humanity? . . . [Letter to Hohenlohe, December 22, 1916]

She had hoped to celebrate her eightieth birthday in 1917 as "the church bells proclaimed peace." She was doomed to disappointment. She knew that discussions about an armistice were taking place, rumor had it that Germany was to concede everything the Allies demanded. She heard a man cry, "Why have we sacrificed our sons?" Cosima wrote in great sadness, "The Wahn monologue said it all." In her little nest, things were quiet: "Nothing has changed except the stride of the soldiers, once strutting, now creeping."

I met in the Court Garden a troop of injured soldiers, then a group of war prisoners. A few paces farther on I saw the funeral of a fallen aviator. When I got to the City Church, I noticed the main window smashed and the pipes of the burned organ strewn all over the square. Suddenly the "sad tune" of *Tristan* sounded in my head and (how wonderfully!) it consoled me. . . .

She was advised to finish her Testament, which she had begun to sketch in 1913. Half of all her possessions had been designated as a gift to her children, each child being given one fifth. As to the other half:

1. Half of Wahnfried with the buildings appertaining to it, as well as the ground, as well as all contents such as furniture, works of art, manuscripts, the library—in short, all movable objects—

2. Half of the Festspielhaus with the buildings appertaining to it, the complete furnishings of these buildings, the entire inventory, as well as whatever may constitute the fund of the Festspiele at that time—

3. Half of all capital and cash, including the sum brought by me into the marriage, as well as the rights of performance and literary rights—are to be inherited by my son Siegfried. His sisters have no part of 1. and 2. As to 3.—S.W. is to grant each of his sisters one fifth. [September 2, 1918]

The Testament is a testament to Cosima's preference for Siegfried. "Fidi" was still something special. Yet none of the children needed to worry: they were wealthy. Right after the end of the war, the Wagner fortune (point 3), invested in stocks and bonds, amounted to no less than seven million marks. The fund (point 2) stood at 700,000 marks.

All this capital, both that of the family and that of the theater, was swept away in the inflation. Yet they were better off than nine out of ten Germans—those who had not converted their capital into dollars or Swiss francs—because they possessed real estate and works of art, which rapidly appreciated in value. Cosima was aware of what was happening. What hurt her most was not the loss, but the inability to resume the festival. Other theaters, she knew, were alight with Wagner, but who could come to Bayreuth when a railroad ticket from nearby Nuremberg today cost as much as a week's supply of food cost yesterday? Mark notes were used as labels for the bottles of "Mark Beer"; that was cheaper than printing the labels. Cosima walked in the woods and pondered. Would Wagner's work sound again on the hill? And when? Would she live to see the day? Was there a future for her mission? Could she forget the present?

CHAPTER XV

Mostly Memories

COSIMA HAD DECREED that nothing in Villa Wahnfried was to be changed, everything had to remain as it had been on the day she and Wagner left for Venice. From there she had brought the couch on which Wagner died, and this she kept in her room. In the *Saal,* the souvenirs and gifts were still displayed, the butterfly collection Wagner had bought from a man in Naples was intact, his spectacles were still in a drawer of his desk, the pianos he and Liszt had used had not been moved an inch; nobody played them. Siegfried had acquired his own piano, a Bechstein, and visitors were allowed to use it.

Siegfried was already forty-six when he brought Winifred home. She was a beautiful English girl of eighteen, and the sisters welcomed the breath of youth. (That was soon to change.) In 1917, Siegfried's first son, Wieland, was born. On the day of his birth, Cosima sat down at the Steinway—for the first time since her husband's death—and remembering the birth of her own son, began to play the *Siegfried Idyll.* She broke off after a few bars—and never touched the piano again.

In March 1920, Cosima was struck by a second attack, more severe than that of 1906. For weeks she was unable to leave her bed. Dr. Schweninger told the family to be prepared for the end. Yet an astonishing strength still pulsed through her eighty-three-year-old body. She could not die while Bayreuth lay barren.

Daniela to Hohenlohe:

Three weeks ago Mama suffered a severe attack which was followed
by a heavy bronchitis and a painful cough which robbed her of sleep
night after night. . . . This means that we will have to nurse her for a
long period and with many deprivations. Unfortunately we get no
help from Bayreuth's climate and its raw winds. What can we do?
There remains solely the escape into the mind. Her mind is lively,
clear, and more profound than ever. She talks much about her youth,
her father, her mother, the great personalities of that epoch, Balzac,
Lamennais, Lamartine, Chopin. She reminisces much about my father,
the intimate friends of our house, and our cause. They emerge
suddenly, Marie Schleinitz above all. Then our artists, the
incomparable performances under her and Siegfried's quiet guidance.
Of the works it is again and again the first act of *Walküre* and the
second act of *Meistersinger* which occupy her thinking. Every day I
read to her some of Mozart's letters. She finds them absolutely
enchanting and is always asking me if I believe that you, dear Prince,
would get pleasure from reading that book. God grant that once again
we have escaped the menacing danger. . . . [Wahnfried, April 1, 1920]

Why was Daniela living in Wahnfried, ready to nurse her mother
"for a long period"? She had returned there because her marriage to
Thode had been a failure. *She* was a failure. Cosima's firstborn, for
whom her mother had hoped great hopes and from whom she had
demanded much, was now, at the age of sixty, a woman without a life
of her own, without independence, feeding on "tradition" as her suste-
nance. Not only had her marriage ended in divorce, but now she hated
Chamberlain—and that of course created a rift with Eva—and soon
she hated Winifred, as the outsider. In *Heritage of Fire,* Winifred's and
Siegfried's daughter, Friedelind, described Daniela:

Daniela was always hating or loving somebody with violence and never
could endure to see anyone happy. If she had lived in another world or
another age she would have made a career in one of the professions for
she had a brilliant mind and a driving energy, but, cramped by Cosima
into the narrow confines of German Society (she was a von Bülow and was
presented at court in spite of Cosima's divorce), she was continually ex-
ploding, wrecking everything about her, continually repenting and flagel-
lating herself for her outbursts.

Both sisters vied with each other in trying to capture Siegfried's
affection; they were united only in their dislike of his wife, who had
made it clear that as soon as Cosima died, she and Siegfried were going
to run Bayreuth, without interference from them. There was no balm
in Wahnfried.

The woman upstairs knew something of what was going on. Yet she
lived in a penumbra in which her true companions were her memo-

ries, become ever more "real," events of long ago and men and women long departed standing around her bed in clear illumination, while the present—her son, her daughters, Siegfried's children— receded behind a veil. What was happening in Germany's internal strife, what was being enacted in the Weimar Republic—or even the question of if, when, and how Bayreuth would be reopened (though to that question she gave the last of her concrete thoughts)—these contemporary matters seemed more remote to her than the night she arrived in Triebschen or the day she had written the letter about Bülow to King Ludwig. When Siegfried apprised her of their financial status, when he spoke to her of the repairs required by the theater, she listened, but the facts did not penetrate, since she dwelled no longer in a world of facts but in a world of feelings. "What we feel is the only thing that exists for us, and we project it into the past, into the future, without letting ourselves be stopped by the fictitious barriers of death," wrote Proust. Cosima's feelings, whether of a positive nature, such as her recollection of the husband forty years dead, or her love for Goethe and Schopenhauer, or whether negative, such as her resentment of Nietzsche, were not held back by the barriers of death. But from those around her she mentally parted. Siegfried's children were taken to call on her at six o'clock in the afternoon when she had had "a good day." Friedelind remembers how frail Cosima looked, as if at any moment she might break in two. Her white hair was still full and beautiful. The visits were uncomfortable: Grandma didn't know what to say and neither did the children. They kissed her cheek gingerly and departed as soon as possible. Fritz Busch, the conductor, was allowed to visit her one day when she was eighty-eight years old. He was introduced to her as the current conductor of *Meistersinger.* The first thing she asked him was what he thought of Hans Richter. Then she wanted his judgment about singers like Brandt, Scaria, and others, all long dead.*

When could Bayreuth be reopened? To bring this about, fresh capital was needed. In 1921, a commission was brought into being—the *Deutsche Festspielstiftung*—which appealed to the nation: "Those who love Germany and want to help its recovery, those who wish to concern themselves with its future as a people of culture, must come to the aid of Bayreuth." They began to sell "Patron Certificates" at 1,000 marks each, just as was done in Wagner's day. The effort was

*Fritz Busch, *Aus dem Leben eines Musikers.*

successful: by the end of 1922, some 5,400 certificates had been sold. Siegfried felt that additional money should be raised abroad, particularly in the United States. Early in 1924, he undertook a concert tour there. It was a failure, partly because the war was still too fresh in America's memory, partly because the press pointed out that "since 1923 there existed a fast friendship between Wahnfried and the Fascist leader Hitler." Siegfried raised $8,000, a mere pittance, but altogether enough money had been collected to assure a somewhat cautious festival in the summer of 1924.*

Siegfried had worked for more than a year to assemble the casts. They used costumes that Daniela had designed long ago and prewar scenery. The seven *Parsifal* performances were conducted by Willibald Kaehler (previously a musical assistant) and by Karl Muck; the *Ring* in two performances by Michael Balling; and *Die Meistersinger* in five performances by Fritz Busch. Though the festival was presented under the aegis of Siegfried, it was Cosima's spirit that still hovered over the performances. Nobody as yet could dispel the spell. Busch, an intellectual musician, analyzed the virtues of the performances: "the unique moments when Richard Wagner's genius became almost tangible to us"; as well as the defects: "a stubborn digging itself fast into a false concept of fidelity . . . an insistence so very contrary to the demands of the eternal Revolutionary to whom Bayreuth owed its existence. . . . If again and again I made critical remarks or offered suggestions, they merely smiled."

The reopening of Bayreuth was important news, and journalists from many countries came to witness it. For some unaccountable reason, Cosima consented to receive an American reporter from the Middle West. He happened to arrive on one of Cosima's good days, the two walked in the garden, he addressed her as "Mother." They had hardly anything to say to each other. Suddenly Cosima made a sound which called a bird she had tamed. The bird flew to her and alighted on her hand. It warbled a couple of notes from *Siegfried* which Cosima had taught it. Then it flew off into the sunset. Cosima looked in the direction of its flight, turned, and returned to the house.†

The doors of the theater had again swung open, the little town had wakened from its decade-long sleep, the visitors, clad in evening dress, again trudged up the hill in broad daylight while the local populace lined up to watch them and to titter, the hotelkeepers were again able

*Facts given by M. Karbaum in *"Studien zur Geschichte der Bayreuther Festspiele."*
†This anecdote was told by Paul Rosenfeld, in *Discoveries of a Music Critic.*

to charge exorbitant prices, while many foreigners lodged with private families, trying to express their wants in broken German. The 1924 season was repeated in 1925; there was a year's pause and then, in '27 and '28, *Tristan* was added to the repertoire—all in "traditional" staging. Only in 1929, a year of no performances, did Siegfried think that the time had arrived for change: he persuaded Toscanini to come and conduct a new staging of *Tannhäuser* in 1930. It was Toscanini who infused new life into the old romantic opera. He took over *Tristan* as well, giving three incandescent performances with Lauritz Melchior and Nanny Larsen-Todsen.

In Cosima's last years she drew closer to Eva, now a widow. The two widows sat together, discussing softly the disposition of the documents locked in the safe of Wahnfried, what was to be published, what suppressed. Cosima transferred to her daughter the task of being archivist and editor of Wagner's story. Cosima's light was dimming, yet sometimes her mind still blazed. Eva, notebook in hand, wrote down what her mother said immediately after she said it.

> Greet Houston [Chamberlain] from me. I feel close to him. I think we met before, on another star. . . . One does not lose such a relationship, but one misses it. [Chamberlain had died two years before.]

> [In connection with the new *Tannhäuser:*] I always felt that secret magicians helped us in our work—as long as we remained honest.

> To know that one has a mission is to know that one has earned grace.

> *Se tenir tranquille et être bon chrétien*—that is what is seemly in a woman.

> I don't know why I dislike female violinists.

> Nothing is unimportant in art. One must treat it like a religion.

> "Life—a dream" [title of a play by Calderón]. One does not lose those who have gone away.

> My best achievement is that I gave birth to you [Eva], my angel.

> [About her diary:] Don't you think that it is a family matter? Not suitable for being published. However, if Wolzogen or Houston wants to glance at it, I have no objection.

> Cosima: Where is Loldi?

> Blandine: In Davos. (Long pause)

> Cosima: But Loldi is dead!

> Blandine: Yes, Mama; long ago she was freed of her suffering.

The last photograph.

Cosima: Where is she buried?

Blandine: In Munich, where she last lived.

Cosima: Yes, I know. In Munich! (Silence)

When I stepped on the stage I felt really and truly at home.

[On the balcony, on a day in July 1929:] I can't tell you how very well I feel. Impressions one cannot describe in words flow toward me in a wave of mysticism. They bring me consolation. Take my thanks for this hour of happiness; it is as if I had never undergone travail. I can say this to you only. . . .

Nothing is more beautiful than a conviction which unites us.

Let's leave nothing to chance. Chance bores me.

Luther was a rare apparition. Oh, God—how he must have suffered! Like Papa.

I love life. Quite simply, that's how I feel.

But as much as I enjoyed having lived, I would rather not be born again.

Where is my father buried? . . . Ah, that is good that he is here; that is providence.

I wanted to ask you—do you *hear* the silence?

His [Wagner's] genius was great, but his kindness even greater.

One ought to read a poem by Goethe every day: that in itself is an education.

I was much occupied with your education. But it never worried me—you were all talented.

For Christmas 1929, Cosima got up; Eva dressed her in her favorite black dress; she put on her pearls and sat at the head of the table. She said that one ought to observe occasions like Christmas because "such days serve to unite people." She asked Siegfried what was to be performed the next summer, and when she heard that *Parsifal* was to be given, along with *Tristan, Tannhäuser,* and the *Ring,* she said: "It is simplicity which accounts for the nobility of *Parsifal.*" But she did not want to see Muck, who was to conduct *Parsifal.*

Cosima lived on until 1930, the year in which Germany had four and a half million unemployed, Hitler swore before the Reich Tribunal that he would observe the country's laws, France was constructing the Maginot Line, and people flocked to see Marlene Dietrich in *The Blue Angel.* By the middle of February, Cosima became weaker. Her speech was not always lucid now, and frequently she would sink into semiconsciousness. Awake again, she would say to Eva: "I feel as if I were no longer here, no longer reachable. I am grateful for that. But I would like to look at the stars once more. Where are we? Are we in Wahnfried?" She was totally blind.

She began to speak of Bülow. She imagined she was still married to him. "What a brilliant man he is. Did you hear how beautifully he conducted the 'Eroica'?" She was drowsy and she mumbled, "Forgive!"

On the 31st of March, when Eva said good night, Cosima replied, "As God wishes. Wonderful." She fell asleep. When Eva entered her room early in the morning, she was dead. The date was April 1, 1930. She had lived more than ninety-two years. She who wanted to die with Wagner had outlived him for forty-seven years—a Titian-like span of life which began when Queen Victoria ascended the British throne and Dickens completed *The Pickwick Papers* and which ended when Mahatma Gandhi instigated his civil disobedience campaign and Freud published *Civilization and Its Discontents*.

She was buried next to Wagner in the Wahnfried garden.

2

Siegfried died in August of the same year, sixty-one years old. Winifred took over the direction of the festival. The toxic traits within the family became acute. Winifred's infatuation with Hitler infuriated Friedelind and Wieland. The inhabitants of Wahnfried shouted at one another.* On one endeavor, however, the family did agree: to burnish the memory of Wagner and Cosima, even if (as mentioned) that necessitated burning letters or smearing over "compromising" passages or pasting pages together. Even before Cosima's death, the official biographers had begun to set her on a refulgent Sibyl's platform, her figure enveloped in steam cooked up in the boiler room of the Festspielhaus.

*Nevertheless, Winifred ran Bayreuth until 1944. After World War II, the American occupation forces permitted the festivals to resume in 1951 only on condition that she take no part in their management. Wieland took over as director—proving himself a brilliant innovator—and won acclaim. He died in 1966. Then his brother Wolfgang became the director. Both Wieland and Wolfgang had broken off relations with their mother, Wolfgang banning her from attending any performances of the 1975 festival. Winifred died on March 5, 1980, eighty-two years old.

Du Moulin Eckart began his two-volume biography by saying: "It was a sacred obligation to raise a monument to the greatest woman of the century"—which rather leaves Marie Curie, Elizabeth Browning, George Sand, etc., out in the cold. Millenkovich-Morold in his biography concluded that "the greatness of Cosima remains unsurpassable."

The reaction was predictable. When her diary was published, the historian Peter Gay wrote:

> Cosima Wagner strains the historian's capacity for detachment. While fanatical Wagnerians will, of course, think otherwise, familiarity with her conduct and her convictions is likely to breed exasperation, even dislike, and require an effort not to turn a review of her writings into a denunciation. . . . They do not make Cosima Wagner less exasperating or, for that matter, less unlovable. They only make her more interesting.

He goes on to say:

> [Yet] Cosima, so long seen as the clever manipulator who guided Wagner in his mendacious and servile correspondence with Ludwig II; as the implacable ideologue who pushed Wagner, the repentant radical, into reactionary chauvinism and antisemitism; as the cool-headed master tactician, half Machiavelli and half Mephistopheles, turns out to be largely a myth. These pages reveal an anxious mother hovering over her embroidery, sobbing about her inadequacies, brooding on her first husband, listening in dumb adoration to Richard Wagner playing Richard Wagner. . . .

After reading the diary, the eminent critic George Steiner remarked that Cosima "continues to fascinate and repel me." She is both "awful and magnificent."

Awful and magnificent—hers was a curious duality. On September 16, 1870—the Franco-Prussian War was in full swing and that day Cosima had received a letter from her mother saying that Marie was hurt by her daughter's "frank judgment of France"—on the evening of that day Wagner and Richter were talking in Wagner's room. Cosima was working in the salon. At frequent intervals, one or the other of the two men appeared in the salon, only to disappear again. Cosima asked what was going on.

> I then learned that they had seen five bats in R.'s room. R. didn't want to tell me, knowing that I was superstitious in that respect. When I heard that I was frightened. Then, taking hold of myself, I prayed: whatever misfortune was menacing me, I wanted to be permitted to fulfill my task as a Christian, a wife, a mother.

This highly educated and worldly-wise woman immediately turned to prayer for protection against bats in the next room. She prayed for the one force that moved her soul and gave joy to her existence: dedication. Wagner used often to write his scores in pencil. Then Cosima would carefully retrace each dot, line, and word in ink. This labor, along with all her other ministrations, is symptomatic of a love which Bernard Levin has called "one of the most intense and beautiful in history." It gave her an inside knowledge of the music. And she understood more than the music. Better than King Ludwig, Liszt, Levi, or anybody else, she understood his wider aims: he hoped for a rebirth of tragedy as he imagined it had been practiced by the Greeks; he wanted to link, as it were, the *Oresteia* to the Nibelungen Saga, the Furies to the Norns, Oedipus to Siegfried, Antigone to Isolde. He wished to use legend as the rostrum from which to speak of crime, wisdom, and love. That he did not succeed entirely is due to his hammering together his own mythology, which was unclear and often out of joint. Wagnerian symbolism has fallen into the sere; the music remains. The idea of Bayreuth was, with all its presumption, a lofty one: the *Gesamtkunstwerk* presented as a people's festival. Cosima saw this clearly: it was not her fault that Bayreuth became a fashion center, a you-must-be-there.

Even in her old age she thought of continuance: she conferred with an architect about modernizing the theater's stage and she searched for new artists, in the course of which she discovered Hans Breuer, who was an incomparable Mime (from 1896 to 1914) and a marvelous David, and Ernest Van Dyck, a tenor who originally wanted to sing Italian roles, whom she persuaded to become a Lohengrin and a Parsifal.

Whatever she did, she did with passion. This is the key to her nature. Nothing about her was halfhearted. Not only were her loves passionate, but so were her prejudices, so were her mistakes. When Daniela went through her unhappy love affair, Cosima wrote that she understood the pain her daughter must be suffering. "You must bear that pain with dignity, freeing yourself of bitterness. If you can understand his action, if you help him to understand himself, you will have won the game of life. If not . . . my child, you will have to undergo other sterile experiences." She, Cosima, had experienced a similar fate when, eleven years after her wedding to Bülow, she went to Triebschen, deeply unhappy but obeying her love without a thought for the future. She had a right now to speak to Daniela, "I who certainly knew love and passion."

The man she loved had to be a genius: that was a need of her nature. She tried with Bülow and failed. Perhaps that was why she succeeded in her second attempt. She was more than the stiff queen of Wahn-fried. "Fame, like Echo, retains only the last syllable," wrote Jean Paul. She was a multisyllabic being, who played a vital role in the life of that prickly genius who was Wagner. One must repeat that without her there would have been no *Siegfried Idyll,* no Bayreuth, and no *Parsifal.*

Appendix

Bibliography

Aldrich, Richard. *Concert Life in New York, 1902–1923.* New York, 1941.

Bahr-Mildenburg, Anna. *Bayreuth.* Leipzig, 1912.

Barth, Henrik, ed. *Internationale Wagner-Bibliographie.* Bayreuth, 1961.

Barth, Herbert, ed. *Der Festspielhügel—Richard Wagners Werk in Bayreuth.* Munich, 1973.

Beecham, Sir Thomas. *A Mingled Chime.* New York, 1943.

Bélart, Hans. *Friedrich Nietzsches Freundschafts-Tragödie mit Richard Wagner und Cosima Wagner-Liszt.* Dresden, 1912.

Blunt, Wilfrid. *The Dream King, Ludwig II.* London, 1970.

Böhm, Gottfried von. *Ludwig II.* Berlin, 1924.

Bory, Robert. *Liszt et ses enfants.* Paris, 1936.

Bülow, Hans von. *Letters.* New York, 1931.

Burbridge, Peter, and Sutton, Richard, eds. *The Wagner Companion.* London, 1979.

Burk, John N. *Letters of Richard Wagner—The Burrell Collection.* New York, 1950.

Burrell, Mary. *Catalogue of Collection, Christie's.* New York, 1978.

Chamberlain, Houston Stewart. *Richard Wagner.* Munich, 1896.

Chamberlain, Houston Stewart. *Richard Wagner.* Translated by G. Ainslie Hight. London, 1897.

Downes, Olin. *Olin Downes on Music.* New York, 1957.

Du Moulin Eckart, Count Richard. *Hans von Bülow.* Munich, 1921.

Du Moulin Eckart, Count Richard. *Cosima Wagner.* 2 vols. New York, 1930.

Gautier, Judith. *Wagner at Home.* London, 1910.

Geissmar, Berta. *Two Worlds of Music.* New York, 1946.

Gersdorff, Freiherr Carl von. *Briefe an Friedrich Nietzsche.* Edited by Karl Schlechta and E. Thierbach. Weimar, 1934–1937.

Gregor-Dellin, Martin. *Wagner Chronik.* Munich, 1972.

Hamerow, Theodore S. *Restoration, Revolution, Reaction.* Princeton, 1966.

Holborn, Hajo. *A History of Modern Germany.* New York, 1964.

Jacobs, Robert L. *Wagner.* London, 1935.

Kapp, Julius. *Richard Wagner in 260 Bildern.* Berlin, 1933.

Kapp, Julius. *The Women in Wagner's Life.* New York, 1931.

Kniese, Julius. *Der Kampf zweier Welten um das Bayreuther Erbe.* Leipzig, 1931.

Kohn, Hans. *The Mind of Germany.* New York, 1960.

Kolodin, Irving. *The Metropolitan Opera.* New York, 1966.

Krehbiel, Henry Edward. *Chapters of Opera.* New York, 1908.

Kreowski, Ernst, and Fuchs, Eduard. *Richard Wagner in der Karikatur.* Berlin, 1907.

Lehmann, Lilli. *Mein Weg.* Leipzig, 1920.

Liszt, Franz. *Correspondance de Liszt et de Mme. D'Agoult.* Edited by D. Ollivier. 2 vols. Paris, 1933–1934.

Liszt, Franz. *Letters to Olga Mayendorff.* Translated by William Tyler. Washington, 1979.

Liszt, Franz, and Bülow, Hans von. *Briefwechsel.* Edited by La Mara. Leipzig, 1898.

Mack, Dietrich. *Bayreuther Festspiele.* Bayreuth, 1976.

Mack, Dietrich. *100 Jahre Bayreuther Festspiele.* Munich, 1978.

Mack, Dietrich, and Voss, Egon. *Richard Wagner Leben und Werk in Daten und Bildern.* Frankfurt, 1978.

Mahler, Alma. *Gustav Mahler, Memories and Letters.* New York, 1969.

Mann, Golo. *The History of Germany Since 1789.* London, 1968.

Mann, Thomas. *Adel des Geistes.* Berlin, 1956.

Millenkovich-Morold, Max. *Cosima Wagner.* Leipzig, 1937.

Morold, Max. *Wagners Kampf und Sieg.* 2 vols. Vienna, 1930.

Mowat, R. B. *The Romantic Age.* London, 1937.

Neumann, Angelo. *Personal Recollections of Wagner.* London, 1909.

Newman, Ernest. *Fact and Fiction About Wagner.* New York, 1931.

Newman, Ernest. *The Life of Richard Wagner.* 4 vols. New York, 1933–1946.

Newman, Ernest. *Wagner as Man and Artist.* New York, 1924.

Newman, Ernest. *The Man Liszt.* New York, 1935.

Perényi, Eleanor. *Liszt.* Boston, 1974.

Praeger, Ferdinand. *Wagner, As I Knew Him.* London, 1892.

Rosenfeld, Paul. *Discoveries of a Music Critic.* New York, 1936.

Santayana, George. *The German Mind.* New York, 1968.

Schenk, H. G. *The Mind of the European Romantics.* New York, 1967.

Schonberg, Harold C. *The Great Conductors.* New York, 1967.

Siegfried, Walther. *Frau Cosima Wagner.* Stuttgart, 1930.

Sitwell, Sacheverell. *Liszt.* Boston, 1934.

Spring, Alexander. *Richard Wagners Weg und Wirken.* Stuttgart, 1933.

Sucher, Rosa. *Aus meinem Leben.* Leipzig, 1914.

Sutherland, Douglas. *Twilight of the Swans.* London, 1973.

Unterer, Verena. *Die Oper in Wien.* Vienna, 1970.

Voss, Egon. *Die Dirigenten der Bayreuther Festspiele.* Regensburg, 1977.

Wagner, Cosima. *Briefe Cosima Wagners an ihre Tochter Daniela von Bülow.* Stuttgart, 1933.

Wagner, Cosima. *Briefwechsel zwischen Cosima Wagner und Fürst Ernst zu Hohenlohe-Langenburg.* Stuttgart, 1937.

Wagner, Cosima. *Cosima Wagner und Houston Stewart Chamberlain im Briefwechsel.* Leipzig, 1934.

Wagner, Cosima. *Cosima Wagner's Diaries.* Translated by Geoffrey Skelton. New York, 1978.

Wagner, Cosima. *Cosima Wagner–Richard Strauss: Ein Briefwechsel.* Tutzing, 1978.

Wagner, Cosima. *Das zweite Leben.* (Letters and Sketches) Edited by Dietrich Mack. Munich, 1980.

Wagner, Cosima. *Die Briefe Cosima Wagners an Friedrich Nietzsche.* Edited by E. Thierbach. Weimar, 1938.

Wagner, Cosima. *Die Tagebücher.* Edited by Martin Gregor-Dellin and Dietrich Mack. Vol. I, 1869–1877; Vol. II, 1878–1883. Munich, 1976–1977.

Wagner, Richard, and Ludwig II. *Briefwechsel.* Edited by Otto Strobel. 5 vols. Karlsruhe, 1936–1939.

Wagner, Richard. *Das Braune Buch.* Zurich, 1975.

Wagner, Richard. *Gesammelte Schriften und Dichtungen.* 5 vols. Leipzig, 1887.

Wagner, Richard. *Letters to Uhlig, Fischer, Heine.* Edited by J. S. Shedlock. New York, 1890.

Wagner, Richard. *My Life.* 2 vols. New York, 1911.

Wagner, Richard. *The Bayreuth Letters of Richard Wagner.* Edited by Caroline V. Kerr. Boston, 1912.

Wagner, Richard. *The Letters of Richard Wagner to Anton Pusinelli.* Edited by Elbert Lenrow. New York, 1932.

Wagner, Richard. *Richard Wagner an Mathilde Wesendonk—Tagebuchblätter und Briefe.* Berlin, 1904.

Wallace, William. *Liszt, Wagner, and the Princess.* London, 1927.

Westernhagen, Curt von. *Wagner.* 2 vols. London, 1978.

Index